Committees and Commissions in India
1979

Concepts in Communication
Informatics & Librarianship-55

General Editor : **S.P. Agrawal**

Committees and Commissions in India 1979

Volume 17

PART B

A Concept's Project

Compiled by a team of professionals
under the guidance of
VIRENDRA KUMAR

CONCEPT PUBLISHING COMPANY, NEW DELHI 110059

ISBN 81-7022-509-4 (Vol. 17, Part B)

First Published 1994

Published and Printed by
Ashok Kumar Mittal
Concept Publishing Company
A/15-16, Commercial Block, Mohan Garden
NEW DELHI 110059 (India)

Lasertypeset by
Printing Express
H-13, Bali Nagar
NEW DELHI 110015

CONTENTS

PART A

PART B

13

WORKING GROUP ON NATIONAL FILM POLICY, 1979 — REPORT[1]

Chairman Dr. K.S. Karanth

Members Shri M. Bhaktavatsala; Shri Shyam Benegal; Shri Tarachand Barjatya; Shri Bikram Singh; Shri Basu Bhattacharya; Shri Manoj Kumar; Shri Ramanand Sagar; Shri Adoor Gopalakrishnan; Shri Tarun Majumdar; Smt. Vijaya Mulay; Dr. Jagdish Parikh; Shri P. Neelakantan; Shri Mrinal Sen; Shri Dilip Jamdar; Sardar Manohar Singh Gill

Co-opted Members Shri D. Ramanujam; Shri D.V.S. Raju; Shri Santosh Singh Jain

M. Secy. Shri S.L. Kapur

Alterations Subsequently, the Government of India vide Resolution dated 20th July, 1979 also nominated Dr. Jagdish Parikh Chairman, Film Finance Corporation, as a member of the Group. Originally Shri R.K. Shastri, the then Joint Secretary in the Ministry of Information and Broadcasting, was nominated as the Member-Secretary of the Working Group. After Shri S.L. Kapur took over as Joint Secretary on July 18, 1979 he was nominated as the Member-Secretary.

Appointment

In pursuance of the recommendation made in the last Conference of State Ministers of Information/Public Relations and after consulting

---

1. Ministry of Information and Broadcasting, Government of India, New Delhi, 1980, 153 p.

the State Governments/Union Territories, it has been decided to appoint a Working Group to study the present state of the Film Industry in areas such as production, distribution, exhibition and taxation and to suggest a National Film Policy which would help the growth of Indian cinema.

Terms of Reference

(a) To enquire into and examine the present state of cinema as an art form and as an instrument of social change, with reference to its role as a medium of information, education and entertainment and to suggest measures for its further promotion and development;

(b) To enquire into all aspects of film making, including technology, raw material, equipment and processing and the whole range of related economic activities, i.e., production, distribution, exhibition and financing and to suggest measures for improvement;

(c) To examine the impact of Government policy and procedures both Central and State — on the film industry with regard to censorship, entertainment tax, excise duties, local taxes, import levies, import and export of films and to suggest modifications consistent with overall objectives of the Government to promote the growth of healthy Indian cinema; and

(d) To suggest measures of State support, where called for to improve Indian cinema in all its forms — feature films, documentary films, news films and TV films.

The Working Group may set up sub-Working Groups where required and co-opt members, if necessary, to provide necessary information and technical expertise.

The Working Group may consult media experts and other sections of interested opinion.

The Working Group will have its headquarters at New Delhi and meet as often as considered necessary, but it may visit such other places in the country as considered necessary for proper and comprehensive study of the matter.

The Working Group may submit its report as soon as possible but within a period of six months from the date of the first meeting.

The membership of this Working Group will be honorary but non-official members will be entitled to travelling and daily allowance in accordance with the Ministry of Finance (Department of Expenditure) Office Memorandum No. 6/26/E. IV/59 dated 5th September, 1960 as amended from time to time.

Contents

Preface; Introduction; Framework for a National Film Policy; Status of Cinema as an Art Form; Production System; Distribution and Exhibition System; Film Technology and Raw Stock; Taxation Policy; Short Films; Children's Films; Import and Export of Films; Promotional Activities of the Central Government; The National Film Development Corporation; Promotional Activities of the State Governments; Censorship; Training Facilities; Labour Legislation and Trade Associations; Implementation: Some Suggestions; Summary of Recommendations; Annexures I to VIII; Report of the Study Group on Film Technology.

Recommendations

Framework for a National Film Policy (Chapter II)

1. Lack of legal powers with the Union Government is one of the major hurdles in laying down a National Film Policy. We recommend that the entire subject of cinema and film industry should be brought within the purview of Central policy and Central control. The subject of cinema should be transferred from the State List to the Union List or Concurrent List. (Paras 2.11 to 2.15)

2. Alternatively the Union Government should consider the possibility of taking over the control of cinema by legislation under Entry 52 of the Union List. (Para 2.16)

3. State Governments should continue to have financial resources to support State level film activity. A fair formula should be evolved to share the entertainment tax revenues between the Central and State Governments. (Para 2.17)

4. The Information and Broadcasting ministry should be expanded and should be called the Ministry of Information, Broadcasting and Cinema. There should be a separate Department of Cinema to be headed by a Secretary. (Para 2.21)

5. The Department of Cinema should develop expertise for dealing with the problems of film industry. It should have a Technology

Cell staffed with technical people and a properly equipped Information Cell which should maintain up-to-date information and statistics. (Para 2.22)

6. The broad objectives of the National Film Policy should be as follows:

(i) To improve the cultural quality of cinema considering its impact upon society;
(ii) To make cinema accessible to the largest number of people throughout the country;
(iii) To help the growth of cinema as a medium of culture, artistic expression, communication, enlightenment and entertainment, and to develop a strategy for the propagation of film appreciation and consciousness;
(iv) To help the Indian cinema by recognising it as an industry of vital importance and extend it the same facility as are available to other important industries;
(v) To encourage the production of short films, information/documentary, educational and scientific films and provide facilities for their exhibition in schools, colleges and community centres in addition to exhibition through theatrical circuits and harness their potential for social progress;
(vi) To provide all facilities for production, distribution and exhibition and exhibition of children's films in all regions of the country;
(vii) To assist in changing the feature film marketing conditions in a manner which provide a fair opportunity for films of aesthetic excellence and social relevance to reach the audience and at the same time reduce marketing pressures on the box-office oriented film which compel it to operate in a speculative environment;
(vii) To regulate and improve the working conditions of film employees;
(ix) To liberalise policies regarding import of equipment and raw stock in line with the need for modernising the technological base of film industry and simultaneously to provide facilities to undertake research and development for indigenisation of film technology and to keep abreast of the latest developments;
(x) To expand training facilities in the creative and technical aspects of cinema, keeping in view the growth of cinema in

India;

(xi) To ensure that the taxation policies are in line with the general objective of encouraging the growth of cinema and that taxation does not contribute to making the market for cinema uncertain and speculative. This implies that the general strategy of generating tax revenues should aim at horizontal expansion of revenue and not vertical rise in taxation levels; and

(xii) To import films reflecting artistic and technical achievements from all over the world with a view to encourage creative interaction between Indian and international cinema, and to fully exploit the foreign exchange earning potential of Indian films by simplifying the procedure for export by providing expert marketing information and organisational support to exporters and by encouraging co-production with foreign film markets. (Paras 2.24 and 2.25)

Status of Cinema as an Art form (Chapter III)

7. Cinema in India has still not been given the status of a major art form which it rightfully deserves. To promote cinema as an art form, on exclusively non-commercial basis, a separate Akademi to be called the Chalachitra Akademi should be set up. The broad functions of the Akademi have been detailed in para 3.10 of the report. These include holding of National Film Festival, selection of Indian films for participation in International Film Festivals, organisation of India Film Weeks in foreign countries and foreign film weeks in India, operating art theatres and assisting similar art theatres in State Capitals, import of art films for non-commercial exploitation, maintaining a National Film Archive and a National Film Museum, propagation of film culture by helping film society movement, operating a Film Educational Advisory Service for introduction of courses in cinema in the educational curriculum, operating a comprehensive Film Information and Documentation Service, organisation of the Indian Panorama Section of the International Film Festival, promoting research in the history and aesthetics of cinema, giving grants for film making to outstanding film makers and operating a Children's Film Centre. (Paras 3.8 to 3.10)

8. The activities of the Directorate of Film Festivals, except the International Film Festival, should be transferred to the Akademi and the Directorate should be wound up. The International Film Festival should be organised by the NFDC. (Para 3.12)

9. The National Film Archive has to function as a 'living' activity and has to be closely involved with the total gamut of activities suggested for the Chalachitra Akademi. The Archive should, therefore, be brought under the proposed Akademi. (Para 3.15)

10. The Government should undertake legislation to introduce a scheme for a compulsory deposit with the Archive of a video copy of every film made in India on the lines of the compulsory deposit scheme for book trade. (Para 3.16)

11. The Akademi will be an entirely non-commercial organisation which will operate on the basis of a grant from the Government. Its functions will be quite distinct from the functions of NFDC which will have to generate its own resources. (Para 3.17)

12. Import of films for the art circuit and children's films should primarily rest with the Akademi. Such imported films as well as films imported for Film Lending Service, National Art Theatre and Film Archive should be exempted from customs duty. All prints taken out by Akademi should be exempted from excise duty. (Paras 3.18 and 3.19)

13. The NFDC being a financing agency for production of films, will naturally have a special interest in promoting its own films. Therefore, the selection of films for participation in foreign film festivals and for the Indian Panorama Section of our International Film Festival should rest with the Akademi and not the NFDC. (Paras 3.20 and 3.21)

14. The local civic bodies should provide land at subsidised rates to film societies for setting up non-commercial exhibition facilities. (Para 3.25)

15. Central and State Governments should give grants to film societies for purchase of mobile vans for exhibition of films. (3.26)

16. The Federation of Film Societies should set up organisation at State levels for better liaison with State Governments. Grants by Central and State Governments may be given directly to regional or State level organisations of film societies. (Para 3.27)

17. All State Governments should exempt film society shows from entertainment tax, show tax, etc. (Para 3.28)

18. To equip school and college students to develop an interest and a critical attitude towards cinema as an art form, comparable with other arts, courses in film appreciation including film history, technique and rediments of film making should be offered at 10 plus stage and the university level. Short-term courses in film appreciation should be offered from Class VIII onwards, special courses in communication including cinema should be developed at the university level. (Paras

3.32 and 3.33)

19. The Film Educational Advisory Service under the Akademi should help in designing teaching programmes and courses in cinema, trained teachers and provide assistance in making the necessary study material available as is being done by the Educational Advisory Service of the British Film Institute. (Para 3.34)

20. The Film Information and Documentation Centre under the Akademi should bring out a monthly journal directed to film criticism and film appreciation. (Para 3.35)

21. The Akademi should receive a substantial grant from the Central Government. It should have its own office-cum-theatre-complex, with several auditoria and space for Archive, Film Museum, Children's Film Centre and Documentation Centre. (Para 3.36)

22. The organisational structure of the Akademi will have to be decided after careful consideration and should provide for active participation of film makers, technicians, film writers and film specialists. As the Akademi grows, it should establish Regional Centres in the major film producing States. State Governments should also set up Chalachitra Akademies with art theatres and branches of National Film Archive at the State level. (Paras 3.37 and 3.38).

Production System (Chapter IV)

23. Film industry as a whole, including the production sector should be recognised as an industry and should be treated on par with atleast the hotel industry for various facilities. (Para 4.22)

24. To free the producers from the clutches of financiers which indirectly adversely affects the quality of films, institutional finance through banks should be given on a fairly large scale for film production. Preference should be given to low budget films. (Para 4.23)

25. The NFDC should concentrate on its specific responsibility of financing good quality and artistic films. Artistic films should be given loan on liberal terms with low rates of interest. Conditions of collateral security should be relaxed and financial allocation should be considerably increased. (Para 4.24)

26. Regulation of film production is necessary only to the extent that there is need to discourage the entry of adventures in film production, to ensure proper pre-planning and to prevent wastage of raw stock in inadequately planned projects. We are definitely against any measures involving prior scrutiny of scripts and pervasive control on

the actual process of film making. We recommend that all film producers should be registered with the NFDC. While allocating raw stock the NFDC should take into account the previous production record of the producer, the state of planning including availability of script, financial plan, actual shooting schedule and signed contracts along with clear indication regarding the availability of dates for main artists and technicians. (Para 4.30, 4.31 and 4.32)

27. All producers should submit a return to the NFDC on completion of film indicating the actual expense on the negative cost of the film. (Para 4.33)

28. The Central and the State Governments and their film development agencies should encourage the formation of film cooperatives. The cooperatives should get preference for loans and other assistance for film making and for setting up production facilities. (Para 4.34)

29. Big budget films indulge in extravagant expenditure are even take pride in this factor. It is necessary that the film industry should recognise the need for operating a sensible budget. (Para 4.36)

Distribution and Exhibition System (Chapter V)

30. An indepth investigation into the system of theatre contractors in cities and towns should be undertaken by the concerned authorities under the MRTP Act. (Para 5.12)

31. The highly speculative nature of the film business is largely on account of the pressures of an unregulated distribution system. An executive division under the Department of Cinema should undertake compulsory licensing of distributors through an appropriate legislative enactment. (Paras 5.14 and 5.16)

32. To discourage saturation release of film, Government should lay down maximum limits of theatres for simultaneous release of films in various centres and also excise duty should be steeply raised beyond 80 prints. (Paras 5.17 and 5.18)

33. Distribution territories should be recognised on a more rational basis, ideally on Statewise basis. (Para 5.19)

34. We strongly feel that increasing the number of cinemas in the country is a matter of urgent necessity, requiring immediate attention on the part of the Government. (Para 5.22)

35. The theatre licensing rules should look at cinema theatres as a place of cultural activity rather than a cause of public nuisance. The

following broad changes in the licensing policy for theatres should made: (i) Detailed conditions applicable to the building of a cinema theatre should be removed from the licensing condition and theatres should adhere to the standard rules applicable to buildings for public assembly. Theatre licence should be based only on a few conditions necessary for proper viewing environment, (ii) Multiple theatres at one place and construction of theatres as part of commercial complexes should be encouraged particularly in major cities; (iii) There should be no condition as to the minimum size of plot; (iv) Building rules should not insist upon liberal parking space; (v) Requirements of fire safety should be revised, as now only safety base films are used; (vi) New theatres of 500 capacity should be eligible for almost automatic licensing for a period of five years; and (vii) Licence once issued should be normally valid for five years. (Paras 5.26 to 5.27)

36. The Central Government should formulate the broad policy parameters for licensing of theatres to be adopted with suitable modifications in all parts of the country. (Para 5.29)

37. Institutional finance through banks and public financial institutions should be made available on a liberal scale for theatre construction. Locational survey for selection of sites for theatres should be done on a scientific basis. (Para 5.31)

38. We suggest the following broad strategy for speeding up theatre construction: (i) Adopting a target construction of 6750 additional theatres by 1985; (ii) The approach should be to provide theatres of 4 to 5 hundred capacity; (iii) Construction and operation of theatres should be recognised as an industrial activity for provision of institutional finance; (iv) Priority treatment for theatre construction on the same lines as given to hotel industryl; (v) Amendment of IDBI Act, 1964 for refinancing theatre construction; (vi) Preference for 16 mm theatres; (vii) Encouragement of open air or semi-permanent theatres; (viii) Special incentives as available to industries in backward areas; (ix) Rural bias for theatre construction; and (x) Inclusion of theatres in town planning schemes and encouragement of travelling/touring theatres. (Para 5.32)

39. Entertainment tax incentives for theatre construction should provide that (i) All new permanent or semi-permanent theatres in rural and semi-urban areas with a population of 25,000 or less should be completely exempted from entertainment tax for five years; (ii) In case of urban centres of more than 25,000 and upto 50,000 population, new theatres should be given entertainment tax exemption upto 50 per cent

for five years; (iii) In case an existing theatre owner undertakes the construction of a new theatre in semi-urban or rural areas of upto 25,000 population, 1/4th of the total entertainment tax collected from his existing theatre for one year subject to a maximum of Rs. 1 lakh should be refunded to him as grant; and (iv) All new theatres with projection facilities in 16 mm should be completely exempted from entertainment tax for five years, irrespective of their location. The exemption should apply to projection in 16 mm only. (Para 5.33)

40. NFDC should take initiative in standardising low cost theatre designs which can be straight away adopted by new entrepreneurs. For rationalising approach towards theatre construction two basic considerations should be kept in view, i.e., mass production based on modular designs and the use of non-formal technology based on local conditions and materials. (Paras 5.34 and 5.35)

41. Formation of theatre cooperatives should be encouraged and these should receive the same preferential treatment as other industrial cooperatives, particularly in the small sector. (Para 5.36)

42. Award winning films in regional languages do not get a national telecast. Doordarshan should arrange to obtain sub-titled prints from producers by paying the cost of sub-titling and make use of sub-titled prints available with the Directorate of Film Festivals. It should use simultaneous character generation techniques during transmission of films and para-dubbing for TV centres meant for rural areas. (Para 5.39)

43. TV offers a very promising outlet for good films which has not been utilised in India. Doordarshan should provide a viable non-theatrical circuit for low budget good quality films. It should be obligatory for Doordarshan to telecast award winning films on all India circuit. Rates of payment for telecasting films should be suitably enhanced. (Para 5.40)

44. Fees for telecast of regional films outside the linguistic zone should be substantially raised. Sub-titled films should be paid at the same rate as Hindi-films. (Para 5.41)

45. Doordarshan should commission making for feature and short films particularly suited for the TV medium. (Para 5.42)

46. Award winning films should be purchased in preference by Armed Forces Organisations, External Publicity Division, Field Publicity Units and Health and Family Welfare Units of Central and State Governments for non-commercial exploitation. (Para 5.44)

47. While giving loans for theatre construction, 25 per cent option

on playing time should be obtained by financing agencies for screening good films. (Para 5.46)

48. Government should acquire, lease or construct one or two small size theatres in important cities and towns for exhibition of good films. (Para 5.47)

Film Technology and Raw Stock (Chapter VI)

49. The Working Group had constituted a separate Study Group on Film Technology. The report of this Study Group should be treated as part of the main report. (Para 6.1)

50. In view of the surplus availability of studio capacity the Government or its agencies should not construct more studios, particularly requiring heavy investment. Instead, the State Film Development Corporations should provide financial assistance for modernisation of existing studios, set up mobile shooting facilities and assist entrepreneurs and film cooperatives for setting up similar facilities. (Para 6.3)

51. Indigenous availability of lighting equipment is generally adequate. However, the import of bulbs and sophisticated dollies should be liberalised. (Para 6.4)

52. Movie cameras available in the country are in unsatisfactory condition. The import of cameras with suitable lenses should be liberalised and maintenance facilities for cameras should be set up. Import of reconditioned cameras should be encouraged. (Para 6.5)

53. There is a shortage of professional sound equipment both of portable and studio variety. The import of this equipment should be liberalised. Some import of 1/4" magnetic tape should be allowed as the indigenous tape is not of professional quality. (Para 6.6.)

54. Inexpensive dubbing theatres of the type established by the Chitralekha Film Cooperative at Trivandrum should be set up which will release sophisticated recording theatres for music recording. Import of equipment for moderning existing recording theatres should be liberalised and the use of crystal motors mounted on cameras should be encouraged. (Para 6.7)

55. Import duties should be reduced on certain sophisticated sound equipments which are not suitable for indigenisation. (Para 6.8)

56. HPF should take up manufacture of sprocketed magnetic tape and consider production of magnetically striped film. (Para 6.9)

57. To encourage indigenous manufacture of editing equipment,

financial support to entrepreneurs should be provided and import of certain component should be permitted. (Para 6.10)

58. There is need to set-up a colour lab in Hyderabad. The proposal of the Films Division for a colour lab in Bombay should be re-examined taking into account the existing availability of lab facilities in Bombay. In the first instance only setting up 16 mm colour lab with direct blow up facility should be considered. (Para 6.12)

59. There is need to improve the technical standards in the labs. Government should insist that labs provide their own generators. Existing labs should be modernised and proposed labs in public sector should provide for latest technology. Existing manufacturers of processing machines in India should be encouraged to take up manufacture of sophisticated colour plants. (Paras 6.13, 6.14 and 6.15)

60. Considerable amount of silver is discharged in the chemical wash during processing of films. About 8 to 10 crores, of Rupees worth of silver per year can be recovered from the chemical bath. It should be compulsory for all labs to set up silver recovery plants. Films Division lab in Delhi should also provide for a silver recovery plant. Standards of silver recovery should be laid down after scientific investigation. Recovered silver should be handed over to HPF and the labs should be reimbursed only the processing cost of silver recovery. HPF should pay an equivalent amount into a Film Development Fund to be set up by the Central Government. Alternatively benefit of recovered silver should be passed on to the producers by reducing the price of HPF raw stock. (Paras 6.16 to 6.18)

61. Films Division should set up a plant for recovery of silver from waste film. (Para 6.19)

62. The norms for wastage allowance of raw stock for labs, recommended by the Expert Committee set up by the Government, should be quickly implemented. (Para 6.20)

63. The sector of labs needs to be regulated from the viewpoint of quality assurance proper raw stock management, elimination of unauthorised prints, prevention of excise evasion and proper accountal of silver recovery. A proper system of licensing for labs should be introduced through the Department of Cinema. This Department should be assisted by a Monitoring Committee of technicians which should undertake periodic checks of labs to ensure quality performance. (Para 6.22)

64. A public sector corporation should be asked to take up development and manufacture of 35 mm and 16 mm projectors in addi-

tion to the present manufacturers. (Para 6.24)

65. There should be a switch over from are carbons to Halogen or Xenon lamps for projectors, which can be developed by the Central Electronics Ltd. Ghaziabad. (Para 6.25)

66. Entire requirement of theatre sound equipment can be met indigenously and no import should be allowed. (Para 6.26)

67. To maintain proper standards of projection, there should be a Standing Committee of independent technicians in every State. The members of this Committee should carry out surprise inspection and report their findings to the State Government. Facilities for training of projectionists employed in theatres should be set up by the local film industry (Exhibitors' Association) either independently or in collaboration with the State Government. (Para 6.27)

68. Cinema today reaches primarily literate audience, therefore, sub-titling is the appropriate technology. A couple of entrepreneurs should be allowed to import modern sub-titling equipment. The possibility of handing over the sub-titling machine lying with the FTII to some private organisation should be explored. (Paras 6.28 and 6.29)

69. The Films Division should take up sub-titling of documentary films or fiction type short films and NFDC of feature length films. The State Film Development Corporations should develop sub-titling technology in the languages of their own regions. (Para 6.30)

70. The organisational and management set up of the HPF should be redesigned on the lines of a corporate structure and segregation of activities into different business groups. (Para 6.33)

71. Immediate action should be taken to set up facilities for manufacture of colour raw stock indigenously. (Para 6.34)

72. NFDC should develop a scientific method for estimating the requirements of raw stock annually as also on a long-term basis. Para 6.35)

73. Import of raw stock under REP licences should be allowed even of the type which is manufactured by HPF and also by producers of award winning films. (Para 6.36)

74. HPF should be brought under the Ministry of Information and Broadcasting instead of Ministry of Industries, as the film industry is the major consumer of HPF products. (6.38)

75. The overall capability demonstrated by even current levels of achievement for indigenous manufacture of film equipment is extremely promising. Financial assistance should be provided to the entrepreneurs by the State Governments, the Central Government and

the NFDC to encourage indigenisation. (Paras 6.39 and 6.40)

76. The 16 mm is the appropriate technology from the view-point of cost, flexibility, need to expand exhibition outlets in semi-urban and rural areas, etc. There are serious gaps in the availability of this technology in India in regard to cameras, re-recording and mixing facilities, processing and blow up facilities, as also projection equipment. The Government should provide all facilities for development of complete infrastructure for making and exhibition of films in 16mm. For this purpose there should be a complete customs holiday for a period of two years for import of 16 mm equipment without customs duty and without import licence. (Paras 6.42 and 6.43)

77. A strategy similar to 16 mm should be adopted for development of complete infrastructure for Super 8 production/reduction and exhibition. (Para 6.45)

78. Video technology has tremendous potential for use in formal education, social education, developmental communication and for making film production more professional and economical. Import of video equipment should be initially allowed for educational institutions, film makers, field publicity units and other specialised agencies involved in community and rural development programmes. Indigenisation of this technology should be considered subsequently. (Paras 6.46 to 6.48)

79. Government should consider granting a complete customs holiday for a limited period of one or two years to import any film equipment which is not manufactured in the country or where the Indian equipment in not of international standard. Since film technology is not an item of mass consumption, the overall requirement of foreign exchange will not be very high. (Para 6.50)

80. A list of items which are being currently manufactured in the country and a list of items which can be taken up for development and manufacture is given in Annexures III and IV of the Report on Film Technology. (Para 6.51)

81. Two separate centres for Research and Development of Film Technology should be established and located in two of the most prolific film making regions of the country. (Para 6.52)

82. For promoting research and development in the area of film technology, a three-tier structure is recommended: (i) A Film Technology Monitoring Cell under the Ministry of I and B; (ii) Two Centres of Film technology; and (iii) Financial and technological support to individual entrepreneurs. Import of latest equipment should continue to

be permitted until the locally producced technology has been marketed and comes up to international standards. (Para 6.53)

82. To keep Indian film makers abreast of the latest developments, an International Cinema Equipment Exhibition should be organised along with India's International Film Festival. This should also help in the export of Indian film equipment. (Para 6.54)

84. All studios, including dubbing theatres and recording theatres, mobile shooting units and equipment hirers should be registered with the NFDC. This will help to monitor overall availability of facilities and also facilitate sponsoring import applications. (Para 6.57)

Taxation Policy (Chapter VII)

85. In formulating entertainment tax policy the following objective should be kept in view:

(i) To encourage construction of small theatres of about 500 seats, preferably with 16 mm projection facility, particularly in semi-urban and rural areas;
(ii) To levy tax keeping in view the capacity to pay;
(iii) To help in the wider circulation of good quality artistic films and children's films;
(iv) To rationalise tax rates and simplify procedures; and
(v) To increase income by expanding theatre network and not by increasing rate of entertainment tax. (Para 7.10)

86. An all inclusive entertainment tax rate should be fixed and no additional taxes such as surcharge, additional surcharge, municipal show tax, etc., should be levied. This all inclusive entertainment tax should be 20, 30, 50, 75 and 100 per cent on basic admission rates of upto Re. 1, Rs. 2, Rs. 3, Rs. 4 and more than Rs. 4 respectively. (Para 7.12)

87. There should be a statutory provision that all theatres should provide at least 20 per cent of the seats in the lowest class or tickets and not more than 20 per cent of the seats in the highest class. (Para 7.14)

88. We strongly recommend that the compounding system of entertainment tax should be adopted in all States for semi-permanent and mobile theatres and for permanent theatres in towns upto 50,000 populations. (Para 7.17)

89. All National and State Award winning films, 'Q' certificate films and children's films should be permanently exempted from entertainment tax instead of exempting them only for a limited period. In granting exemption there should be no insistence to reduce the basic admission rates, except to the extent of excluding entertainment tax. (Para 7.18)

90. All theatres run by the Chalachitra Akademi, the State Film Akademies or any other body specifically devoted to the promotion of cinema as an art form should be permanently exempted from entertainment tax. (Para 7.19)

91. The rates of entertainment tax should in no case be discriminatory on the basis of 'U' or 'A' nature of the Censor Certificate or on the basis of a film being in black and white or in colour. (Para 7.20)

92. We support the recommendation made by the earlier Committees that 10 per cent of the entertainment tax should be earmarked for the development of the film industry. (Para 7.21)

93. There should be no separate show tax or local tax in addition to an all inclusive entertainment tax. State may share a part of their receipts with the local bodies. (Para 7.22)

94. A downward revision of excise duty on prints should be undertaken. In such a revision the following points should be kept in view:

(i) The number of exempted prints should be increased from 12 to 20;

(ii) Excise duty on additional prints should be fixed on slabs of 20 prints and the rates should be kept low upto 80 prints. The rates should be steeply raised for more than 80 prints which will be only required by big budget films;

(iii) The enhanced exemption limit of 20 prints should operate irrespective of the period within which the prints are taken out. The rule of charging low rates of excise duty after one year should apply only for more than 20 prints;

(iv) Difference in the rate of excise duty on colour prints and black and white prints should be reduced by bringing down the excise on colour prints;

(v) To promote good quality artistic films, the prints of National and State Award winning films should be exempted from excise duty;

(vi) Prints of films with 'Q' certificate should be charged duty at 50 per cent of the normal rate;

(vii) All prints of 16 mm and smaller formats should be exempted from excise duty;

(viii) The principle of levying higher rates of excise duty on prints of more than 4000 feet length should be retained to discourage production of unduly long films; and

(ix) All prints required by the National Film Archive, the Central and the State Akademies and the Children's Film Centres should be exempted from excise duty. (Para 7.26)

95. As a general principle all short films except advertisement films and trailers should be exempted from excise duty on prints. If for some reason this basic change in principle is not acceptable, at least short films which are approved for compulsory release should be completely exempted from excise duty. (Para 7.29)

96. As suggested in the case of 16 mm feature films, prints of 16 mm short films, except advertisement films and trailers, should be exempted from excise duty. (Para 7.30)

97. All Short films/non-fiction films produced or sponsored by educational and cultural institutions, scientific and training establishments, research organisations, etc., which may not be meant for theatrical circulation should be exempted from excise duty whether made in 35 mm or 16 mm. (Para 7.31)

98. Excise duty on film equipment manufactured in India ranges from 25 to 40 per cent and is quite reasonable. Excise exemption of 16 mm and smaller projectors should continue. (Para 7.32)

99. There should be a customs holiday for import of any film equipment not manufactured in India for at least one or two years and particularly a customs holiday for all 16 mm equipment for a period of two years for building of 16 mm infrastructure. This will mean exemption from customs and permission to import on OGL basis. (Para 7.35)

100. On a general consideration the overall rates of customs duty on film equipment should not exceed 40 per cent. (Para 7.36)

101. There is a case for reduction of customs duty on jumbo rolls as excise duty is again charged on this raw stock when prints of films are taken out. (Para 7.37)

102. Art films for non-commercial exploitation and children's films should be exempted from customs. Customs exemption for films imported by the National Film Archive should continue. (Para) 7.38

103. Deduction of a percentage of the capital employed in new industries for income-tax purposes, as admissible for other industries, should be extended to the film Industry. (Para 7.40)

104. Income-tax rebate by way of investment allowance or development allowance on 25 per cent of the cost on new machinery, as given to other industries, should be given to all sectors of the film industry. (Para 7.41)

105. Fully paid annuity policies are now taken into account for wealth-tax assessment. Perhaps a better approach would be to add the annual premium equivalent of the annuity policy to the taxable income of the concerned artiste/technician and exempt the policy from wealth-tax. (Para 7.43)

Short Films (Chapter VIII)

106. For effective use of film medium for development, the film making activity of the Films Division should be decentralised. The film making process and the film maker should be brought closer to the people at the grassroot level where developmental activities are taking place. (Para 8.11)

107. The overall role of the Films Division as a producer of short films should be redefined. Films Division should be converted into an organisation of facilities which should be made available for short film making in all the regions. Almost the entire production of short films should be assigned by the Films Division to independent film makers. The existing personnel of the Films Division should be diverted to specialised tasks such as need assessment studies identification of projects, collection of information, preparation of an outline and estimates and collection of feed-back information. (Paras 8.21 and 8.22)

108. The panel of film makers maintained by the Films Division should be enlarged and made more representative. (Para 8.23)

109. The rates of payment for independent film makers engaged by the Films Division should be re-fixed on a realistic basis taking into account the time value of the talent employed. The cost of films should be determined by negotiations and the tender system should be abolished. (Para 8.24)

110. In drawing up the annual production programme, people involved in developmental activities and film makers should be activity involved. A proper need assessment organisation under the Films Division should be created, which should undertake research in regard to

the needs of not only the urban theatrical audience but more so for the rural audience. For such studies help of Field Publicity Units, University Extension Services and the research theses available in the universities should be taken. (Para 8.25)

111. The annual production programme should be widely advertised and made available to organisations of film makers. (Para 8.26)

112. The present attitude of mainly relying upon suggestions from various Ministries for designing production programme should end. If specific Ministries insist upon making films to met their own needs, the cost of production should be borne by the concerned Ministries. (Para 8.27)

113. There should be in an audience Research Cell in the Films Division for continuously monitoring reaction to its own films. This should be an addition to the periodic evaluation being done by the Department of Evaluation Studies. (Para 8.28)

114. The number of short films being produced by the Films Division should be substantially increased and specially localised films meant for the rural audience for circulation through non-commercial circuits. The number of prints per film may be reduced. Most subjects of immediate rural concern cannot be treated effectively in films designed for national release. (Para 8.29)

115. For making films for the rural audience appropriate technology such as 16 mm or Super 8 should be employed. (Para 8.30)

116. Films Division should opt for a genuine federal structure and production branches, along with production facilities should be set up in all the regions where film making talent is available. These branches should have the authority to engage local talent for film making without referring to the Head Office. (Para 8.31)

117. Available time of 20 minutes in theatrical circuits should be fully utilised. Licensing rules should require that the approved film is shown immediately before the feature film. (Para 8.32)

118. The Central Field Publicity set up should be vastly expanded and closely coordinated with the State set up. The State Government should pay for the cost of prints supplied by the Films Division. (Para 8.33)

119. Exhibition outlets exclusively devoted for screening of short films at railway stations and bus terminals should be set up and the outlets of educational institutions and factories should be fully utilised. (Para 8.34)

120. The major expansion of developmental communication in fu-

ture is likely to be through television. There should be close coordination between the Films Division and the Doordarshan for production of films and TV features for rural audience. The Films Division should also make short films particularly suited for telecast. (Para 8.35)

121. The overall style and format of documentary films should change from a single language commentary and greater use of dialogues should be made. For this purpose Films Division should switch over to sub-titling of dialogues of films in regional languages for different circuits rather than relying upon single language commentary. (Para 8.36)

122. The Films Division should continue to make films of sensitive nature for the Ministry of Defence and the Ministry of External Affairs. It should also make specialised films which require long period of observation. (Para 8.37)

123. Films Division should change over from Weekly News Review to Weekly News Magazine. It should treat topical items in depth as is done in feature articles in newspapers. Features on contemporary subjects from film makers should be incorporated in New Magazines. (Para 8.38)

124. Immediate steps should be taken by the Films Division to develop expertise for the production of scientific and educational films in collaboration with educational and scientific establishments. A Research Cell should be created which should assess the requirements of films for educational institutions. (Para 8.39)

125. Films Division should create necessary infrastructure for experimentation and development of animation and analogous technology, acquire the latest equipment and train personnel in this technology. (Para 8.40)

126. The functions of film Advisory Board should be merged with the Censor Board. (Para 8.41)

127. The scope of the scheme for compulsory exhibition of films should be enlarged to include all types of artistic short films, films of social relevance and even short fiction films. (Para 8.42)

128. Apart from the role of short films as medium of conveying social message, its status as a creative art form should be recognised. The purchase of short films from independent film makers by the Films Division should be increased and should cover not only message oriented films but all categories of artistic short films. (Para 8.43)

Children's Films (Chapter IX)

129. After surveying the work done by the Children's Film Society (CFS) and the present state of children's films in India the Group feels that the children's film movement cannot grow in isolation and should be brought under a much larger central organisation, with parallel organisations at the State level such as the Chalachitra Akademi. The Akademi should set up and operate a Children's Film Centre and similar Centres should be set up under the State Akademies at State level. (Paras 9.11 and 9.12)

130. The Centre under the Central Chalachitra Akademi should not directly produce children's films but should aim at promoting the production, distribution and exhibition of children's films. It should undertake research into the requirements of films for Indian children and help to expand the scope of this genre. It should import films for children, export and exchange children's films with other countries, and undertake sub-titling of children's films in regional languages including foreign films in Indian languages. (Paras 9.13 and 9.14)

131. The Centre should hold a separate annual Children's Film Festival and Children's International Film Festival periodically. The Akademi should provide for a separate section in the Documentation Centre and the National Films Archive devoted to children's films. (Para 9.15)

132. The Centre under the Central Akademi should maintain an extensive lending library of films which should be made available to the Centres in the State Akademies, schools, colleges and other organisations involved with children's activities. It should run regular shows for children at its own theatres as also be hiring outside auditoria. (Para 9.16)

133. The Children's Film Centres should work in close coordination with educational agencies, distinguished people engaged in the non-formal education and creative people from all over the country. It should resist exclusive involvement with urbanisation and should not be allowed to be monopolised by socialites. The Centre should run primarily on the basis of a grant from the Government but should supplement its resources from the distribution and exhibition activity. (Para 9.17)

134. It is impossible for any single organisation to reach a significant section of the children population. Therefore, every State should set up Children's Film Centre under the State Film Akademies.

For this purpose Central Government should give a matching grant to the State Governments. The Chalachitra Akademi should have the right to nominate an agreed percentage of members on the Management Committees of the State Children's Film Centres. (Paras 9.18 and 9.19)

135. The State level Centres should perform all activities indicated for the Centre under the Chalachitra Akademi except import, export and preservation of films. State Centres should undertake production of children's films by assigning films to independent film makers and by involving people from different fields who are connected with children's activities. (Paras 9.20 and 9.21)

136. The Children's Films Centres should maintain film equipment to give participative demonstration and for recording feed-back of children's reactions to the films. (Para 9.22)

137. Children's Films Centre should be screened in special auditoria attached in the Centres. However, generally the films would have to be taken to the schools and screened in consultation with the school authorities. For this purpose, the Centre should have mobile projection vans. (Para 9.23)

138. TV offers tremendous potential for the exhibition of children's films. Children's Film Centres should coordinate with the television for production of children's films suited for telecasting and the Government should give directions to TV for providing greater exposure to children's films. (Para 9.24)

139. For reaching non-school going children in the villages, exhibition facilities available with Field Publicity Units of the Central and State Governments, voluntary and semi-Government organisations engaged in children's fields should be utilised. (Paras 9.25)

140. Considering the exhibition outlets, children's films should be primarily produced in 16 mm format. (Para 9.26)

141. There should be no excise duty, entertainment tax, show tax or any other local tax on the shows of children's films. Exemption should be automatic on the Censor Board classifying a film as "children's film". (Para 9.27)

142. The Children's Films Society should be wound up and its activity should be transferred to the proposed Centre under the Akademi. This Centre should be located at Delhi. The project for setting up a children's complex, including the studio in Bombay, under the CPS, should be immediately stopped. (Para 9.28)

Import and Export of Films (Chapter X)

143. The basic policy objective of importing films should be to import films of artistic and technical achievements from all over the world. A secondary objective should be to allow import to the extent it is linked with export of Indian films. (Para 10.2)

144. (i) Import canalisation of feature films should continue and NFDC should remain the canalising agency. A limited quota of imported films should be given to exporters or producer-exporters to import films from the countries to which Indian films are exported;

(ii) There should be an overall limit on the number of films to be imported. The films being imported from MPEAA sources should be substantially reduced and the import by NFDC and other agencies from other film making countries, including the Third World, should be increased;

(iii) Quality considerations should apply to the import of all films. Government should constitute a Screening Committee consisting of film makers, film critics, representatives of Chalachitra Akademi, NFDC, Censor Board, and Ministry of I&B to preview films before import;

(iv) Import of art films for non-commercial exploitation and import of children's films should be primarily handled by the Chalachitra Akademi; and

(v) The NFDC should continue to collect canalising charges on imported films except on non-commercial art films and children's films imported by the Chalachitra Akademi and its agencies. The canalising fee should be levied not on the C.I.F. value but on the market value of imported films. (Para 10.11)

145. The NFDC should obtain TV exhibition rights for India on an option basis while importing films. (Para 10.12)

146. There should be no customs duty on import of art films by the Chalachitra Akademi, the National Film Archive and also NFDC in case NFDC also imports films exclusively for non-commercial circulation. (Para 10.13)

147. Free import of short films under OGL should continue. (Para 10.14)

148. The policy objective for export of Indian films should be to fully exploit the foreign exchange earning potential. There is no need for special censorship for export of films. (Paras 10.16 and 10.17)

149. Canalisation of export of Indian feature films should continue as it has reduced malpractices, helped to monitor export markets and

resulted in increasing the sale price per film. (Para 10.19)

150. In addition to being a canaliser of export, the main function of NFDC should be promotion of exports. For this purpose NFDC should set up Regional Marketing Centres in important foreign markets for Indian films which should handle both import of foreign films and export of Indian films. These Centres should be staffed by a specialised cadre and provide help and advice to Indian exporters. (Para 10.22)

151. The Regional Marketing Centres of NFDC should enter the field of exhibition in some important countries such as U.K., Indonesia and Latin America to create a regular show window of Indian cinema. Indian exporters and producers should be encouraged to operate theatres in foreign countries. (Para 10.23)

152. NFDC should create facilities in India for quality sub-titling in foreign languages to provide sub-titled prints of Indian films for export. (Para 10.24)

153. Co-productions with foreign countries should be encouraged and procedural restrictions should be simplified. A fixed foreign exchange allowance per member of the film unit should be given for shooting abroad. (Para 10.25)

154. For exploitation of TV outlets abroad it is necessary to concentrate on the artistic films from India. NFDC should help to prepare shorter versions of such films which can fit into TV slots. Export contracts should have a separate clause providing for additional payment if TV rights are exploited. (Para 10.26)

155. In addition to the Films Division, NFDC should also export short films which have a huge market on the foreign TV circuits. (Para 10.27)

156. A small inter-ministerial committee should examine the existing export procedures for films with a view to simplifying the same. (Para 10.28)

157. The additional commission levied by the NFDC for direct export of films should be reduced from 15 per cent to 10 per cent. In case of territories exclusively handled by NFDC, third party deals should be under-written by levying a commission of 5 per cent in addition to canalisation charges. (Para 10.29)

158. The opportunity offered by India's International Film Festival for promoting export of Indian films should be properly utilised. Market Section should provide support facilities for marketing of Indian films by independent exporters. The expenditure of the Market Section should be met from the canalisation charges collected by the

NFDC. (Para 10.30)

159. To promote the export of regional films, NFDC should set up full-fledged in film making regions with full authority to clear contracts for export. (Para 10.31)

160. The sale of video right for foreign buyers along with the export of Indian films should be allowed. NFDC should itself set up a pilot plant for transferring Indian feature films to video cassettes for export. In addition one or two manufacturers should be licensed for manufacture of video cassettes of Indian films exclusively for export. (Para 10.34)

Promotional Activities of the Central Government (Chapter XI)

161. We envisage that a complete review of the National Film Awards scheme will be under-taken once this activity is transferred to the Akademi. In the intervening period action should be taken on the following lines to make the Awards scheme more attractive:

(i) The National Awards for Children's Films should be held separately so that the children's films receive proper national attention. The number of awards should be expanded to include Best Educational Film for Children, best Original Story Idea for Children's Film, the Best Music Score for Children's Film and the Best Short Film for Children. In view of the present shortage of films for children the cash award should be substantially increased;

(ii) The Award for the Best Feature Film with Mass Appeal, Wholesome Entertainment and Aesthetic Value should be replaced by an Award for the Second Best Feature Film. Awards for Best Feature Film on National Integration and Best Playback Singers should be discontinued;

(ii) The value of cash awards for the Best Feature Film, Second Best Feature Film and Best Regional Films should be substantially raised;

(iv) A new award for the First Feature Film of a Director should be introduced;

(v) Cash value of the awards for individual distinction should be of the same as for Best Acting and Best Music Direction;

(vi) There should be a separate Jury Award to cover any special distinction which may not be covered by the scheme of awards;

(vii) The Award for the Best Sound Recording should be re-designated as the Award for Best Audiography and should be shared by the Recordist and Re-recordist;

(viii) While giving the Award for the Best Cinematography, a Certificate of Merit should be given to the concerned laboratory; and

(ix) In case of short films, the cash award to the Producer and the Director should be the same and the award money should be suitably increased. (Para 11.4)

162. The Jury for feature and short films should be drawn from people who are exclusively concerned with cinema. In the Jury for short films, an educationist should be included in view of the award for the Best Educational Film. The Jury should be constituted well in advance of the screenings. (Para 11.5)

163. Effort should be made to take full advantage of Cultural Agreements with foreign countries and the number of Film Weeks being organised in India and abroad should be substantially increased. Foreign film delegations should be brought in contact with the Indian film makers. Indian film makers should be included in the delegations which accompany Indian films to be presented as Film Weeks in foreign countries. (Para 11.7)

164. A proper machinery for ensuring prompt return of prints should be set up. This should be the specific responsibility of the official who accompanies the delegation. Help of the Indian Missions abroad should be effectively enlisted. (Para 11.8)

165. Regional Selection Panels for selection of films for foreign film festivals should be discontinued and all the offered films should be scrutinised by the Central Panel. (Paras 11.9 and 11.10)

166. Participation in foreign film festivals should be considerably increased. A careful short-listing of important film festivals, specialised film festivals and others should be done. The Central Panel should recommend films only for important general category festivals. Apart from the official entry, producers should be free to send their films to any festival. (Para 11.11)

167. It should be the specific responsibility of the agency sponsoring Indian films in foreign festivals to actively promote works of lesser known film makers, so that the number of internationally known Indian film makers gradually expands. (Para 11.12)

168. Participation of Indian film makers and exporters in foreign film festivals at their own expenses should be encouraged. The number

of civil servants going with official delegations should be reduced. (Para 11.13)

169. The Competitive International Film Festival of India does not provide any intrinsic advantage in terms of quality of films, promotion of Indian cinema, interaction between film makers, etc., over a non-competitive film festival. Even third world countries prefer to send their best films to competitive festivals in the West. India should, therefore, hold only a non-competitive film festival every year on the lines of a 'Festival of Festivals'. Within this concept, a more systematic effort should be made to provide for a strong Third World representation. (Paras 11.14 to 11.16)

170. The market forum of the International Film Festival should be systematically used to promote the export of Indian films. The NFDC should purchase most of the imported films through the market. Third party deals in the market should be promoted. (Para 11.17)

171. Selections films for the Indian Panorama should be done by the same Central Panel which selects films for participation in foreign film festivals. Until the Akademi becomes operational, the responsibility for putting together the Indian Panorama should continue to rest with the Directorate of Film Festivals. (Para 11.18)

172. In addition to the Panorama of artistic films there should be a separate Market Panorama. This should be organised with adequate publicity and fanfare by the NFDC with the film industry. (Para 11.19)

173. The Festival should provide a good standard of hospitality to delegates but the 5-star concept should be given up. The number of Indian and foreign delegates should be increased and admission rates to theatres should be kept low. Festivals everywhere run at a loss and receive financial help. Indian Festival should also receive financial support from the Government or the NFDC. Festival should be organised by the NFDC as already recommended in Chapter III. Para 11.20 to 11.22)

174. As already suggested in Chapter VI, there should be a Film Equipment Bazaar in our International Film Festival which should display the film equipment available in foreign countries as also the equipment manufactured in India. (Para 11.23)

175. In organising the International Film Festival, NFDC must involve all sectors of the Indian film industry and organisations like the Chalachitra Akademi. (Para 11.24)

176. There is need for a number of specialised International Film Festivals in addition to an annual major event, such as International

Children's Film Festival, International/Festival for Short Films, specialised market film festivals and Film Weeks. (Para 11.25)

National Film Development Corporation (NFDC) (Chapter XII)

177. The overall chapter of the NFDC should be to help in the general development of the film industry and to particularly help in the development of good cinema in the country. NFDC should be a financially viable organisation but because of its developmental role, the should not aim at profit maximisation. (Para 12.7)

178. NFDC should specifically undertake the following activities:

(i) Financing of low budget good quality films and production of films of high artistic intent by commissioning deserving film makers;
(ii) Development of distribution and exhibition facilities for films which it finances as also other good films;
(iii) Financing of theatre construction preferably small theatres equipped with 16 mm, with lien on a part of the playing time and directly owning or managing theatres wherever advisable and necessary;
(iv) Registration of producers, studios, and equipment hirers;
(v) Encourage formation of film cooperatives for film production and exhibition;
(vi) Canalising import of films, direct import of good quality films;
(vii) Canalising export of films, research in export market, development of non-traditional markets, general promotion of export of films, special attention to the export of low budget good quality films in regional languages and export of short films;
(viii) Represent technology and equipment requirements of the industry to the Government and sponsor applications for import of equipment without canalisation. It should continue to canalise import of raw stock and regulate its distribution;
(ix) Financial assistance to entrepreneurs engaged in indigenisation and manufacture of him equipment;
(x) Development of sub-titling facilities for Indian films in foreign languages and foreign films in Indian languages;
(xi) Loans for setting up and modernisation of studios, labs and other allied facilities;
(xii) Coordination with State Film Development Corporations;

(xiii) Helping the growth of proper representative organisations/ associations of film industry; and

(xiv) Organisation of the International Film Festival of India and also specialised festivals for short films and marketing of films. (Para 12.8)

179. The Management Board of the NFDC should consist of 50 per cent of the Directors drawn from the representatives of the Central and the State Governments and the remaining 50 per cent to be drawn from the film industry. The latter should include adequate representation to film makers and technician who are generally identified with artistic cinema. (Para 12.9)

180. NFDC must opt for a genuine federal structure and set up proper regional organisations with specific fund allocation and clear authority for decision-making. For this purpose the Board of Management should function in important film making regions. (Para 12.10)

Promotional Activities of the State Governments (Chapter XIII)

181. Though a large number of States are involved in film promotional activities, there is a general lack of clear strategy and well defined perspective for undertaking development of film industry and helping the growth of good cinema. There should be a State Chalachitra Akademi/State Film Akademi in every major State for promotion of cinema as an art form on an entirely non-commercial basis and a State Film Development Corporation to provide financial help and infrastructural support for the development of film industry and good cinema. (Paras 13.28 and 13.29)

182. The broad range of activities of the State Film Akademies should include State Film Awards, operation of art theatres, maintaining a film lending service, helping film society movement, introduction of courses in film appreciation in schools and colleges, holding festivals of Indian films and Film Weeks of foreign films, operating film information and Documentation Centre, and running a Children's Film Centre. Provision should be made to accommodate branches of the National Film Archive. (Para 13.30)

183. The State Film Development Corporations should broadly follow the range of activities suggested for the NFDC except important export of films and canalisation of raw stock. The Corporation should advise State Governments on the simplification of cinema licensing

rules and development of incentive scheme for exemption from entertainment tax. (Paras 13.31 and 13.32)

184. The State Corporation should assist in getting equipment import applications sponsored through the NFDC and monitor the export of films from the State. It should intervene with the NFDC in case the export of films from the State does not receive enough support from the NFDC. The Corporation should enter into bilateral arrangement with Corporations of other States for the exhibition of its films in other States and vice versa. It should provide preferential treatment to artistic films in every sphere. (Para 13.33)

185. The State Corporations should make investments in those areas of film technology such as animation in which private entrepreneurs may not be interested to make investment. It should not undertake heavy capital intensive projects such as studio complexes which are likely to be beyond the reach of low budget film makers. Instead it should provide inexpensive mobile shooting facilities. The concept of low budget must permeate the total activities of the corporation. Formation of film cooperatives should be encouraged. (Para 13.34)

186. In major film producing States, the State Corporations should set up equipment maintenance and repair facilities, either directly or by financially assisting independent entrepreneurs. (Para 13.35)

187. The State Corporations and State Akademies should receive adequate financial resources from the State Governments. As in the case of NFDC, the State Corporations should operate on the basis of financial self-sufficiency but not profit-maximisation. Ten per cent of the revenues earned by the State by way of taxes on the film industry should be earmarked for providing resources to the State Film Academies and the State film Development Corporations. (Para 13.36)

188. The organisations at the State level must maintain close coordination with the organisations at the Central level, i.e., the NFDC and the Chalachitra Akademi. The State level organisations should visualise their role in the overall perspective of developing good cinema on a national basis. (Para 13.37)

Censorship (Chapter XIV)

189. Statutory pre-censorship of films should continue. (Para 14.6)

190. Government must lay down clear guidelines for the appointment of the Chairman and members of the Censor Board, which should keep in view the broad qualifications recommended by the Khosla Committee. The guidelines should provide for adequate representation

of people draw from the film industry including those involved in the creative aspects of film making. (Para 14.9)

191. In Section 5(B)(1) of the Indian Cinematograph Act which follows Article 19(2) of the Constitution the words "the Sovereignty and integrity of India" appear to have been left out. The Act should be suitably amended. (Paras 14.12 and 14.13)

192. The power of the Central Government to give detailed guidelines to the Censor Board erodes the independence and authority of the Censor Board. The Censor Board should have the freedom to evolve its own code and guidelines within Article 19(2) of the Constitution as suggested by the Khosla Committee. (Paras 14.5 and 14.16)

193. The Cinematograph Act should be amended to take away the revisional and appellate powers of the Central Government over the decisions of the Censor Board in all cases except where issues are involved which have a bearing on (i) the sovereignty and integrity of India, (ii) the security of the State, and (iii) friendly relations with foreign States. (Para 14.19)

194. Government should set up a Standing Tribunal to be headed by a person with judicial background to hear appeals against the decisions of the Censor Board. The Tribunal should include an eminent film maker while hearing appeals. Appeal should lie with the Tribunal in all cases except in the three specific areas mentioned in para 14.19 where the revisional and appellate powers will rest with the Central Government. (Para 14.20)

195. An intermediary censor classification should be introduced which may be designated as 'UA'. This will indicate that the film is approved for universal exhibition but contains material which the parents may not like children upto the age of 12 to see. This certificate will be purely advisory. (Para 14.24)

196. In granting 'A' certificate a puritanical approach towards depiction of six should not be adopted but a stricter view should be taken regarding the depiction of excessive, sadistic and debasive violence. (Paras 14.25 and 14.26)

197. Censor Board has generally adopted a rigid approach regarding the exposure of corruption in relation to established authority such as police, political government, etc. Cinema like literature has to be given the freedom for social and political comment. (Para 14.27)

198. Censor Board should give a 'Q' certificate indicating that a film has definite artistic quality. This should be supported by exemption from entertainment tax and excise duty for such films. This certifi-

cate should be recommended by a separate committee attached to the Censor Board consisting primarily of film makers, film critics and people from allied arts. Only those films should be considered for 'Q' certificate where the producers specially request for such a consideration. (Paras 14.28 and 14.29)

199. All nominations to the Advisory Panels of the Censor Board should be made by the Censor Board itself and not by the Central Government and these should provide adequate representation to film makers and artistes other fields. (Para 14.30)

200. The membership of the Censor Board should be suitably enlarged. Each Regional Office should be headed by a full time member to be called Regional Chairman and there should be at least 2 or 3 non-official members in each region. Every Examining Committee should include either the Regional Chairman or a non-official member of the Board. The Regional Chairman should have full authority to grant censorship certificate so long as the decision is not contested by the applicant. In case the decision is contested, the present procedure of a Revising Committee should be followed. (Para 14.32)

201. The Regional Officers of the Censor Board should not function in an insulated atmosphere. There should be an Advisory Committee largely drawn from the film industry, to assist the Regional Chairman in resolving procedural and policy problems. (Para 14.33)

202. Considering the fact that Karnataka, Kerala and Andhra Pradesh are now producing a large number of feature films every year, there is need to set up Censor Board Offices in Bangalore, Hyderabad and Trivandrum. Similarly as and when film making activity expands in other regions, suitable expansion of the Censorship machinery should be considered. (Para 14.34)

203. The autonomy of the Censor Board should be statutorily guaranteed and it should cease to function as a department of the Ministry of Information and Broadcasting. The Chairman and members should be appointed for a fixed minimum tenure of three years. (Para 14.35)

204. The status of the Chairman of the Board should be at least of the rank of Secretary to the Government of India and of the full time members of at least Joint Secretary to the Government of India. (Para 14.36)

205. The Board should be given a fixed budget and should be left free to manage its own affairs. The Censorship function is basically in the nature of policing function and it is the responsibility of the Government to meet the expenditure of the Board. (Para 14.37)

206. To discourage violation of censorship, the Censor Board should maintain a video copy of the censored films and have a nucleus cell of enforcement staff to carry out spot checks. It must be a legal responsibility of the labs that except for the print required for censorship no other prints of a film are prepared until the films have been censored. (Para 14.38)

Training Facilities (Chapter XV)

207. Government should constitute an Expert Committee which should undertake a scientific study of the overall training requirements in different disciplines of film making and suggest a long-term training plan. (Para 15.9)

208. The Expert Committee should also examine the reasons for low acceptability of FTII graduates, suggest ways and means for improving the rapport between the industry and the FTII without weakening the role of FTII as a catalyst of change. (Para 15.10)

209. There is an urgent need for the FTII to consider expansion of its training facilities. The FTII should aim at developing into an institute of excellence not only for meeting our needs but also for providing advanced training to students from Asian and Third World countries. (Para 15.12)

210. The FTII should take up advanced training in film processing, production management and in specialised techniques such as animation, miniaturisation, special effects, high speed photography, under water photography, process photography, etc. Refresher courses for working technicians in the advanced technique of film making should be started at the earliest. (Para 15.13)

211. The FTII should develop proper machinery for monitoring the latest developments in film technology. Its library should be expanded to become a proper information and documentation service. (Para 15.14)

212. A section of the Institute should work on the lines of an open university which should offer capsule courses in specialised areas to any person who fulfils the basic minimum qualification and who is willing to pay the cost of the course. (Para 15.15)

213. The FTII should develop a proper student exchange and a teacher exchange programme with foreign training institutes. (Para 15.16)

214. The present approach to involve film makers and film tech-

nicians as guest lecturers should be further extended. (Para 15.17)

215. To reduce the cost of training, the number of non-teaching staff should be gradually brought down and the intake of students should be gradually increased. (Para 15.18)

216. The possibility of extending the Apprentices Act, 1961 to the organised sectors of the film industry such as laboratories, studios, etc., both in the private and public sector should be explored. The Films Division's apprenticeship scheme should be revived and should cover FTII students as also apprentices directly taken from the market. (Para 15.20)

217. The posts of Cameraman, Editors, Sound Recordists, etc., in the Doordarshan should be straightaway filled by the FTII graduates. (Para 15.21)

218. The Expert Committee to assess the training requirements should also examine the level of training facilities to the existing training institutes and identify areas where standards need to be upgraded, and the kind of funding required. The Central Government should earmark funds for upgradation of standards in the State Training Institutes. In case the standards still do not come up, the Central Government should consider take over of such Institutes. (Para 15.24)

219. The objectives of the State level institutes should be to provide graduate or diploma level training. These should also take up new areas of training such as theatre management and production designing. (Para 15.25)

220. The State Governments should consider setting up of Training Institutes in Calcutta and Trivandrum. Central Government should provide financial assistance to these Institutes for training in selected areas. (Para 15.26)

221. The course content for repairs and maintenance of the equipment as a part of the technical courses should be suitably enlarged. (Para 15.27)

Labour Legislation and Trade Associations (Chapter XVI)

222. While the need for special legislation to regulate the working conditions of cine workers has been recognised since long, appropriate legislation has still not been enacted. We recommend that the Central Government should take urgent steps to immediately introduce an appropriate legislation for regulating the employment conditions of cine workers. (Paras 16.13 and 16.14)

223. The proposed legislation should cover cine employees in all sectors of the film industry, i.e., production, distribution and exhibition. It should cover all categories of employees with special protection to be provided for casual, daily rated or contractual workers. There should be written contracts for a casual or contractual employment. (Para 16.15)

224. In case of production sector, the legislation should provide for an affidavit to be furnished by the producer, while applying for a censor certificate, containing a declaration that either the producer has already made full payment to all workers or a mutually acceptable agreement with the workers has been reached to make the payment by an agreed date. (Para 16.16)

225. The Government should take steps to set up a Welfare Fund to help cine employees, artistes and technicians in indigent circumstances. To finance this fund, the Government should collect an amount of Rs. 20 on every print of a feature film and make a matching grant out of its own resources. (Para 16.19)

226. The Government should take immediate steps to bring movie stunt artistes under accident risk insurance scheme. (Para 16.20)

227. The Government and the film industry should adopt the following broad approach for establishing proper associations in the film industry:

(i) Every person working in the film industry should belong to an association relating to his own trade or craft;

(ii) No person should be member of more than one association of the same discipline in one region;

(iii) Government at different levels should deal with only one association which represents the majority;

(iv) Membership of the different associations should be periodically verified; and

(v) Local associations should be federally organised into State or Zonal associations which through their representatives should form the All India apex body. (Para 16.25)

228. For forming trade associations, Government should recognise the categories of (1) Producers, (2) Distributors, (3) Exhibitors, (4) Studia and Equipment Owners, (5) Laboratories, (6) Directors, (7) Technicians including cameraman, editors, sound recordists, musicians, etc. (8) Artistes, (9) General Cine employees, and (10) Exporters. (Para 16.26)

229. There should be a legal requirement that membership of associations is freely available to anybody who fulfils the basic qualification so that the associations do not work as "closed shop" establishments. (Para 16.27)

Implementation: Some Suggestions (Chapter XVII)

230. In processing the report, is should be kept in view that most of the recommendations are inter-linked and unless the whole package of measures suggested for a particular area is accepted and implemented, the desired policy objectives are not likely to be fully achieved. (Para 17.2)

231. It is necessary that a special cell is created in the Ministry of I&B which should be exclusively concerned with the processing and implementation of te recommendations. Several recommendations will require enactment of special legislation, consultations with other Ministries and State Governments and monitoring of progress over a long period. Existing machinery in the I&B Ministry will not be able to find time to devote such attention to the Report. (Para 17.6)

14

RAILWAY ACCIDENT INVESTIGATION REPORT ON THE COLLISION BETWEEN NO. 82 UP TRIVANDRUM-BOMBAY JAYANTI JANATA EXPRESS TRAIN AND A TOURIST BUS NO. 1755 AT UNMANNED LEVEL CROSSING AT KM.80/12-13 BETWEEN ALWAYE AND ANGAMALI STATIONS OF SOUTHERN RAILWAY ON MAY 9, 1979 – REPORT[1]

One Man Commission Shri B.P. Sastry

Appointment

The Commission was constituted Under Ministry of Tourism and Civil Aviation (Commission of Railway Safety) in accordance with Rule 4 of the Statutory Investigation into Railway Accidents Rules, 1973 Vide Notification No RS-13-T (8)/71 dated April 19, 1973 on May 9, 1979.

Terms of Reference

To enquire into the Collision between No. 82 Up Trivandrum-Bombay Jayanti Janata Express Train and a Tourist Bus No. 1755 at Unmanned level crossing at Km. 80/12-13 between Alwaye and Angamali Stations of Southern Railway on May 9, 1979.

Contents

Summary; Inspection and Inquiry; Relief Measures; The Train and the Road Vehicle; Local Features; Summary of Evidence; Tests and

---

1. Delhi, Controller of Publications, 1983, 14 p.

Observations; Discussion; Conclusions; Remarks and Recommendations; Annexures; Railway Boards Comments on Various Paras of the Report.

Conclusions

Cause

The collision between No. 82 "Trivandrum-Bombay Jayanthi Janata Express" and tourist bus bearing Registration No. TMX 1755 at the unmanned level crossing No. 64 located at KM. 80/12-13 between Alwaye and Angamali stations of Southern Railway on the afternoon of the 9th May, 1979 was caused on account of the road vehicle entering the level crossing with a view to cross the Railway track in the face of the approaching train.

Responsibility

The driver of the bus (deceased Shri Murugesan) who failed to stop short of the crossing and make sure that it was safe for him to cross the track and the Conductor Shri V.B. Vittal, who failed to discharge his functions as a Conductor and failed to stop the vehicle short of the crossing were responsible for the accident.

Both had violated the provisions of Rule 100-2(f) of the "Law of Motor Vehicles" of Kerala State.

No Railway official is considered responsible for the accident.

Relief Measures

Relief measures were satisfactory. The promptness with which local Doctors of Angamali responded to the emergency, on being informed, is commendable. The way in which the injured were taken care of by the authorities of the District Hospitals at Alwaye and Ernakulam also deserves a mention.

Although the Railway Medical Vans were not called into action, the fact that the one from Ernakulam could not even be ordered to be turned out for over 40 minutes due to failure of communication facilities and the one from Shoranur could not move within the scheduled time in spite of its being ordered to be turned out during the day shift when all concerned were expected to be alert, requires a probe by Southern Railway Administration to avoid similar situations.

Recommendations

9.1 The provisions in the Motor Vehicles Rules of various States which stipulate that the road vehicle driver should stop short of an unmanned level crossing, look towards the track on both sides carefully and then cross the track when it is safe to do so is seen to be observed more in its breach than incompliance. It is very necessary that State Governments gear up their enforcement machinery to ensure strict observance of this important rule, the disregard of which is mostly responsible for accidents at unmanned level crossings. Railway Administrations which have also a degree of moral responsibility in the matter should co-ordinate with the Police Authorities in a greater measure than at present, to conduct ambush checks to bring the offenders of the rule to book. Government of India may also lend a helping hand in bringing about this co-ordination.

9.2 Provision of speed breakers in the approaches of level crossings, when properly designed and sited in a sure means of slowing down the road vehicle driver to be reminded of the rule which requires him to stop and look out on both sides of the track before attempting to cross. There should be no delay on the part of the State Governments in implementing this important safety measure at all unmanned level crossings as directed in the Ministry of Shipping and Transport's letter No. TGS/21/75 dated 6-1-1978. Railway Administrations in their own interest should closely watch the implementation of this directive and take appropriate and timely steps towards its early completion.

9.3 Once an unmanned level crossing is considered to be qualifying for manning, there should be no delay in giving effect to it. It is strongly suggested that the Government of India may take the initiative to bring about the necessary understanding between the State Governments and the Railway Administrations towards achieving this objective. In the scheme of things which could be called satisfactory the Railway Administrations should have the authority to man a level crossing once the need is established, without getting bogged down by considerations of apportionment of the expenditure between the Railways and State Governments concerned. The question of apportionment should be left to be decided and financial adjustments made subsequent to its implementation.

9.4 State Government should exercise a degree of control to

ensure that private vehicle owners observe the ours of Employment Rules of the Staff they employ on long distance routes or Contract Carriages with a view to ensure optimum hours of duty and proper rest to them which will go a long way in reducing accidents of this nature.

Railway Board's Comments on Various Paras of the Report

Paras 9.1, 9.2 and 9.4: The Railway Administration have addressed the Chief Secretaries of the concerned State Governments for implementation of these recommendations, and are also keeping a watch to ensure their compliance.

Para 9.3: The Railway Ministry are already seized of the importance of expeditious manning of unmanned level crossings once the need for their manning is established. Though, as per rules, in such cases the initial cost is to be borne by the State Governments (Road Authority) and their acceptance of the proposal for manning is necessary, the Railway Ministry have taken the following steps to assist them and to expedite the process:

(i) A Railway Safety Works Fund had been constituted with effect from 1-4-1966. The State Government's share of cost is reimbursable to them from this fund; and
(ii) Ten per cent of this Fund had been earmarked for direct expenditure on manning/upgradation of level crossing. This has been raised to 20 per cent with effect from 1-4-1978. For level crossing manned out of 10 per cent (now 20 per cent) of Railway Safety Works Fund, the State Governments are not required to spend any money or even to make any deposit.

In addition to above, it has been decided to man such of the unmanned level crossings, as are potential hazards to the safety of passengers, in a phased manner, entirely at the cost of the Railways. Under this scheme, during the current year, manning of about 61 unmanned level crossings at Railways' cost has been approved by the Railway Ministry.

However, as suggested by the Commissioner of Railway Safety, for the level crossings to be manned out of 10 per cent (now 20 per cent) Railways Safety Works Fund, the matter will be taken up with the State Governments to permit Railways to go ahead with the manning once the need therefore has been established, without waiting for the formal acceptance of the former.

Relief Measures

Para 8.3: It is noted that relief measures were satisfactory in this case. Regarding delay in ordering/turning out of the medical vans from Ernakulam and Shoranur, the Railway Administration are taking necessary action against the staff held blame-worth.

As for Chief Commissioner of Railway Safety's suggestion that the ARME van at Ernakulam should be stabled on a siding with points taking off from Shoranur/Quilon sides' the railway is being asked to examine the proposal and take action as necessary.

RAILWAY ACCIDENT INVESTIGATION REPORT ON DERAILMENT OF 3 PN UP (PATHANKOT-NAGROTA) PASSENGER TRAIN AT KM. 37/5-6 BETWEEN TALARA AND JAWANWALA SHAHR STATIONS ON PATHANKOT JOGINDER NAGAR NARROW GAUGE SECTION IN FIROZEPUR DIVISION OF NORTHERN RAILWAY AT ABOUT 20.30 HOURS ON MAY 12, 1979 – REPORT[1]

One Man Commission Shri A.A. Rego

Appointment

The Commission was constituted under Ministry of Tourism and Civil Aviation (Commission of Railway Safety) in accordance with Rule 4 of the Statutory Investigation into Railway Accidents Rules, 1973 Vide Notification No. RS. 13-T(8)/71 dated April 19, 1973.

Terms of Reference

To enquire into the derailment of 3 PN Up (Pathankot-Nagrota) Passenger train at km. 37/5-6 between Talara and Jawanwala Shahr Stations on Pathankot Joginder Nagar Narrow Gauge Section in Firozepur Division of Northern Railway at about 20.30 hours on May 12, 1979.

Contents

Summary; Inspection and Inquiry; Relief measures; Train and Damage; Local Features; Summary of Evidence; Observations and Tests; Discussions; Conclusions; Remarks and Recommendations;

1. Delhi, Controller of Publications, 1988, 19 p.

Remarks of the Railway Board on Various Parts of the Report.

Conclusions

Cause

On full consideration of the factual, material and circumstantial evidence, I have come to the conclusion that the derailment of 3 PN Up passenger train which occurred at km. 37/5-6 between Talara and Jawanwala Shahr on Pathankot-Nagrota-Joginder Nagar Narrow Gauge section in the Firozepur Division of Northern Railway at 20.30 hrs. on 12-5-1979, was due to the over turning of the over crowded coaches with passengers standing on the foot boards and sitting on the roofs of the said train. The breakage of the flawed rear draw bar of the coupling of the 3rd coach and over speeding of the train contributed to the over turning.

Responsibility

(a) Shri Prabhu Ram, Driver of 3 PN Up passenger train, is held responsible* for exceeding the maximum sanctioned speed of 35 kmph. He violated the provisions of General Rule No. 89/(a) and (b) and Subsidiary Rule No. 89/1.

(b) The responsibility for passing a defective draw bar may be fixed by the Railway Administration, if possible.

Service record of persons held responsible

Shri Prabhu Ram, Driver joined service as a Cleaner on 29-8-1945. He was promoted as Fireman on 13-7-1952, Driver 'C' grade on 02-11-1973 and Driver Gr. 'B' on 01-11-1976, in which grade he was working on the day of the accident. He had an accident free service.

Relief Measures

(a) Avoidable delays have taken place (vide para 2.2), in–

* Since acquitted by the Court.

(i) the departure of the Accident Relief Train from Pathankot,

(ii) the departure of the ADMO Pathankot by Road from Pathankot; and

(iii) the intimation given by the Amritsar Control to the DMO Amritsar and the departure of the DMO by road from Amritsar.

(b) It is also unfortunate that the Railway Ambulance was lying out of order from 12-3-1979 in the Deputy Chief Mechanical Engineer's Workshop at Amritsar and could not be commissioned for shifting the injured persons from one Hospital to the other after the accident.

(c) The Railway administration will take note of the delays/ shortcomings in rushing medical aid to the site of accident and fix responsibility for failure of various persons. Instructions may be issued to the Workshop to give the highest priority hereafter to repairs to Ambulance Vans so that they are available for use in serious accidents.

(d) I hasten to add that these delays/shortcomings did not affect the medical attention given to the injured passengers, who were rushed by road to the nearest Civil Dispensary and rendered necessary medical aid before and after the arrival of the Railway Doctors from Pathankot.

Recommendations

9.1 Because of the inherent instability of Narrow Gauge coaches, the Railway administration should frame rules enjoining on Drivers and Guards of passenger trains to reduce speeds when passengers travel on the foot boards and roofs of Narrow gauge trains. The speed in such cases should no exceed 25 kmph in sections with sharp curves on down gradients subject to other local restrictions.

9.2 It came to light during the Inquiry that brake power certificates in form OPRS-22 were being issued in duplicate for goods trains and in triplicate for passenger trains in terms of para 5 of the Railway's Carriage and Wagon Circular No. 15. Due to shortage of printed books, various abuses have crept in. In this case, the 2 foils of the same printed number were used for different trains and carbon copies were made on blank paper and issued to the Driver and the Guard. Elsewhere I have seen certificates with different printed numbers issued to the Driver and Guard of the same train from one book and over writing of figures. A drive may be instituted to ensure that the rules laid down for issue of brake power certificates are strictly enforced as correctness of this certificate has a vital bearing on safety. The principle of one printed number for one train and printing the copies in triplicate for the Driver and the Guard may be considered. Over-writing must be banned and corrections if necessary done by scoring out the original entry and writing alongside the revised figure under a clear signature.

9.3 (a) Joint track measurements under load were not taken after the accident in this case as required vide para 1408(c) of Indian Railways Way and Works Manual. A plea was put forward that due to the inadequate space available under Narrow Gauge stock, it is not possible to do so. This is not acceptable. As track measurements under load give an important indication of the behaviour of the track under traffic, they must be invariably recorded after an accident (unless operating conditions make this loading impracticable). Northern Railway may reiterate these instructions.

(b) None took a note of the marks on the inside of the left rail, dog spikes, bearing plates and fish bolts till the same were pointed out by me on 15-5-1979, 3 days after the accident. In fact, an impression was given to me that, other than the rubbing marks on the outside shoulders of the ballast and drag marks on the side of the cutting, there were no other marks whatsoever on the track. As all marks on the track give important clues to arrive at a correct conclusion, Northern Railway may please issue instructions that Engineers must keep a proper note and careful record of all such marks observed on the track and rolling stock immediately after an accident and this record should preferably be countersigned and accepted as correct by an official of another department.

9.4 The Railway has been unable to trace till nor the source of supply of the culprit draw bar fitted in coach No. 229 as no draw bars have been purchased for many years in the past. Currently the Railway is procuring rolling stock parts by inviting quotations on the basis of drawings and specifications and inspection is carried out by RDSO/RITES on the basis of these specifications. Apart from checking of specification of material and other prescribed tests for composition of the raw material, only dimensional and visual examination is now carried out. The Railway is presently examining a suggestion to introduce stamping the name of the supplier, contract number, etc., so as to identify the draw bar in future. The feasibility of introducing ultra-sonic testing to detect such internal flaws is also under consideration. The results of this examination may be expedited and expeditious action taken to trace the source of the culprit draw bar.

Railway Board's Comments on Various Paras of the Report

Para 9.1: Accepted. Necessary instructions on the subject have been issued to all the Railways (Copy enclosed).

Para 9.2: Accepted. A safety drive was launched by the Railway to ensure correct filling up of brake power certificates in form OP/RS-22, which yielded good results.

Para 9.3: This has been accepted by the Railway Administration who have already issued necessary instructions in compliance with this recommendation.

Para 9.3: This has been accepted by the Railway. Necessary instructions on the subject are being issued to all the Railways.

Para 9.4: The system of stamping the manufacturer's name will not be of much use as these draw bars will be in service for a number of years and it will be incorrect to fix responsibility on the manufacturer if the breakage takes place after a few years. The proper course would be to go for periodical testing of the draw bar to expose any inherent defects, cracks or any deterioration in the material, like corrosion, etc. Periodical proof testing, say at the time of POH, will serve the purpose adequately. This matter will need examination by RDSO and suitable instructions will be issued to all the Railways after a scheme for proof testing is finalised.

Relief Measures

Para 8.4: Regarding delay in the departure of the accident relief train from Pathankot, ADMO, Pathankot/DMO, Amritsar by road, and the Ambulance Car at Amritsar laying out of order, the matter has been examined by the railway administration and the position is given below:

1. *Departure of the ART, Pathankot*

The information about the accident was conveyed by the Guard of the train to the Section Controller, Amritsar at 20.45 hrs. The ART/Pathankot was ordered at 20.47 hrs. and it left for the site at 22.00 hrs., i.e., after a period of 73 minutes against a target of 45 minutes.

The Railway Administration has taken up with the defaulting staff.

2. *Departure of ADMO, Pathankot by Road*

Normally the medical aid is sent to the site by the nominated medical relief van. However, in this case, no accident relief medical van for narrow gauge was based at Pathankot. The first medical team, therefore, collected the materials from Pathankot Health Unit and left for the site by the Accident Relief Train. In view of the heavy casualties reported, the ADMO thought it proper to take additional men and materials also with him by road to assist the first medical team which had already left by the ART. Thus the medical team which left by road later was actually the second medical team; the first medical team having left earlier by the accident relief train. However, both the medical teams arrived at site of the accident almost all the same time, and so the purpose for which the second medical team was sent, was fully served. It may also be mentioned that the travelling time from Pathankot to the site of the accident was about 1 hour. During this period the injured persons had already been shifted to Civil Dispensary, Jawali. Both the railway medical teams assisted and supplemented the resources at Jawali Civil Dispensary so as to provide better medical attention to the injured persons.

Keeping in view the action taken by the ADMO, Pathankot to collect additional materials and take the second medical team with him, his late departure by road from Pathankot (but simultaneous arrival with relief train at the site of the accident) would appear to be in consonance with the practical requirements of the situation.

3. *Intimation by Amritsar Control of DMO, Amritsar and his Departure*

The Amritsar Control received information of the accident at 20.45 hrs. and ordered Medical Van, Baijnath Paprola and the Relief Train, Pathankot and also alerted various first-aid agencies in the area at 20.47 hrs. At 20.55 hrs., ADMO, Pathankot was instructed to carry sufficient first-aid material to the site. At 21.00 hrs., the ADMO/Line was also advised to proceed to the site of the accident with sufficient first-aid materials. DMO, Amritsar was advised at 22.20 hrs. It would be appreciated that wherever the site of the accident is too far away from the Divisional Headquarters, the visit of the DMO is more in the nature of a follow-up action to see that the injured persons are receiving the best possible medical attention. The travelling time from Amritsar to

Pathankot by road is by about 6 hours and since DMO, Amritsar was not expected to be part of the team to manage the injured cases at the site of the accident, the time of his departure from Amritsar was of no consequence so far as the attention to the injured persons was concerned. When DMO, Amritsar reached the site, he visited all the injured persons in different hospitals, and satisfied himself about the treatment being given to them. In view of the fact that due to the long distance from Amritsar, DMO was not expected to reach the site of accident for actual management of injured cases and no delay in the actual management of injured cases had taken place as they had already been attended to by the Civil and other Medical Officers, the time lag between the accident and advice to DMO, Amritsar was utilised by Amritsar Control in chasing doctors at Jawanwala Shahr, Nurpur Road and Pathankot to rush immediate first-aid to the injured persons, which was the foremost basic necessity at that time.

4. *Railway Ambulance Car lying out of order*

As regards the local ambulance car lying out of order, it may be mentioned that the vehicle was under repairs from 12-3-1979 after receipt of inspection report of Motors Vehicles Inspector, Punjab State Government. The delay in its repairs was on account of non-availability of imported spare parts. Instructions have been issued to Workshops to give priority to the repairs of the ambulance vans.

It may be mentioned here that according to the Commissioner of Railway Safety, slight delays/short comings did not affect the medical attention given to the injured persons. In this connection observations made in para 8.4(d) of the report of Commissioner of Railway Safety, reproduced below, are relevant;

> "I hasten to add that these delays/short comings did not affect the medical attention given to the injured passengers, who were rushed by road to the nearest Civil Dispensary and rendered necessary medical aid before and after arrival of the Railway Doctors from Pathankot".

RAILWAY ACCIDENT INVESTIGATION REPORT ON COLLISION OF K 121 UP HOWRAH-KHARAGPUR LOCAL WITH THE REAR OF 3 UP HOWRAH-MADRAS MAIL AT KM. 25/25-27 ON THE UP LINE BETWEEN BAURIA AND CHENGAIL STATIONS ON HOWRAH-KHARAGPUR ELECTRIFIED TRIPLE LINE SECTION IN KHARAGPUR DIVISION OF SOUTH EASTERN RAILWAY AT 21-04 HOURS ON MAY 18, 1979 – REPORT[1]

One Man Commission Shri K. Ganapati

Appointment

The Commission was constituted under Ministry of Tourism and Civil Aviation (Commission of Railway Safety) in accordance with the Rule 4 of the Statutory Investigation into Railway Accidents Rules, 1973 Vide Notification No. RS. 13-T(8)/71 dated April 19, 1973.

Terms of Reference

To enquire into the collision of K 121 Up Howrah-Kharagpur Local with the rear of 3 Up Howrah-Madras mail at km. 25/25-27 on the Up line between Bauria and Chengail stations on Howrah-Kharagpur electrified triple line section in Kharagpur Division of South Eastern Railway at 21-04 hours on May 18, 1979.

Contents

Summary; Inspection and Inquiry; Relief Measures; The Trains; Local

1. Delhi, Controller of Publications, 1982, 47 p.

conditions; Summary of Evidence; Observations and Tests; Discussion; Conclusions; Remarks and Recommendations; A Note on the Brake System of 25 KV AC BG EMU Stock; Annexures; Railway Board's Comments on Various Paras of the Report.

Conclusions

On careful consideration of the factual, material and circumstantial evidence, I have come to the conclusion that the rear end collision of K. 121 EMU Howrah-Kharagpur local with the rear of 3 Up Howrah-Madras Mail at km. 25/25-27 between Bauria and Chengail stations, on the Up line on Howrah-Kharagpur Electrified Section, Kharagpur Division of S.E. Railway at 21.04 hours on 18-5-1979 was caused by the Motorman of K. 121 Up EMU Local not having exercised great caution after having passed the Automatic Starter Signal 74/75 of Up line at Bauria station in the 'on' position.

Responsibility

Shri P.B. Dey, Deceased Motorman of K. 121 Up EMU Local is mainly responsible for not having exercised great caution after having passed automatic signal 74/75 in the 'ON' position. He violated G.R. 277 and 279. In addition he also violated G. Rs. 83, 99 and 122.

Lapses of other Railway Staff

Name of Staff	*Specific lapse*	*Violation of rule*
Shri Abdul Gafur Guard of 3 Up	Failure to protect the train which halted at outside Home signal, Chengail.	G.R. 125 & G.R. 280(1)
	Failure to ensure safety of public.	G.R. 163(a)(i)
Shri J.M. Roy, Guard of K. 121	Failure to stop K. 121 proceedings as a speed of 65 km/h after passing the Starter signal in the 'ON' position.	G.Rs. 121, 126 & 163(a)(i)

Relief Measures and Medical Attention

(a) Evidence has come on record that relief measures were delayed unduly. Witnesses were very sore on this point and gave evidence with lot of emotion. The accident occurred at 21.04 hours and thc 1st medical van from Santragachi arrived at the site of accident at 23.20 hours only. Some sort of first aid appears to have been given by the local doctors but here again there was conflicting evidence, and the local doctors seemed to have arrived very late. In the meantime local volunteers and villagers sent many of the injured passengers by truck and other means to the Jute Mill Hospital and also the Civil and ESI Hospital at Uluberia. In this process belongings of passengers are reported to have been snatched by unsocial elements.

(b) The Railway should probe further to ascertain the reasons for:

(i) Late receipt of accident message at the stations of ARME Vans.
(ii) Late start of ARME Vans.
(iii) Late arrival of ARME Vans at the site of accident.
(iv) Non-arrival of a doctor by road vehicle at the site of accident fix responsibility, and take suitable follow up and remedial action to avoid recurrence.

(c) I, however, hasten to add that once the ARME Vans reached the site, excellent medical attention and succour were provided to the injured passengers by the railway medical team under the guidance of CMO who was personally supervising the operations at site. The follow up action and treatment given to the injured passengers in the railway hospital under his guidance is also of a high order.

Recommendations

Immediate Recommendation and Compliance

65. After conclusion of the inquiry an immediate recommendation was sent to the Railway to disconnect the 'A' marker of Starter signal of 74/75 of the Up line at Bauria station forthwith to ensure that a third accident does not occur at the same spot. The Railway after examining the case agreed with my suggestion and disconnected the 'A' marker at 19.00 hours on 26-5-1979.

Permanent Remedial Measures

66. I have carefully gone through the various suggestions put forward by public during the course of the inquiry regarding the permanent remedial measures to prevent a recurrence of an accident at the same spot. I, however, do not find any of these suggestions suitable or feasible. The Railway did not tender any evidence regarding this matter. I, therefore, come to the conclusion that the disconnection of 'A' market of the Starter Signal 74/75 at Bauria should continue as a temporary measure till the Railway is able to suggest a better alternative.

Installation of Automatic Train Control System

67. It is hardly necessary to overemphasise the need for automatic train control system on the Howrah-Kharagpur suburban section by which the speed of a train passing a red signal in Automatic section is restricted to a preset limit. Efforts may be made for the installation of the same as early as possible.

Improvement in Rear Warning System

68. Time and again the Commission has pointed out the inadequacy of the present tail lamp and the necessity of providing a rear end warning system suitable to present day speeds and traffic. Para 102 of Naini Accident report may be referred to for details.

Doctors to Proceed by Road Vehicles where Possible

69. South Eastern Railway may review all stations where road vehicles belonging to the Railway are available and issue instructions nominating road vehicles for the emergency use of doctors in the case of the accidents.

Adequacy of Ambush Checks

70. The position of ambush checks conducted by the Division during 1978 and 1979 is indicated below: –

Year	Checks to be conducted by	Quota prescribed	No. of checks actually done	Shortfall
1978	D.S.O. Safety	24	22	2
	Counsellor (Optg.)	24	18	6
	Safety Counsellor (Mech.)	24	14	10
1979 (from Jan. to April 1979	D.S.O.	8	4	4
	Safety Counsellor (Optg.)	8	8	0
	Safety Counsellor (Mech.)	8	4	4

There has been some shortfall in the quota of ambush checks. The Railway should further probe and tighten up the procedure for ensuring minimum number of ambush checks and also take up with the staff for deficiency. Head office may also organise ambush checks independently.

Probe into cause of delay in the arrival of 1st ARME Vans

71. South Eastern Railway to probe into the cause of delay in the arrival of 1st ARME Vans, fix responsibility and take suitable remedial measures to avoid recurrence.

Changes in General Rule 277, 280 and 125

72. Board may consider changes in General Rules 277, 280 and 125 as suggested in para 60 and also seek the advice of R.A.E.C. 1978 in this connection.

Crash worthiness of EMU stock to be improved by suitable changes in design as brought out in the Naigaon accident on 18-4-1978 on the Western Railway.

ANNEXURE-I

Braking Distance Trial conducted by DEE (RS), SDI/Tikiapara and others

Date: 23-5-1979 Train – Trial Spl. (Empty train)

Units: 526/527 Motorman: Shri N. Rama Rao, Load – 8.20=280 Tonnes

Srl. No.	Speed in Kmph	Brake Cylinder pressure	Time taken	Distance	Remarks
1.	20-0	3.4 KG/CM^2	4.5 sec.	13.1 m	**Emergency application with EP supply "NO"**
2.	40-0	3.4 KG/CM^2	9.0 sec.	56 m	-do-
3.	60-0	3.4 KG/CM^2	14.5 sec.	127.5m	-do-
4.	80-0	3.4 KG/CM^2	24.0 sec.	283.5m	-do-
5.	20-0	3.2 KG/CM^2	6.5 sec.	23.5m	**Emergency application without EP supply.**
6.	40-0	3.2 KG/CM^2	10.0 sec.	58.5 m	-do-
7.	60-0	3.4 KG/CM^2	20.0 sec.	196.5m	-do-
8.	80-0	3.4 KG/CM^2	30.0 sec.	365 m	-do-
9.	40-0	3.3 KG/CM^2	13.0 sec.	87 m	**Emergency application by releasing deadman handle**

Sd/-
DEE (RS)/Tikiapara

Sd/-
SDI/Tikiapara

ANNEXURE-II

A Note on the Brake System of 25 KV AC BG EMU Stock

EMU stocks are equipped with compressed Air Brake system by providing a Brake Controller in driving cab and an electro-pneumatic brake unit (E.P. Unit) in individual coaches of a rake. The brake is applied as well as released simultaneously in all coaches of a rake by actuating the brake controller handle. The magnitude of brake depends on the movement of brake controller handle.

The "Service Brake" of EMU is the E.P. brake application which is generally used. In this system the desired braking effort is achieved by simply actuating the brake controller handle which in turn through a brake relay, connects the holding and application magnetic coils in all the E.P. units in all coaches through train line wire with 11OV DC supply to admit the compressed air from main reservoir under air pressure of 6 to 7 kg per CM^2 to brake cylinder after closing the exhaust part of the brake cylinders. The maximum brake cylinder pressure is limited to 3.5 kg per CM^2 which is self-lapped. The brake is released by bringing the brake controller handle to normal (release) position. Thus, application magnet coil is de-energised and it does not allow further admission of Air to the brake cylinders and holding coil also de-energises which opens the exhaust port of brake cylinders as well, so that whatever air pressure is available in the brake cylinders that vents to the atmosphere.

The "Standby Brake" is the automatic brake which is always available but is generally used when the electric supply to the brake system fails. In this system braking efforts for brake application is achieved as desired, by destroying brake pipe pressure, air rushes to the brake cylinders from Aux. reservoirs under 5 kg per CM^2 pressure. The brake cylinder pressure is lapped and controlled in application at any pressure from '0' to 3.5 kg per CM^2. The maximum brake cylinder pressure of 3.5 kg per CM^2 depends on the brake pipe pressure which is normally 5 kg per CM^2. Brakes on all the coaches are initiated at a time. Brake is released, by putting back the handle at normal (release) position, as soon as the brake pipe is re-charged. By any chance is the brake pipe pressure comes down there will be auto brake application on the rake.

"Emergency Brake" is the most reliable brake which is the combination of E.P. and Auto Brakes. It is applied by moving Brake Controller handle to the last position. Electric supply is connected to the holding and application coil of all E.P. units and open the Brake pipe pressure directly to the atmosphere to vent at a time causing compressed air from both sides, i.e., from Main reservoir Aux. reservoir to rush to the brake cylinders; hence brake cylinder pressure goes up to 3.9 kg/sq. CM quickly. This type of brake after application is also released when the brake controller handle is brought to normal (release) position. Hence, this brake is more effective and quicker than E.P. and Auto brake. The emergency brake application is also actuated by releasing the dead man's device on the power controller with reverser in either forward or reverse position. In this type of application the power supply is also automatically cut off.

The normal leakage of air pressures from brake cylinder is at the rate of 1.5 kg/CM^2 per hour.

After meeting with accident the driving cab was completely smashed cutting off all electrical connections. This resulted in lowering of the pantograph of unit No. 516 (KGP end unit). Main compressor of this unit also stopped functioning. Heavy air leakage from air pipe couplers between C & D coaches of unit 516 was noticed. Normally, with the permissible leakages of brake cylinder pressure once the brakes are applied and the unit is de-energised and the supply of air pressure from main compressor is cut off, the brake cylinder pressure will exhaust and release the brakes in 3 hrs. time. In this case, however, it is expected that brakes would have been released earlier due to damage to the cab equipment and air pipe couplers.

ANNEXURE-III

List of Collision cases on Howrah-Kharagpur Suburban Section, S.E. Railway

Sl. No.	Date of accident	Accident	Cause/Remarks
1.	7-6-1977	Collision between Dn. steam TPKR Spl. and M/38 EMU local at Andul station.	Inquiry was done by Railway.
2.	8-2-1976	Collision between P-4 Dn. and 84 Dn. Express between Santragachi and Tikiapara stations.	Driver of 84 Dn. not exercising great caution after passing Auto signal at danger.
3.	12-5-1974	Collision between K. 119 Up and 83 Up at Sankrail station.	Inquiry was done by Railway.
4.	15-8-1973	Collision of M/29 Up Local with Up Electric Kharagpur Spl. between Bauria and Chengail stations.	Failure of Motorman of M/29 Up in not exercising great caution after passing Bauria Starter in 'ON' position.
5.	24-2-1973	Collision between M/6 Dn. EMU local and 324 Dn. at Tikiapara station.	Violation of G.R. 277 by Motorman.
6.	5-12-1971	Collision between 316 Dn. and 324 Dn. at Panskura station.	324 Dn. having passed Dn. Home signal of Panskura in the 'ON' position.
7.	27-11-1970	Collision between 38 Down and empty rake of K-101 A at Uluberia station.	Motorman of K-101A violating G.R. 277.
8.	19-2-1969	Collision between Up Mechada Local and Material Train between Santragachi and Andul stations.	Violation of G.R. 277 by Motorman.
9.	21-2-1968	Side-collision between 8 Up and Up Special Goods at Mechada station.	Driver of 8 Up passing Main Home signal at danger.
10.	27-8-1947	Collision of 18 Up with 14 up at Kolaghat station.	Driver of 14 Up passing signal at danger.

ANNEXURE-IV

Extracts of Rules Violated

G.R.83: Precautions when view of signal is obstructed – If in consequence of a fog or storm or for any other reason, the view of signals is obstructed, the Driver shall take every possible precaution, especially when approaching a station or an Intermediate Block Post or junction, so as to have the train well under control.

G.R. 99: Riding on engine or tender – Except in accordance with special instructions no person other than the Driver and Fireman shall ride on the engine or tender.

G.R. 121: Guard to keep a good look out – During the journey including halts at stations, every Guard shall keep a good look out except under special instructions and satisfy himself from time to time that the tail-board and brake-van lamps are in position and that all break-van lamps, if required, are burning brightly, that the train is complete in every respect and is proceeding in safe and proper manner.

G.R. 122: Driver and Fireman to keep a good look-out – Every Driver shall keep a good look-out while the train is in motion, and every Fireman shall also do so when he is not necessarily otherwise engaged.

G.R. 125: Train waiting at Outer or Home signal – When a train has without apparent cause been kept standing at an Outer or Home signal for five minutes, the Driver shall sound his whistle to warn the Guard, and the Brakesman shall proceed to the cabin or station to warn the Station Master. If there is no Brakesman, the driver shall depute a Fireman to proceed to the cabin or station to warn the Station Master. The Brakesman or the Fireman proceeding to the cabin or station shall show a danger signal towards the station. The Guard shall as soon as the train is stopped at an Outer and Home signal, check up the tail board/light is correctly exhibited and shall maintain a vigilant attitude in the rear of the train. After 15 minutes or such less time as may be prescribed by special instructions, the Guard shall irrespective of whether the cause is apparent or not proceed to protect the rear of the train in accordance with instructions, laid down in Rule 166. If in the meantime the signal is taken 'off' or the Driver receives necessary authority to pass the signal in the 'on' position he shall sound his whistle to recall the Guard and exchange hand signal with him before starting the train.

S.R. 125/1 (i) * * * *

(ii) Should the cause of the signal being 'on' be not apparent, the usual brake whistle must be used after 5 minutes' halt, whereupon Brakes or Fireman should proceed to the station or cabin. After 15 minutes' halt, if the signal has not been taken "off", and no information has been received, the Driver will sound his whistle repeatedly until the Guard acknowledges by waving a read hand signal up and down. Having done so, the Guard will proceed to protect the train in rear as per G.R.I. 166 and Subsidiary Rules thereto.

G.R. 126: Attracting attention of Driver — (a) If any Guard sees reason to apprehend danger, or considers it necessary for any reason to stop the train, he shall use his best endeavours to attract the attention of the Driver.

(b) In the absence of other means of communication with the engine, a Guard desiring to attract the Driver's attention shall apply his hand-brake sharply and as suddenly release it.

(c) When the attention of the Driver has been attracted, the necessary danger signal shall be shown.

(d) If the train is fitted with a continuous brake, the Guard may, in case of emergency, apply such brake to stop the train.

G.R. 163: Duty securing safety (a) Every railway servant shall: –

(i) See that every exertion is made for ensuring the safety of the public.

G.R. 277: Driver's duty when Automatic Stop Signal is "on".

(1) When a driver finds an Automatic Stop signal with an 'A' marker at "on" he must bring has train to a stop in the rear of that signal. After bringing his train to a stop in the rear of the signal, the Driver shall wait there for one minute by day and two minutes by night. If after waiting for this period the signal continues to remain at "on", he shall give on long whistle and exchange signals with the Guard and then proceed ahead, as far as the line is clear, towards the next stop signal in advance, exercising great caution so as to stop short of any obstruction.

(2) Where owing to the curvature of the line, fog, dust storm, engine working the train pushing it, or other cause, the line ahead cannot be

seen clearly, the driver shall proceed at a very slow speed, which shall under no circumstances exceed 8 kilometres per hour. The Driver if he considers necessary may seek the assistance of the Guard by giving the prescribed code of whistle.

G.R. 279: Precautions after passing Automatic Stop Signal at "on" — When an Automatic Stop signal has been passed at "on" the Driver shall proceed with great caution until the next Stop signal is reached. Even if this signal display 'Caution' or 'Attention' or 'Clear' aspects, the Driver must continue to look out for any possible obstruction short of the same. He shall proceed cautiously up to that signal and shall act upon its indication only after he has reached it.

G.R. 280: Protection of a train stopped in an Automatic Signalling Section — (1) When a train is stopped in an Automatic Signalling section, the Guard shall immediately exhibit a 'Danger' hand signal towards the rear and check up that the tail board or tail light is correctly exhibited.

(2) If the stoppage is on account of accident, failure or obstruction and the train cannot proceed, the Driver shall sound the prescribed code of whistle and the train shall be protected immediately as per rule 166 except that for the protection of the occupied line, one detonator shall be placed at 90 metres from the train on the way out and similarly two detonators, 10 metres apart, not-less-than 180 metres from the train or at such distance as has been fixed by special instructions.

Railway Board's Comments on Various Paras of the Report

Para 65 and 66: Recommendations noted. While the provision of 4th aspect in the automatic signalling section between Tikiapara and Haur section is carried out the signal shall be re-spaced for providing for closer headway. Only the 'A' marker on the semi-automatic starter signal 74/75 of Bauria station was disconnected on the recommendation of the Commissioner of Railway Safety, the same is being reinstated as there is nothing special about this particular signal and also the main cause of the accident was non-observance of speed restriction as per GR 277.

Para 67: As per recommendations of the Railway Accidents Inquiry Committee — 68, the work of providing Automatic Warning System is being progressed in a phased manner with the following priorities:

(a) Suburban sections.
(b) Trunk routes where the speed of train exceeds 120 kmph.
(c) Other trunk routes and main lines.

At present, the works for automatic warning system are sanctioned for Howrah-Mughalsarai, Mughalsarai-Delhi section and for the suburban sections of the Western and Central Railway. As for installation of Automatic warning System on the Howrah-Kharagpur section, the survey is under progress.

Para 68: The matter is already receiving attention of the R.D.S.O. For use on the Mail/Express and Passenger trains, the electric tail lamp of 24 V auto bulb or refractor assembly, which uses power from the train battery, has been developed by the D.S.O. This would give much better visibility and is expected to give sufficient warning to the drivers of approaching trains to enable them to control their trains in time. The tail lamp developed has given a good account in preliminary trial. Further trials under various adverse conditions are being planned and it would be possible to arrive at the decision only after these trials are completed. As for goods trains, the development of a suitable tail lamp by drawing energy from the portable lead acid rechargeable battery is in progress. It may also be mentioned that the development of flasher unit for tail light is also under consideration of RDSO.

It may also be mentioned that instructions indicating the measures to improve visibility of rear-end of trains have been issued to RDSO/Railways vide Board's circular letter No. 77/Elec (TRS)/445/20 dated 26-3-1980.

Para 69: As correctly observed by the Chief Commissioner of Railway Safety, doctors are expected to go to site of serious accidents by the quickest possible means and to make use of the available road vehicles belonging to the railways. Nominations of the road vehicles for use by doctors in an emergency may provide an excuse for not finding alternative means of transport in the event of the nominated vehicle being no readily available.

It is seen that Chief Commissioner of Railway Safety has withdrawn this recommendation.

Para 70: The observations of the Commissioner of Railway Safety with regard to adequacy of ambush checks in the automatic signal territories have been taken not of by the Railway Administration who have intensified such checks. These checks are also being organised by the head office independently.

The short fall noticed by the Commissioner of Railway Safety in inspection quota was due to vacancies. This has since been put right.

Para 71: Remarks of this Ministry are set out in the Annexure enclosed.

Para 72: Herein the Commissioner of Railway Safety have made certain suggestions with regard to amendment of GRs 277, 280 and 125. These are given below along with views of this Ministry therein juxta-position.

Suggestions *G.R. 277*	*Views of Ministry of Railways* *(i) to (iii)*
(i) The maximum speed of trains at night should invariably be limited to 15 km. per hr. under GR 277(1); (ii) The speed limit of 15 kmph should also apply during day time on sections where visibility is generally poor due to cuttings, curves, down gradients, etc. (This is in addition to 8 kmph restriction prescribed in GR 277(2); (iii) In all cases after passing the automatic signals in the 'on' position the driver shall so adjust his speed that he can being his train to a stop within half the distance up to which the line ahead can be seen clearly.	The issue of imposition of a general speed restriction after passing the automatic signal in the 'on' position has come up for consideration of this Ministry more than once in the past. The issue was raised by the Commissioner of Railway Safety in the case of collision which took place at Delhi Shahdara on 12-2-1974, and again the Annual Report of the Commissioner of Railway Safety for the year 1975-1976 and also in the Inquiry Reports on the collision between Vikhroli and Kanjur Marg stations of Central Railway on 24-5-1976 and collision of Down Durgapur Special with Asansol Special between Rajkharswan and Mahali Marup station of South Eastern. Railway on 1.12.1978. In this connection this Ministry's O.Ms. No. 76 Safety (A&R) /11/1 dated 23-3-77. No. 76 Safety (A&R) 1/11, dated 19-9-1977 and No. 79 Safety (A&R) 29/10 dated 10-9-1979 would be relevant. This Ministry would wish to reiterate that the existing rules are quite clear and adequate. These rules enjoined on the driver to exercise a great caution after passing the automatic signal at 'on' and to so regulate his speed as to stop short of any obstruction. Further a speed restriction of 8 kmph which is applicable both during the day and the night has been legislated when the visibility is restricted either due to curves cuttings, dust storms, etc., and the line can not be seen clearly. The driver is also authorised to seek the

assistance of the guard, if he considers necessary. There is hardly any idea for prescribing a speed limit at night, specially when the visibility is good either due to illumination of the adjacent locality or due to a moonlit night.

The suggestions for imposition of a speed limit of 15 kmph during day on the sections where visibility is poor due to cuttings, curves, etc., gets vitiated and nullified by the fact that the existing rules specify a much lower speed limit of 8 kmph when the visibility is obstructed on any section and at any time.

The driver who cannot decide the circumstances under which he has to reduce the speed to 8 kmph, and also at what speed he should proceed under varying circumstances, is not fit to be kept at the foot-plate. This is the primary and basic quality required of a driver.

In view of the position explained above, no imposition of a general speed restriction after passing the automatic stop signal in the 'ON' position is called for. In this connection, it will be significant to note that the Chief Commissioner of Railway Safety in his noting on the Inquiry report of the Commissioner of Railway Safety on the collision of 47 Up suburban train with 563 Up Manmad-Kacheguda Passenger train between Malkajgiri and Secunderabad stations of South Central Railway on 6-11-1978 has observed that the following recommendations of the Commissioner of Railway Safety may be treated as withdrawn.

"General Rule 277(1) does not prescribe a minimum speed at present. I suggest, therefore, that the words 'speed not to exceed 10 kmph in any case' be added at the end of this para......."

(iv) The stoppage of two minutes at night at the automatic signal in the 'on' may be reduced to one minute to compensate for any time loss on account of the reduced speed.

(v) A push-button may be provided in the Driving Cabs of EMUs'/Locomotives in automatic block working of system so that when the same is pressed by the driver on passing the signal at danger, the speed is automatically restricted to 15 km. per hr. The second push-button provided in the Guard's Cab in case of EMUs would serve the same purpose — this can act as a second line of defence in the event of Driver not pressing the button.

(iv) & (v): Since no imposition of a general speed limit is considered necessary after passing the automatic signal in the 'on' position, reduction of time interval in waiting at the signal and provision of push button, as suggested, is not warranted. Regarding provision of push-button in EMUs, it may also be mentioned that the responsibility to watch the aspects of the signals and exercise a great caution after passing the automatic stop signal at danger, depending upon the visibility conditions squarely rests with the driver/motorman, and this responsibility in any manner should not be diluted or diffused.

Suggestions
G.R. 280

The GR 280, as existed earlier, should be restored so that a stopping train is protected not only in the case of an accident, failure or obstructions but also in other cases when detention exceeds 5 minutes for any reason.

Views of Ministry of Railways
(i) to (iii)

While furnishing their comments or the revised General Rules, the Commissioner of Railway Safety vide their D.O. letter No. RS.3-T(4)/74 dated 16-1-1975 categorically stated that the question of protecting a train in the automatic block system should not normally arise, as it is impracticable and dilutes the responsibility of the driver who become complacent and gets a false sense of safety. The Commission considered that it should be made clear that the entire responsibility in such cases rests squarely on the driver/motorman. The General Rules, have, therefore, been amended to stipulate that protection will be restored to only when the train stops in a automatic block signal section on account of accidents, failure or obstruction, and the train cannot proceed. If the train stops in automatic signal section for short duration for any other reason, there is no need to protect the train. Under the circumstances no amendment of GR 280 is considered necessary.

Suggestions	*Views of Ministry of Railways*
G.R. 125	
This rule should be amended to cater for a time interval of 5 minutes for protection of train in automatic signalling territories.	As rightly pointed out by the Chief Commissioner of Railway Safety, GR 125 is not applicable to automatic block territories.

Para 73: This has been examined by RDSO and it has been found that it would not be possible to increase the crash-worthiness of EMU stock without increase in tare weight/or reduction in carrying capacity as the maximum load or which the EMU coaches have been designed are already exceeded under actual loading conditions during the peak hours in Bombay area. However, RDSO has been asked to make further efforts at achieving weight reduction.

Additional Recommendations of CCRS;
No. 1

(a) This is covered up in para 68 of the report. Remarks of this Ministry against that para may please be seen.

(b) (i) to (iii) & (v)

These are regarding imposition of a speed limit and other safeguards after passing the automatic stop signal at 'ON' Remarks of this Ministry against para 72 above may please-be referred to.

(b) (vi)

The need for providing the 4th aspect in automatic signalling section is accepted. However, the spacing of signals will be uniform as far as possible consistent with line capacity required and local conditions.

(c) This is regarding amendment of GR 280. Remarks given against para 72 would refer.

(d) This relates to improvement in crash-worthiness of EMU stock. This has been dealt with in para 73.

(e) Remarks of this Ministry against para 70 of the report may please be seen.

(f) The Central and Western Railways follow a periodical programme of counselling the Drivers/Motormen at prescribed intervals of time. Instructions also exist on the railways vide Board's letter No. 73 Safety-1/24/1 dated 29-11-1973 that the competency certificates should be issued to the drivers/motormen in their knowledge of rules relating to automatic signalling sections by qualified inspectors after periods not exceeding one year, and that the drivers/motormen should not be allowed to operate unless they are in possession of such certificates. Instructions in this regard have been re-iterated to the Railways.

Additional Recommendation of CCRS No. 2

At present there are about 4170 coaches with doors at extreme ends on the Indian Railways. This is too large a number to be excluded from being treated as anti-telescopic coaches. However, this type of coaches are not being manufactured now. It is hoped that these coaches would be gradually phased out from Mail/Express trains in a period of 10 years.

D.A. As above.

17

COMMITTEE TO REVIEW THE WORKING OF LIC, 1979 — REPORT[1]

Chairman Shri Era Sezhiyan

Members Prof. V.M. Dandekar; Shri A. Rajagopalan; Dr. S.K. Chakraborty; Dr. D.P. Singh; Shri R.M. Mehta; Shri S. Ramanathan

M. Secy. Shri A. Srinivasan

Appointment

The Working of the Life Insurance Corporation of India (LIC) has been the subject of Review from time to time by a number of Parliamentary and other Committees. The Estimates Committee of Parliament (1960-61) was the first to examine its working. It submitted its report (134th Report of the Second Lok Sabha) in April 1961. It was followed by another Parliamentary Committee, the Committee on Public Undertakings (1964-65) which submitted its report in March 1965 (4th Report of the Third Lok Sabha). The next to examine the working of the LIC was the Working Group on Life Insurance Administration Constituted by the Administrative Reforms Commission in August 1967. The Group submitted its report in October 1968 which was incorporated in the Report of the Commission submitted in December 1968. The last was a Committee under the Chairmanship of Shri R.R. Morarka "to investigate into the causes of the present high level of expenses of the Corporation as indicated by its renewal expense ratio and to recommend measures, administrative or otherwise to bring it down to reasonable levels so as to subserve the Maximum interest of the policyholders". This Committee submitted its report in April 1969.

Announcing the appointment of the present Committee in the Lok

1. Delhi, Controller of Publications, 1981, 261 p.

Sabha/Rajya Sabha on May 16, 1979 the then Dy. Prime Minister (Finance) stated as under:

> "With the growth of life insurance, however, expectations in respect of service and benefits to the policy-holders have gone up considerably, and, both in Parliament and outside, demands have been made for more economic management, better return and improvement in the service to policy-holders and reorientation of the investment policy. Suggestions have also been made to the effect that the present organisational set up of the Corporation calls for a radical change for achieving the desired objectives. That apart, after the Corporation was established, there have been vast changes in the economic scene and national priorities, and increasing emphasis is now being laid on rural development, removal of unemployment and provision of essential social services. It is necessary, therefore, that the life insurance industry's structure, business operations and investment policy are geared to meet the changing requirements of the insuring public and the national economy".

The Government of India, Ministry of Finance (Department of Economic Affairs) constituted the Committee to Review the Working of LIC Vide Resolution No.F. No. 98(3) Ins.II/78 dated May 18, 1979.

Terms of Reference

(a) to review the progress of the Life Insurance since nationalisation, to assess the potential for its growth, particularly in the rural areas and to suggest steps for accelerating the development of the business;

(b) to examine the organisation of the Corporation at different levels including the set up of the field force and to suggest such changes as may bad to greater efficiency and economy in operations;

(c) to recommended measures for improving the quality of service to policy-holders;

(d) to examine the existing pattern of investment of the life fund and to suggest such changes, as may be considered necessary, for improving the return on the investments consistent with the safety of the capital and the national priorities; and

(e) to make any other recommendations which will contribute to more effective management of life insurance business.

Contents

Recommendations

Development of Life Insurance Business

1. From the analysis of some of the important issues affecting life insurance business, the following broad conclusions emerge.

(i) The cost of providing life insurance through individual life insurance policies is high and beyond the means of a large section of the population both in urban and rural areas;

(ii) In pursuance of one of its basic objectives, namely, mobilisation of savings through life insurance, the LIC has been concentrating its efforts mainly on that section of population which has a regular income and savings potential. The obligatory linking of life insurance to savings inherent in the conventional individual assurance plans and the LIC's concentration on this type of business have together and the effect of denying life insurance cover to the vast section of the people who do not have a regular income and whose savings potential is low;

(iii) As a result of the above, only about 10 per cent of the insurable male lives in the country have been provided cover against death. Even among those covered, the concentration has hitherto been on the salary earning classes and persons in the higher income groups who take out life insurance mainly because of the tax relief available. The coverage of persons in rural areas and of those employed in the unorganised sector in the urban areas is meagre;

(iv) Though a beginning has been made by the LIC in providing insurance cover against death at reasonable cost through the group term insurance plan, such coverage has again been confined mainly to the salary earning classes and very little progress is noticeable in extending this type of cover to the rural areas and to the unorganised sector in the urban areas;

(v) Because of the relatively low yield on the life fund and the high level of expenses, life insurance has ceased to be aviable savings medium and this is the reason why the share of life insurance in domestic savings has been declining; and

(vi) Life insurance in India can still be a viable savings medium, as it is in U.K., provided the LIC is enabled to improve substantially the yield on its investments and to control effectively its expenses of management. (Para 13.1)

2. Group term insurance is the best method of providing life insurance protection to large numbers at a low cost, as it avoids the cost of individual selling and individual policy administration. Also, as it precludes individual selection, it is possible to provide insurance cover to large numbers who would not be eligible for insurance under individual insurance plans. Therefore, the best way to ensure that life insurance is spread much more widely and in particular in the rural areas and among the socially and economically backward classes is through a wider spread of group term insurance. At present the LIC's Group Term Insurance business is confined mainly to salaried classes as it is easier to deal with them as a group. It is, however, necessary to extend this business to other classes as well. The LIC should, therefore, adopts as the principal plank in its development programme, promotion of group term insurance extensively to the people in rural areas and to the unorganised sectors in the urban areas. (Para 13.3)

3. An agency through which life insurance coverage can be extended to the rural people is the Central Co-operative Bank or the Regional Rural Bank. All these Banks advance short-term loans to farmers for their agricultural needs. Insurance cover could provide a collateral security for the Bank loan and the cost of insurance can be combined with the interest charged by the Bank. The group policy can

be issued to the Bank itself covering all persons to whom loans have been granted, the insurancc cover being the amount of the loan. The Committee recommends that the LIC should consult the Reserve Bank and explore the possibility of making such group insurance compulsory for all farm loans granted. (Para 13.6)

4. The Committee recommends that the LIC should lay down every year definite targets regarding the number of lives to be covered through group schemes in the rural areas and in the unorganised urban sector by each Division and create the necessary organisational framework for achieving them. (Para 13.8)

5. A large proportion of lives insured under individual assurances as well as under group schemes belong to the salaried class. The Committee is of the view that the best way of providing life insurance cover at minimum cost to them would be through a compulsory insurance scheme. The Committee has noted that some form of compulsory insurance already exists for this class under the Deposit Linked Insurance Schemes, which is a part of the Employees' Provident Fund Scheme. However, the risk cover offered under this Scheme is low. The Committee, therefore, recommends that a compulsory insurance scheme which will provide a cover equal to 2.5 times the annual salary of the employee subject to a maximum of Rs. 50,000 should be introduced for all employees covered through various Provident Fund Schemes. (Para 13.9)

6. As regards salaries employees who are not covered by a Provident Fund, another approach for providing a compulsory insurance cover can be considered. The LIC has already submitted a proposal to the Gujarat State Government to provide, as a social security measure, some basic insurance cover to employees of Shops and Establishments with less than 10 employees. The proposal is to make a small beginning. The premium would be only Re. 1 per month of which 50 paise would be paid by the employee and 50 paise by the employer. The amount of contribution would be collected by the Municipal Corporation along with the Registration Fees under the Shops and Establishments Act. All the records necessary for the purpose of insurance would be available with the authorities administering the Shops and Establishments Act and the same authorities can be authorised to pay the death claims. The Committee understands that the Gujarat Government has accepted the proposal and has decided to make it operative in the four cities of the State with Municipal Corporation. The Committee recommends that other State Governments

should also be approached for introducing similar schemes. (Para 13.10)

7. Besides the compulsory insurance scheme suggested for all salary earners contributing to a Provident Fund, the Committee recommends that the LIC should continue its efforts to extend Group Insurance coverage linked with savings to the salary earning classes through its Group Term-*cum*-Savings Schemes. Under this scheme the LIC is at present allowing accumulation of the contributions at 6 per cent only. It should be noted that the LIC is currently earning on its new investments a rate of interest of over 8 per cent. If the funds pertaining to such group scheme are invested separately and if a rate of interest 1/2 per cent to 1 per cent less than the actual rate earned on the LIC's funds, depending on the size of the group, is allowed, the scheme will prove more attractive than at present. The Committee is of the view that the difference between the interest actually earned and the interest allowed on the accumulation of contribution as suggested would be adequate to meet the expenses of administration of the Schemes. (Para 13.11)

8. The Committee is informed that under its existing Group Term-*cum*-Savings Schemes the maximum amount of cover that the LIC allows is Rs. 12,000 and that it has recently decided that under all new group schemes, the cover should be restricted to Rs. 10,000 only. The Committee is of the view that the even the present limit of Rs. 12,000 is too low and that the limit should be increased to Rs. 50,000 which is the maximum limit suggested for the proposed compulsory insurance scheme. . . . The Committee is convinced that the Group Term-*cum*-Savings Scheme re-designed on the lines suggested would be found attractive by a large number of employee groups and will help the LIC both in spreading insurance coverage and in mobilisation of savings at minimum cost. (Para 13.12)

9. The Committee appreciates that introduction of compulsory insurance schemes and wider extension of Group Term-*cum*-Saving Schemes for salaried employees may affect LIC's direct business adversely as currently a very large proportion of its business is being secured from salaried employees. The Committee, however, feels that there is enough potential in the country for development of life insurance business and if to an extent the potential from salary earning class is reduced, it would stimulate the LIC to concentrate on other classes who have till now been relatively neglected, and thus help in greater spread of life insurance business in the country as a whole. The

Committee also believes that even after introduction of compulsory insurance schemes and extension of Group Term-*cum*-Saving Schemes to large sections of salaried employees, there will still be scope for selling individual savings linked life insurance policies to the salaried class, provided steps are taken to make life insurance a viable savings medium. (Para 13.13)

10. In considering life insurance as a savings medium the difference in the return (taking into account the tax reliefs obtainable) obtained by those in the higher income brackets and by those who pay little or no tax has to be considered. This difference in the return obviously involves serious lack of equity. The Committee would, therefore, like to recommend an alternative approach on the lines of the suggestion made in the report of the Committee of Actuaries which involves establishment of a separate fund for policies on which on income-tax relief would be available and on which the Government would allow a substantially higher rate of interest. The broad outlines of the plan are given hereunder :

(i) Only one type of policy will be issued under this Fund which will be Endowment with Profits Policy for terms 15, 20 and 25 years and maturing not beyond age 60;

(ii) The maximum amount of annual premium that can be paid under all policies taken under this plan by an individual would be Rs. 1,000. The proponent would be required to give details in the proposal form, of policies already taken out by him under this plan and the amount of premium he is paying under such policies. He should also be required to give a declaration that if the information given is false or inaccurate and he had, in fact, taken out other policies under this plan, any premium paid in excess of Rs. 1,000 per annum under such policies would stand forfeited and the sum assured would be reduced correspondingly;

(iii) Premiums paid under these policies would not be eligible for any income-tax relief. This will by itself ensure that such a policy will be mainly availed of by persons who are not liable for high rates of income-tax;

(iv) This fund will be invested in a special Deposit Account as directed by the Government. The rate of interest on this fund should be at least 2 per cent higher than the rate of interest on 7 Year National Savings Certificates where the current rate of interest is 10.75 per cent compound. The 2 per cent difference in yield is to cover outgo by way of expenses of management so that the net yield obtained by the policyholder is the same as on investments in National Savings;

(v) In determining the LIC's liability for income-tax, the surplus of this fund would be excluded from the total surplus;

(vi) The entire surplus of this fund disclosed by periodical actuarial valuations should be available for distribution to the policy-holders and no share will be reserved for the Government; and

(vii) A separate account of this fund should be maintained and all premiums and other income relating to this fund should be accounted for separately. All expenses should be allocated between the Ordinary Life Fund and this Fund in proportion to the respective premium income of the two funds. (Para 13.15)

11. Various suggestions have been made to the Committee for introduction of new plans of insurance to meet the needs of the rural population. . . . After considering the various suggestions received, the Committee recommends examination of the following two suggestions for special plans rural:

(i) As the population do not have regular income, any special plan for rural population should permit variations in premium from year to year. To meet this, particular problem, the Committee suggests that the LIC should consider issuing single premium Endowment policies under which the risk cover would be double the amount payable on maturity. The cost of servicing such policy would be small. As the full premium is paid in one instalment and would be available for immediate investment, it should be possible to assume a much higher rate of interest in the calculation of premium than under the ordinary Endowment plan. A variation of this plan would be to have a single policy contract, with a Pass Book issued to the policy-holder, under which option would be given to the policy-holder to pay additional premium at any time and obtain additional cover merely by way of an endorsement in the Pass Book. As both the original cover as well as additional covers would be on the basis of single premium contracts, it may be possible to issue all such policies on non-medical basis, subject of course to certain limits on the maximum sum assured. To ensure that agents take interest in persuading the policy-holders to go in for periodical additions to such policies, commission at reasonable rates should be paid to the agent each time an additional cover is availed of. It should be possible to work out a suitable scheme on the above lines with would permit considerable flexibility and still be simple to administer;

(ii) In rural areas there are often periods which may extend from one to three years when the policy-holder is unable to pay the premium because of drought or other natural calamities. The LIC should, therefore, consider issuing an ordinary endowment policy under which a small term insurance premium would be collected along with the first premium which would provide risk cover for a period up to three years in case the policy-holder is unable to pay, the premium for some time after two years' premia have been paid. Any time within the three years' period during which risk cover is provided without payment of the normal annual premium, the policyholder will have the option to pay off the arrears of premium with interest for continuation of the policy beyond the three-year period. Risk premium already paid would then again become available for covering further defaults in future. Though the risk premium would increase with the age, as the amount at risk will go on reducing with the duration of the policy, it should be possible to determine, at the outset, the amount of risk premium to be collected along with the first premium which could provided risk cover for defaults in payment of premium up to three years throughout the term of the policy. (Para 13.16)

12. There is one other plan which the Committee feels the LIC ought to introduce and that is a level premium term insurance plan. The Committee has noted that the Committee of Actuaries had recommended introduction of such a plan. The Committee understands that the LIC has not yet taken any decision on this recommendation. As a monopoly organisation, it is the LIC's obligation to provide all types of life insurance cover which are actuarially sound and are generally offered by insurers in other countries. The Committee, therefore, recommends that the LIC should introduce this scheme. (Para 13.18)

13. The Committee is strongly of the view that the present restriction on the operation of approved Pension Funds is not at all justified and all approved Pension Funds should be given freedom from the provisions of the LIC Act, as was the case before nationalisation. At the same time, the LIC should itself re-examine its methods of operating its pension schemes and should urgently consider introduction of the managed fund concept which is recommended by the Committee of Actuaries in the report, so that they are able to offer terms which are competitive with those which privately managed pension funds can give to their members. . . . The Committee, therefore, recommends that:

(i) The LIC Act should be suitably amended, so that exemption is granted to all Pension Funds from the operation of the LIC Act, on par with the exemption granted to the Funds existing as on 1-9-1956 under Section 44(f) of the LIC Act, subject to their working being supervised by the Controller of Insurance; and

(ii) The LIC should urgently re-examine its present pattern of working of Pension Schemes and introduce the managed fund concept, so that it is able to offer terms which are competitive with those that can be offered to their members by privately managed Pension Funds. (Para 13.20)

Marketing Organisation and Development Planning

14. We believe that if life insurance business is to grow on healthy lines a strong agency organisation consisting of trained professional agents should be the corner-stone of the LIC's marketing organisation. (Para 14.4)

15. There should be a pre-recruitment training and test before an agent is appointed. The LIC should devise appropriate aptitude tests as well as tests for the basic knowledge required by an agent and selection should be made on the basis of such tests and after interview by the Branch Manager, who should be made responsible for proper selection of agents. He should ensure that only such persons as are likely to continue in the insurance agency career are recruited and in no case a "Benami" is given an agency. (Para 14.5)

16. The Committee is of the view that renewal commission should be viewed as payment for services required to be rendered and

not as a deferred compensation for just selling a policy. It is, therefore, necessary to ensure that agents render essential services to policy-holders. Though the Committee appreciates that there would be practical difficulties in strictly enforcing any such rule, it suggests laying down some broad criteria for this purpose such as follows:

(i) The agent should be required to maintain certain essential records which should be periodically verified by the Branch Manager; and

(ii) Whenever there is default in payment of premiums the agent should be required to give the reasons for non-payment.

The suggestions made above are only illustrative. The Committee is of the view that it would be possible for the LIC to evolve on the basis of practical experience, methods of ensuring that agents do maintain contacts with policy-holders and render essential services to them to entitle them to payment of renewal commission. (Para 14.7)

17. To enable the agent to render these services, proper post-recruitment training is essential. The Committee recommends that the training should be at three levels. The first will be the pre-recruitment training, which will be given by the Development Officer who recruits the agent and which would give him basic knowledge of life insurance plans and selling techniques to enable him to start working as an agent. The second stage is the post recruitment training given by trained instructors covering all aspects of policy servicing and giving more detailed guidance in selling techniques. This stage would also include field training by the Development Officer through joint calls on prospects. Servicing of "orphaned policies", that is policies where the original agent has ceased to work as an agent, can also form part of such field training. The third will be advanced training if a high standard for professional agents, provided through special courses designed by the Federation of Insurance Institutes leading to the grant of a diploma on passing an examination. Agents who have obtained the diploma should receive recognition as professional agents and holding of the diploma should after a transition period, be made a condition for membership of various clubs. (Para 14.8)

18. At present the LIC classifies its agents into three categories—inactive, active and qualified agents. None of these classifications gives any indications as to whether the agent is working effectively throughout the year. The Committee, therefore, recommends

that a new classification of "effective agents" be introduced the criterion being that the agent insures a minimum of 2 lives for a sum assured of Rs. 10,000 every month for at least 10 months in the year and his total business during the year is not-less-than 25 lives and a sum assured of Rs. 2 lakhs. Efforts of the Development Officials should be concentrated on increasing the number of such "effective" agents from year to year. (Para 14.9)

19. After careful consideration, the Committee has come to the conclusion that if the LIC is to get the right type of person to work as agents particularly in the rural areas and untapped segments of urban areas, it would be necessary to retain the existing levels of agency commission. The Committee also feels that any re-scheduling of commission rates between first year and renewal would not be of great practical utility. (Para 14.10)

20. As the Committee is of the view that renewal commission should be considered as payment for services required to be rendered by the agent and not deferred compensation for selling of life insurance policies, it is necessary that the present rule regarding continuation of renewal commission after termination of agency should also be modified.

The Committee recommends that continuation of renewal commission after cessation of the agency should be allowed only if the agent has worked for at least 15 years out of which for at least 10 years he should have completed the minimum qualifying business required in accordance with the Agents' Regulations. (Para 14.11)

21. As regards payment of "hereditary" commission, the Committee is of the view that there is no justification for payment of commission after the death of an agent. However, to give protection to the families of agents who die during their agency career, a more generous term insurance benefit should be allowed. The Committee recommends that the present term insurance scheme for agents may be modified to cover all agents who have completed the minimum qualifying business for a period of at least five years and the quantum of cover fixed at five times the renewal commission earned by the agent in the agency year preceding his death. (Para 14.12)

22. In order to bring down in the high incidence of early lapses certain changes are necessary in the agent's commissions schedule. The Committee recommends that commission on first year's premium should be paid only on receipt of the full first year's premium. Further, bonus commission should be based on the first year's premia after

deducting therefrom the premia on policies which have lapsed during the year in question without acquiring surrender value. The Committee realises that such a change in the method of payment of bonus commission may be difficult to implement with the existing data processing machines and that it will be possible to give effect to it only after the existing data processing system is replaced by a more versatile system as recommended by us. (Para 14.13)

23. Regarding Development Officers the Committee recommends that their functions should be redefined. At present, though the Development Officer is expected to recruit, train, motivate and supervise the agents, his work is appraised mainly on the basis of the sum assured and premium income secured through his organisation. This has resulted in the neglect of the essential function of the Development Officer, namely creation of a stable agency organisation. The Committee, therefore, recommends that the Development Officer's functions should be clearly defined as that of recruitment and training of agents and supervision of the working of the agents recruited by him. It should be his responsibility to see that the right type of persons are chosen as agents and given pre-recruitment training before appointment and they are given detailed training, guidance and motivation in the field after recruitment so that they develop into "effective" agents. The work of a Development Officer should be appraised solely on the basis of his success in developing an organisation of "effective" agents. His targets should be fixed in terms of the number of agents to be recruited by him, the proportion of recruited agents to be made "effective" and the increase in the number of "effective" agents. (Para 14.14)

24. The Committee accepts that for employees whose work will be completely in the field, a scheme of incentives and disincentives should constitute an essential part of their remuneration. However, the incentives and disincentives should be linked to the performance in creating an "effective" agency organisation and not to "cost ratio". (Para 14.14)

25. The Committee recommends that all agents who have worked as "effective" agents for a period of at least 3 years and who are in a position to work on their own should be detached from the Development Officer and made direct agents. This, however, will not affect the appraisal of the Development Officer as his work is to be judged mainly on the basis of the new agents he is able to recruit and make "effective". (Para 14.14)

26. The cadre of Assistant Branch Manager (Development) should be treated as a selection grade for the Development Officers and not as an intermediary between the Development Officer and Branch Manager. In the urban areas the ABM(D) will look after all agents who have been made direct. It will be his responsibility to see that the direct agents continue to remain "effective" and their productivity continues to increase. In the rural areas where a Development Officer is in exclusive charge of a certain area, it may not be practicable to detach from the Development Officer, agents who have worked as "effective" agents for three years. However, in such areas where a Development Officer has been able to create a fairly large organisation of "effective" agents, he should be considered for promotion to the cadre of Assistant Branch Manager (Development). After such promotion also, he will continue to look after his whole area and it will be his responsibility to see that the whenever any gaps occur in the agency organisation by termination of any existing agent, the vacancy is filled by recruitment of a new agent. (Para 14.15)

27. The Committee makes the following recommendations with regard to the marketing organisation for the expansion of the group scheme business and its administration:

(i) The decision already taken by the LIC to set up full-fledged Group and Superannuation Department in all the Divisions should be implemented at an early date;

(ii) In each Branch office, particularly in the rural areas, at least one Officer from the cadre of Assistant Branch Manager (Development) and one Higher Grade Assistant should be given thorough training in the sale and administration of group insurance business so that they are able to initiate and conduct negotiations for the sake of group business under the overall guidance of the Divisional Office;

(iii) The Committee recommends that the officer and staff posted in the proposed development-cum-servicing centres should also be given training in the special problems of development of group business in the rural areas, so that they can take the initiative in developing group business in these areas;

(iv) Though group schemes should continue to be canvassed mainly by the officials, professional agents who have received specialised training in this behalf and passed a prescribed test may be allowed to play a limited role in selling this business.

They should, however, be restricted to rural areas and to the unorganised sector in the urban areas. They may also be allowed to play a limited role in the sale of group gratuity schemes and pension schemes with large employers in the urban areas. The Commission to the agent will, however, be restricted to a small percentage which will not add materially to the cost of group cover; and

(v) A scheme of incentives should be introduced for officers in charge of group business for outstanding performance in the development of such business. However, the scale of incentives should be so fixed that it does not add materially to the cost of the group cover. (Para 14.20)

28. From a review of the operations of the LIC in the area of Development planning, the following conclusions emerge:

(i) Though the LIC realised the need for planning based on market survey and statistics relating to the economic potential of the area and its manuals provided for the same in practice these were not implemented. Instead the easier method of fixing *ad hoc* targets of new business in terms of sun assured was adopted;

(ii) While a large number of agents were recruited year after year, almost an equal number had to be terminated as they failed to complete the minimum business guarantee. These were merely spotters with no sustained interest in the agency work. Consequently growth of a stable and professional agency force was inhibited;

(iii) In the earlier years a large number of development officers were recruited without any regard for their aptitude. The performance of most of them was poor, the remuneration paid to them exceeded in some cases even the premium income brought by them;

(iv) The stress on new business sum assured has led to an organisational culture where success was measured solely by new business sum assured, and other aspects of organisational functioning were virtually ignored; and

(v) Since volume of new business was the major yardstick for measuring the progress, the entire organisation gears itself to fulfil the target set before it during the closing period of the accounting year. Heavy new business in the last month of the accounting year has been in evidence even during the years before nationalisation and the LIC is no exception. There was heavy concentration of business in December when the accounting year ended in December and now, when the accounting year ends in March, the concentration has shifted to March. This has resulted in (a) delays in the adjustment of amounts received towards premium, (b) delays in the issuing of policies (c) non-issue of premium notices, particularly in the case of quarterly and half-yearly mode of premium and the consequential lapsation, revivals, etc., etc. (Para 5.16)

29. The LIC should fix targets every year for the number of lives to be covered through group insurance schemes in the rural areas and in the unorganised sector in the urban areas. To start with, such targets may be fixed for the Division as a whole. Later it may be possible to fix targets Branch-wise as well. Separate targets may also be fixed or the number of lives to be covered and the amount of savings to be mobilised through group term-cum-savings plan and through group gratuity schemes and group pension schemes. The work of the Development Officials concerned with this business should get recognition at all-India levels through competitions and awards. In its internal and external publicity, increasing stress should be paid by the LIC of the role of these schemes in extending insurance coverage. (Para 14.21)

30. As regards planning for development of individual life insurance business. The basic planning should be in terms of growth of organisation as represented by the number of "effective" agents. Planning should start with locating all the centres in the rural areas which have the potential for supporting an "effective" agent, which may be termed an "agency block". The plan would take into consideration the number of such blocks where "effective" agents are already working and the number of blocks which lack such agents. The aim of the plan should be to ensue that the proportion of agency blocks where there are "effective" agents should steadily increase. (Para 14.22)

31. As regards urban areas, the Committee has noted that at present there is no effective planning to ensure that the agency organisation cover all important sectors of the urban centre. The Branches are at present located on the basis of availability of premises and convenience of the development personnel. As, till recently, the

City Branch Offices were not handling any service to policy-holders, the convenience of the policy-holders did not arise. Further, in the recruitment of agents no efforts are made to see that all the important sectors of the population are covered. The Committee suggests that the LIC should undertake an complete review of its present policy in the matter of location of Branch Offices and recruitment of agents in the large cities. It should take steps to disperse the Branch Offices over the city with a view to locating the Branches near the policy-holders' place of work or residence. It should also plan its agents' recruitment in such a manner that all important sectors classified on the basis of geographical location, economic activity or community-wise are covered. (Para 14.23)

32. As regards overall targets for the Branches, Divisions and the LIC as a whole, the Committee recommends that these targets should be fixed not in terms of new business, but in terms of the increase in the business in force as represented by the number of lives covered, sum assured and premium income and also in terms of the increase in the number of "effective" agents. (Para 14.24)

33. One of the terms of reference of the Committee is to assess the potential for growth of life insurance particularly in the rural areas and suggest steps for accelerating the development of business. The existence of a vast potential for development of life insurance business is obvious from the fact that only 10 per cent of the insurable population has so far been covered by the LIC and 90 per cent still remains to be covered. The main reason for the LIC's failure in extending the coverage to the rural areas and to the weaker sections of the community has been its concentration on savings linked individual insurance business which is beyond the reach of large sections of the community. The Committee has, therefore, recommended a wider spread of group insurance business which would enable the LIC to extend the coverage of life insurance to those neglected sections. As for the potential of life insurance as a means of mobilising savings, this depends on restoring viability of life insurance as a savings medium. The Committee has, therefore, concentrated its attention on the steps to be taken to make life insurance viable as a savings medium in the face of other competing savings media. If the recommendations made by the Committee in both these areas are accepted and early action taken thereon, the Committee is convinced that the LIC will be able to extend the coverage of life insurance at a much faster rate than at present and thus tap the potential for life insurance in the country, which is indeed

vast, in an increasing measure. (Para 14.25)

Service to Policy-holders

34. The main problems in the area of underwriting and issue of policies is the delay in issue of policies particularly in respect of proposals completed in the peak month of March. Such delays have serious adverse consequences on the other aspects of policy servicing as well. The Committee expects that if the concept of "effective" agent and the change in emphasis in fixation of targets from new business to increase in the business in force are accepted, they should go a long way in ensuring a more even spread of business. Meanwhile, the LIC should consider ways of ensuring expeditious issue of policies. (Para 15.2)

35. Preparation of advance receipts involves considerable amount of work and cost. Further, control over them at the branch offices is also not quite satisfactory and instances have been reported where receipts have been misused and premium collections misappropriated. A suggestion has been made that instead of preparing receipts in advance the premium notice form itself should contain a small counterpart which could serve as a receipt. The branch office which is responsible for receiving premiums and issuing receipts should be supplied with Cash Register Machines which would endorse receipts of premium on the counterpart of the notice and simultaneously print out the details of the receipt on a scroll which would serve the purpose of a cash book. Such a system, it has been represented, would not only reduce considerably the work-load at the cash counter but would also provide stricter control on cash collections. The Committee recommends that the LIC should introduce such an alternative system on an experimental basis in one of its Divisions so that, on the basis of actual experience, it can decide whether the system is workable and if so consider its extension to all the Offices. (Para 15.3)

36. The Committee recommends that in all important rural centres where a full-fledged branch office would not be economically viable, the LIC should open small offices which may be termed Development-*cum*-Servicing Centres. Such offices should have a small complement of staff consisting of an Officer-in-charge in the cadre of ABM, with one or two assistants in the HGA's cadre. These offices would be responsible for development of business as well as collection of premium and rendering of certain essential services to policy-

holders. (Para 15.4)

37. The Committee believes that one of the main causes of the large proportion of collections going into deposit is the lack of contact between the agent and the policy-holder after sale. If the Committee's recommendations on the agents role in the service to the policy-holders are accepted and agent's help is sought in ensuring that premiums are paid in time and with full particulars and also in obtaining the necessary requirements for clearance of deposits, it should be possible for the LIC to reduce the amounts of collections going into deposit. (Para 15.5)

38. To improve the LIC's performance in regard to grant of policy loans, action will be required in the following areas:

(i) Completion of decentralisation of policy servicing functions to branch offices, including settlement of all policy loans;

(ii) Extending the decentralisation programme to city branch offices; and

(iii) Reorganisation of the work relating to servicing of SSS business. (Para 15.6)

39. A large proportion of applications for policy loans are for very small amounts particularly under SSS policies. Since this work entails fairly high administrative cost, the Committee recommends that apart from raising the minimum amount of loan that could be sanctioned under a policy from Rs. 150 to Rs. 250, no loan should be granted within three years of a previous loan and not more than three loans in all during the currency of a policy. (Para 15.7)

40. As loans are availed of by only a section of policy-holders, equity demands that the net rate of interest obtained by the LIC on its policy loans, that is, after allowing for administrative costs for servicing such loans, is not lower than what is obtained on its investments generally. The Committee recommends that the LIC should immediately undertake a study of the unit cost of the operation involved and revise the rate of interest accordingly. (Para 15.8)

41. The LIC has shown a substantial improvement in the matter of claim settlement during the last ten years, and its performance compares favourably with that of leading Indian companies before nationalisation and even of U.S. insurance companies today. (Para 15.9)

42. The two major problems in the area of maturity claims are

firstly to ensure that maturity intimations are sent in time and are accurate and secondly that the following up by the field staff of maturity claims remaining outstanding for more than three months is made more effective. As regards the first, the problem is due mainly to the defective data processing system. As regards the second, the Committee recommends that the LIC should make a thorough review of its present scheme of servicing of outstanding claims by its field staff through issue of Claim Particular Sheets (CPS) and take all possible steps to make the scheme more effective. The action taken on CPS and the number of outstanding claims settled through such follow-up action should be suitably included as one of the indices in appraisal of performance of the development officials. (Para 15.10)

43. As regards death claims, two major areas where improvements are necessary are firstly with regard to investigation of early claims and secondly in dealing with repudiation of claims........ considerable delay still occurs in investigation of early claims and also in taking decisions quickly. To reduce these delays to the minimum, the present machinery for claims investigation will have to be strengthened and the decision-making process speeded up. According to the procedure laid down by the LIC the investigation can be entrusted to field officials and wherever necessary to members of the staff specially trained for the purpose. In practice the work seems to be entrusted to the former category only. The Committee recommends that the LIC reviews the present system, ascertains reasons for the delays and evolves necessary machinery as well as sanctions to ensure that the time limit it has laid down for completing the investigation is not exceeded and decisions are taken without delay. (Para 15.11)

44. We recommend that a Committee consisting of a Managing Director of the LIC, the Controller of Insurance and an Actuary not currently in the service of the LIC should go into all the cases of repudiated claims where the courts have decided against the LIC or where the LIC has decided to compromise the case. In the light of a review of these cases, the said Committee should make specific recommendations regarding the policy to be followed in the matter of repudiation of claims. (Para 15.12)

45. The Committee notes that under Section 47A of the Insurance Act a provision already exists for referring disputes regarding claims up to Rs. 2000 to the Controller of Insurance. The Committee recommends that this section may be amended to increase the limit to Rs. 25,000 sum assured. (Para 15.13)

46. The Committee notes that currently the LIC pays interest at the rate of 6 per cent for delay in settlement of claims, where the delay is attributable to the LIC only. The Committee recommends that the rate of interest for such delayed payment of claims should be the same is the rate the LIC charges for delays in payment of premia. (Para 15.14)

47. Though the procedure laid down for dealing with complaints are generally satisfactory, in actual practice they are not proving effective. The Committee recommends that the LIC should find out the reasons for this and take appropriate steps to see that the existing machinery is made more effective. (Para 15.15)

48. The Salary Savings Schemes provides the salaried class the most convenient method of payment of premium. The scheme is, therefore, becoming increasingly popular among this class. However, in actual working it has thrown up a number of administrative problems and a result the service to the policy-holders is far from satisfactory. (Para 15.16)

49. The Committee recommends stricter enforcement of the conditions laid down by the LIC at the time of introduction of a salary savings scheme with a new employer. The responsibility should be fixed on the Divisional Manager/Branch Manager to see that all instructions are strictly complied with. Further, in respect of existing salary savings scheme, if it transpires that the employer is unable to comply with the conditions prescribed, the LIC should consider withdrawal of the scheme after giving due notice. (Para 15.17)

50. The Committee further recommends that the LIC must exercise strict control on the timely remittance of the premium deductions by the employer (in respect of policies under salary savings scheme) and whenever there is delay in remittance of premium by the employer interest at the rate usually charged on bank borrowing for working capital should be collected. (Para 15.18)

51. Under the SSS as it is operated at present, after issue of the policy, the agent has practically no role in servicing. Therefore, there appears to be no justification for payment of renewal commission to the agent. The Committee recommends that commission under SSS should be restricted to the first three years. Such commission should also be paid only after the full year's premium is paid in each of the three years. (Para 15.19)

52 The Committee also suggests consideration of another approach which is to restrict canvassing of policies under SSS in respect

of each Paying Authority to a selected professional agent who will be responsible for both selling and servicing the policies. Entitlement to commission would then be conditional on the agent ensuring that premiums are remitted by the authority in time, with necessary supporting reconciliation statements. Such an arrangement would improve the administration of SSS business and also make the operation of commission settlement much simpler. (Para 15.20)

53. The Committee recommends that the LIC should undertake a detailed study of the cost of administration of SSS policies and if it is established that it is substantially higher than on ordinary policies, the extra charge for monthly payment should be made applicable to salary savings scheme policies also. (Para 15.21)

54. The Committee recommends that the minimum amount of instalment of premium under SSS should be fixed at, say, Rs. 10 per month. (Para 15.22)

55. As regards, payment of commission on the existing policies under SSS, the Committee recommends that the payment should be released on yearly basis after receipts of the whole year's premium. (Para 15.23)

56. The Committee recommends that the LIC should pursue its policy of decentralisation of servicing functions to branch offices and ensure full coverage of all mofussil and city branch offices with a time bound programme. (Para 15.24)

57. The Committee also recommends that the LIC should open a number of Development-*cum*-servicing centres in the more important rural blocks where it does not have a Branch office and where the present potential for business is not enough to support a full-fledged branch office. These offices besides looking after development of business and agency organisation will also attend to certain essential servicing functions like collection of premium. This would help considerably in improving service facilities in rural areas and also help in spreading life insurance coverage both through individual assurances and group schemes to the rural areas. The Committee recommends that the LIC should draw up a definite programme for opening such offices, so that over a ten year period there is at least one such office in each Community Development Block. The Committee appreciates that opening of a large number of such small offices may increase the overall costs of administration at least initially. As this step is suggested in pursuance of the LIC's social objective of spreading life insurance business in rural areas, the Committee recommends that a part of these

costs should be reimbursed by the Government from the share of valuation surplus at present being allotted to it. (Para 15.25)

58. Due to the inherent limitations of unit record-*cum*-adrema based data processing system, as also due to the increasing frequency of the breakdowns of the unit record machines, there is an increasing deterioration in the standard of service now being rendered to the policy-holders as also in the financial and other controls on the LIC's various servicing operations. Some of these are listed below:

(i) Because of the inaccuracies in the premium master card and adrema files, omissions in issue of premium notices and preparation of premium receipts are becoming more frequent leading to serious complaints from the policy-holders;

(ii) The work of issue of first default notices has to be handled manually because of the inadequacy of the present data processing system. Having regard to the volume of work, manual handling of this job is becoming increasingly difficult and in many of the offices this work is not being attended to at all;

(iii) The premium posting on policy ledger sheets has been discontinued in some of the Divisional Offices as a result of decentralisation and the Divisional Office has to entirely depend on Branch records to know the status of the policy. This involves some risk as the Branch Office records can be easily tampered with. Also if the records at the Branch Office are lost in any natural calamity like fire or flood, there is not alternative source to fall back upon. Under the unit record system, it is not possible to maintain premium payment particulars in the machine card files. The consequence is that even with the complete decentralisation of servicing responsibility to the Branch Offices, the Divisional Office will either have to continue with the premium postings on policy ledgers involving considerable amount of duplication of work or alternatively to discontinue the same and face the risks referred to above;

(iv) The Commission billing system also is becoming increasingly unreliable. Adequate controls are not exercised in stopping payment of commission to terminated agents and there is a possibility of diversion of such commission to other agents by a tampering with unit record card files. Further, reconciliation of monthly commission payments with premium collections, as also verifying the accuracy of commission paid by sorting the payment by policy year or commission year controls basis, which are the controls envisaged on commission payment under the existing Machine Department Manual procedures is becoming increasingly difficult and such reconciliation has been discontinued in most of the Divisional Offices. This again increases the risks of wrong payment of commission;

(v) It will not be possible under the present unit record system to provide for any further changes in commission rate pattern or commission payment procedures;

(vi) Settlement of bonus commission to agents is at present done manually at the Branch Office and there is practically no control on such payments. In the interest of adequate financial control, it is necessary to mechanise this work but it is not possible to do so on the present unit record system. Further, if the bonus commission procedure is to be changed on the lines suggested by us these changes cannot be given effect to in the unit record system or even on the present manual system;

(vii) Due to lack of proper controls on updating card files the list of maturities, survival benefits cases under anticipated endowment plan and other automatic changes to be incorporated in the policies are becoming increasingly unreliable. Many omissions are noticed in the lists prepared by the machine department, leading to inefficient service to policy-holders, and delays in the matter of settlement of maturity claims and survival benefits under anticipated endowment policies;

(viii) At present the machine departments are not able to generate timely and meaningful statistics about policy lapsation such as agent, development officer or Branch-wise lapse statements, analysis of lapses according to plan of policy, mode of payment of premium, month of issue of policy, etc. In the absence of such statistics it becomes difficult to decide upon appropriate policies to prevent or minimise lapsation or to take appropriate follow-up action for revival of lapsed policies;

(ix) Though the Machine Department manual of the LIC visualises mechanisation of a number of jobs like policy deposit accounting, loan accounting and foreclosure action, etc., most of the Divisional Offices do not find it possible to undertake these jobs on the machines because of the inadequacy of machines. As handling these jobs manually is very difficult because of the large volume of work requiring to be handled, these jobs are either not being done at all or are being done very inadequately;

(x) Because of the inadequacy of the present data processing system, salary savings scheme servicing has become extremely unsatisfactory as well as uneconomic; and

(xi) Above all, the increasing failures of financial controls arising out of the inadequacies of the existing data processing system are opening up a fertile ground for possible frauds. (Para 7.63)

59. It will be seen that the existing unit record machines as well as the whole data processing system of the LIC have become totally obsolete, which is a major cause for the serious deterioration in the standard of policy-holders' servicing in the LIC. The deterioration in the functioning of the data processing system is of such serious magnitude, that unless very urgent action is taken to replace the existing system by a more modern and reliable system, the LIC may have to face a complete breakdown in its data processing system in the not too distant future with very serious consequences on its service to policy-holders as well as on its overall financial working. (Para 7.64)

60. The Committee strongly recommends that the LIC should arrange for a complete change over from the existing data processing system based on the Unit Record and Adrema machines to a versatile and modern system as early as possible. The system that the Committee recommends for consideration of the LIC is one based on installation of micro-processors at the large Branch Offices and mini-computers at the Divisional Offices. The micro-processors at the Branch Offices will attend to the work relating to premium billing and premium and commission accounting, and will also replace the policy and the loan ledgers at the branch level. A consolidated data of the policy would be available on the floppy disc or the magnetic tape attachment to the micro-processor. The new system will replace the multiple file system obtaining at present where records of the policy are spread over a number of files such as premium ledger, loan lodger, premium master card and demand receipt cards, valuation master cards, adrema plates, etc., by a single consolidated record maintained on the magnetic tape or floppy disc. The same consolidated record of the policy will also be available on the mini-computer at the Divisional Office which will exercise automatic control on all the operations of

the Branch Offices. The mini-computer will also act as a servicing medium for the smaller branches which will not be in a position to install a micro-processor and for the still smaller Development-*cum*-Servicing centres in the rural areas. The smaller Branch Offices will continue to maintain individual policy ledgers but all premium and commission billing work will be handled by the Divisional Office. The Development-*cum*-Servicing centres will not maintain any policy ledgers or other records but they will still be able to render essential services to the policy-holders on the basis of updated status cards supplied by the Divisional Office. (Para 15.26)

61. Some of the important advantages of the new system in improving the service to the policy-holders are indicated below:

(i) Apart from being more reliable and regular, the premium notices would be more in the nature of a statement of account and will include particulars of loan and interest dues, other outstanding dues like "X-charges", outstanding deposits, etc.;

(ii) It will make it easier for the LIC to change the present system of preparing receipts in advance along with the premium notices, leading to substantial saving in cost;

(iii) It will enable the LIC to take automatic loan foreclosure action in cases where such foreclosure becomes necessary in accordance with the condition of loan bond;

(iv) It will enable the LIC to exercise stricter control on all agency commission payments including bonus commission payments and also enable the LIC to effect a change over in the commission payment system on the lines recommended by the Committee or in any other manner;

(v) It will ensure timely issue of maturity intimations and thus help expeditious settlement of maturity claims;

(vi) It will help considerably in improving the servicing of SSS business and reducing substantially the cost of its servicing;

(vii) It will eliminate duplication of functions and records between the Branch Offices and the Divisional Offices, which still obtains to a great extent, and provide automatic controls on branch operations;

(viii) It will make it possible for the proposed small Development-*cum*-Servicing offices in the rural centres to provide most of the essential services; and

(ix) The financial control system in the LIC are not at all working effectively leading to increasing mistakes involving losses to the LIC and also opening up possibilities of large scale frauds. A change over in the data processing system will help considerably in tightening up the financial controls and thus preventing losses. (Para 15.27)

62. The Committee is satisfied that such a change over would not reduce employment opportunities in the LIC. As the LIC is now functioning life insurance has ceased to be viable as a savings medium and unless urgent steps are taken to restore its economic viability, the business is bound to be grievously affected with serious effect on the employment opportunities in the LIC. On the other hand, if the LIC is enabled to restore the economic viability of life insurance as a savings medium, and also to improve its services to the policy-holders, it would result in increased business, with consequent increase in employment opportunities. (Para 15.28)

Expenses of Management

63. Taking all the aspects into considerations, it will be readily accepted that if life insurance is to remain as a viable saving medium, it is essential that the level of expenses of the LIC should be brought down to a level substantially lower than the present statutorily prescribed maximum level. (Para 8.14)

64. Though the number of staff per lakh of policies in force has been continuously going down, the staff salaries have been rising somewhat steeply. A part of this increase is undoubtedly due to inflationary trend and the continuous increase in the consumer price index. However, the staff salaries have increased far in excess of the rise in the consumer price index. (Para 8.24)

65. While expenses on administrative staff salaries per in-force policy has gone up in a proportion higher than the corresponding increases in the consumer price index, the expenses under other major heads have one up a much lower extent. If the corresponding increases in the sum assured and premium per in-force policy are also taken into consideration, then it would appear that all other expenses expressed as a percentage of premium have remained more or less steady and if the renewal expense ratio has gone up, it is mainly due to the increase in the administrative staff, staff salaries on the one hand and increase in the development officers' salaries and other development costs on the

other. The remedy for the increase in the expense ratio will, therefore, have to be found in tackling the problem of expenses under those two heads. (Para 8.30)

66. During an inflationary period staff salaries will inevitably increase more rapidly than the premium per policy in-force, and to prevent the cost of servicing becoming burden some to the policy-holder, it would be necessary to improve the productivity of the state so that the same staff can service a larger number of policies in force. The Committee therefore, recommends that the LIC should continually review:

(i) its administrative procedures;
(ii) its data processing techniques;
(iii) its method of organising work; and
(iv) its general personnel policies as affecting staff attitudes and motivations, so as to improve the overall productivity of the staff and to enable it to control effectively the number of staff required to service its business. (Para 16.2)

67. The Committee also recommends that decentralisation of servicing functions to Branch Offices should be completed soon. This should be accompanied by introduction of a more efficient data processing system for ensuring effective control on the functioning of the Branch Offices. This would also eliminate duplication of work and records between Branch Offices and Divisional Offices, which exists at present, and would thus help in reducing costs. (Para 16.3)

68. In respect of the other major head of expenses, namely, development officers' salaries and other development costs, the changes suggested in the pattern of field organisation involving elimination of one tier between the agent and the Branch, and the suggestions made for professionalisation of the agency organisation would help in reducing the number of Development Officers required by the LIC and thus help in reducing the total costs under this head. (Para 16.4)

69. As regards agent's commission......the Committee is of the view that the change suggested by it namely linking payment of commissioner to the agent's obligation to render certain services to the policy-holders, would help in avoiding payment of renewal commission to a number of non-functioning agents, and thus help in reducing the total outgo under the head of commission. Further, controls on pay-

ment of commission to agents are not working satisfactorily at present and a number of cases of excess payments and payments where none are due are being reported. The Committee is convinced that introduction of a more efficient data processing system will ensure stricter control on commission payments and thus help in reducing the cost under this head. (Para 16.5)

70. The Committee further recommends that the LIC should undertake, on a continuing basis, a cost benefit analysis of various services rendered to the policy-holders. Where it is found that the cost of a particular service has over the years increased substantially and it is not a contractual obligation and is availed of only by a small minority of policy-holders, the LIC may consider whether it is essential to continue this service and, if so, whether any specific fee can be charged for such service. Instances of some of the services for which special charge can be considered are given below:

(i) For certain types of alterations in policy contracts, the LIC now charges either a quotation fee of Rs. 5 or an alteration fee of the same amount. These charges were fixed at a time when the actual cost of these operations was low. The LIC should re-examine the fees now being charged in the light of the actual direct costs involved and consider whether and to what extent the existing fees should be increased;

(ii) At present, the practice is to insist on age proof being submitted along with the proposal. However, in a number of cases this is not being done. There are also a large number of old policies where the age has not been proved and admitted. When proof of age is received after issue of the policy and it transpires that the age originally given is wrong, a considerable amount of work is involved in endorsing the policy for appropriate changes and collecting or refunding the difference. In all such cases it would be justifiable to charge a fee, the amount of which can be decided on the basis of an analysis of the unit cost of this operation;

(iii) In certain types of cases the LIC permits an existing policy to be substituted by a new policy under the Married Women's Property Act. At present, the LIC charges only a nominal fee of Rs. 5 plus the actual policy stamps charges for giving effect to a such a change. Considering the amount of work involved in giving effect to such a change, the fee charged by the LIC would appear to be inadequate and the LIC should consider increasing the fee suitably; and

(iv) At present, a policy-holder is allowed to have his policy records transferred from one Branch or Division to another on his changing his residence. The work and cost involved in effecting the transfer are substantial. The LIC should, therefore, consider charging an appropriate fee for such transfers of policies. In his connection it may be noted that the policy-holders has the option to remit his premium by cheque to the original branch and the LIC accepts all outstation cheques at par. Therefore, a policy-holder who has a bank account will in practice suffer no inconvenience even if the policy records are not transferred. (Para 16.6)

71. Suggestions made under Para 16.6 are only by way of illustrations and are not intended to be exhaustive. Decision should be taken by the LIC after examining all aspects of the problem. In general, the LIC should undertake detailed cost benefit analysis of all such servicing operations to enable it to control the costs of policy servicing and to preserve equity different groups of policy-holders. (Para 16.7)

72. The Committee recommends consideration of the following further suggestions:

(i) Cost of servicing a policy with half yearly mode of payment is substantially higher than that of a policy with yearly mode and the cost of servicing a policy with quarterly or monthly mode is higher still. In the Committee's view, the present rebate for mode does not reflect adequately the difference in cost of servicing of policies with different modes of payment of premiums. The Committee, therefore, suggests that the rebate for yearly mode, which at present is Re. 0.75 per Rs. 1000 sum assured, should be increased to at least Re. 1 per Rs. 1000 sum assured and suitable extras charged where premiums are paid quarterly or monthly.

(ii) The cost of servicing depends on the number of policies serviced. It is, therefore, in the interest of the LIC that a policy-holder insuring for a large sum is persuaded to take out a single policy for that sum and not split it up into a number of policies for smaller sums. For this purpose, the LIC is already allowing a rebate of Re. 1 per Rs. 1000 sum assured for policies of Rs. 25,000 or more. The result of this is that a policy-holder insuring for Rs. 1 lakh and over, is advised by the agent to take out several policies of Rs. 25,000 each. The Committee, therefore, suggests allowing higher rebates for policies of Rs. 50,000 to Rs. 1 lakh.

(iii) At present, the LIC is charging interest at 7.5 per cent for late payment of premium. As the LIC is today earning a gross rate of interest of over 7.5 per cent on its existing investment and about 8.9 per cent on its new investments, the Committee recommends that the rate of interest charged for late payment of premium should be increased to a minimum of 9 per cent. The Committee has also noted from an analysis of the Internal Audit reports that there is a considerable amount of laxity in many of the offices of the LIC in collection of interest for late payments. The Committee, therefore, recommends a stricter enforcement of the rules regarding collection of late fees in all cases; and

(iv) At present, the LIC is required to affix on each policy a stamp of a value depending on the amount of the policy. This task is tedious, time consuming and in addition involves keeping control on the stock of stamps. The LIC has, therefore, taken up with the Government a proposal that it may be permitted to pay a consolidated stamp duty and exempted from individual stamping. The proposal is still pending with Government. There is another matter which bears on the rate of stamp duty itself. Now stamp duty is levied on Group Insurance policies on the same basis as on individual long term life insurance policies, that is, on the sum assured. As Group insurance provides only year to year risk cover at a very low rate, the stamp duty bears heavily on the scheme. Group insurance policies are likely General Insurance policies where the cover is from year to year and the LIC has represented to Government to change the duty on group insurance policies to bring them on par with General Insurance policies. This proposal is also still under the consideration of the Government. The Committee recommends that the proposals of the LIC should be considered favourably and appropriate action taken early. (Para 16.8)

73. Apart from the above suggestions the Committee recommends

that the LIC should undertaken on a continuing basis a study of the unit cost incurred by the branch and the divisional offices for the various operations required to be undertaken in the normal course of servicing separately for each office. The Committee has noted that there are large unexplained differences in the expenses ratios of the various divisions. This study would, therefore, enable the LIC to investigate into the reasons for the wide differences and take appropriate corrective action wherever it is found that in certain offices unit cost of particular operation is unduly high. The study will also help in evolving simpler procedures based on practices of offices with low unit cost which can then be adopted by other offices. (Para 16.9)

74. Section 40B of the Insurance Act itself provides that in prescribing the limit on the expenses of management "regard shall be had to the size and age of the insurer and to the provision generally made for expenses of management in the premium rates of insurers". . . . On the assumption underlying these premium rates and taking the average sum assured per policy and average premium per policy both in respect of new business and business in force on the basis of the actual distribution of business in the year 1978-79, the limit on the renewal expense ratio on the basis that it does not exceed the provisions in the premiums, works out to about 12.13 per cent. From the point of view of size and age, the LIC must be considered as a giant insurer and that too with the advantage of monopoly. The limit on the expenses of the LIC should, therefore, be nearer to 12 per cent and in any case substantially lower than 15 per cent. (Para 8.10)

The Committee would like to reiterate the urgent need for control on the expenses of management by keeping a watch on the trend of expenses and the level of expenditure of all the Divisional and Branch Offices. The Committee is of the view that the adjusted renewal expense ratio may be accepted as a practical guide to judge the trend in the level of expenses of management of the LIC and that all efforts should be made to bring this ratio down to 12.5 per cent or less. (Para 16.10)

Investment

75. The Committee feels that the statutory framework laid down for investment of life insurance funds is not in conformity with the basic principles that should govern the investment of life insurance funds . . . and also the objectives accepted by the Corporation relating

to investment of its funds. In recent years, the LIC has had to face severe competition from other savings media such as Bank Deposits, Company Deposits, Unit Trust and National Savings. By its very nature, life insurance business will involve a higher level of selling and administrative costs than other savings media. Therefore, if life insurance business has to compete with other savings media, the return on the investments of life insurance funds has to be higher than that available on their savings media. (Para 9.12)

76. The LIC has so far been able to mobilise large amounts for savings which have been available to Government for its various plans and for other socially oriented projects. The annual accretions to the LIC funds now exceed Rs. 700 crores. Such mobilisation has been possible hither to mainly due to the high pressure salesmanship of the LIC's field force on the one hand and the lack of awareness of other options among the public on the other. This situation is not likely to continue and unless early steps are taken to make life insurance viable as a savings medium, we are afraid that the LIC will no longer be able to play its vital role in mobilisation of savings. (Para 17.1)

77. At present, the major avenues of long-term investments in India are Government securities and term loans to State Governments and to public and private sector institutions for their development projects. As these investments do not provide any hedge against inflation, the only way the long-term investors can protect themselves against the effect of inflation, is by introducing the concept of a variable rate of interest, a concept which has already been introduced by the LIC in respect of its mortgage loans and loans to State Electricity Boards. The Committee, therefore, recommends that the Government should review its policy insofar as the LIC is concerned regarding rates of interest on Government and approved securities and on long-term loans for private and public sector projects and consider allowing a variable rate of interest linked to a suitable index on all such long term financial in investments, where the possibility of any capital gain to offset the effect of inflation is not there. The nature of the linkage will inevitably have to be different for different forms of financial investments and is a matter to be decided by the Government and the Reserve Bank. (Para 17.3)

78. If the yield to the policy-holder on his investments in savings linked life insurance policies is to be comparable to the investment in Public Provident Fund the gross yield on the life insurance fund should be at least 10 per cent. At present the LIC is able to obtain a gross yield

of about 8.9 per cent on the average on its new investments. It would, therefore, be necessary to change the pattern of investment of the LIC in such a manner that the LIC is enabled to earn at least 1.1 per cent more on its total investments to enable it to compete with other savings media like Public Provident Fund. (Para 17.4)

79. The Committee submits the following recommendations for consideration of the Government:

(i) At present, The LIC is required to invest about 50 per cent of its total investments in Government and other approved marketable securities. The Committee has noted that approved trust funds like provident funds and gratuity funds are required to invest only 40 per cent of their total investments in such securities. The Committee, therefore, recommends that for the LIC also this percentage should be reduced to 40 per cent, 20 per cent in Government Securities and 20 per cent in other approved marketable securities; and

(ii) In respect of the 25 per cent of the investible funds which at present are required to be invested in socially oriented projects, different rates of interest are offered on loans to Government, loans which are guaranteed by Government and loans which are granted to public sector institutions like the State Electricity Board on the security of a mortgage. The Committee is of the view that this distinction is unjustifiable and it recommends that all such loans should be granted at the market rates of interest for such term loans, which also is determined from time to time by the Controller of Capital Issues in case of debentures and by the consortium of financial institutions in case of term loans. At best, a differential of half a per cent may be retained for loans to Government, and also to semi-Government institutions, because of the implied Government guarantee;

(iii) As for the LIC's investment in the private corporate sector, the Committee has already noted that the LIC's investments by purchases from the market have been generally very satisfactory and the capital appreciation on such investments has enabled the LIC to offset the depreciation on its investments in Government Securities. However, the LIC's experience in underwriting of equities of new projects has not been satisfactory. The Committee, therefore, recommends that the LIC should restrict its participation in financing of new projects in the corporate sector to term loans and that too after closely examining the financial viability of the project. This should not preclude the LIC considering cases where an existing company, well-managed and successful, goes in for further equity capital for financing an expansion or new project where equity participation may be considered on individual merits. In short, the LIC should not be viewed as a developmental organisation;

(iv) So far as the balance of the funds is concerned, the Committee recommends that the LIC should consider increasing its investment in the housing field, both residential and commercial housing, subject to the condition that the net return on such investments after taking into consideration the expenses involved, is not-less-than what is obtainable on comparable investments in the socially oriented sector. (Para 17.5)

80. As regards the special Fund proposed by the Committee to be set up by the LIC for policies which will not be eligible for income-tax relief, the Committee recommends that the whole of this fund should be placed in a special deposit account with the Government carrying a rate of interest of 2 per cent more than what is at present available on National Savings Certificates of Seven Year term. Here again, the Committee would like to suggest that the rate of interest on such deposits should be variable and as and when the rate of interest on National Savings is changed, a similar change should also be made in the rate of interest available on this fund, subject to a certain minimum rate of interest being guaranteed. (Para 17.6)

81. As regards the ordinary life fund, a suggestions has been made to the Committee that whole of this fund, except for portion to be retained for loans to policy-holders, should be handed over to the Government who would guarantee a reasonable rate of interest on the fund. The Committee is unable to agree with this suggestion because of various considerations discussed in the report. The Committee is of the view that the LIC should be allowed to continue the management of its investment function, subject to the modifications in the investment policy suggested by it. (Para 17.7)

Management Information and Controls

82. The Committee has noted that the LIC has been making continuous efforts for improving its management information and control system, so that a close watch can be kept on the performance of the various Offices. The main problems in this area are the delays in obtaining the information as well as the unreliability or inadequacy of the information itself. These are due to the defective data processing system. (Para 18.1)

83. With the present data processing system, the LIC is unable to compile many items of essential information like the number of lives covered through individual assurances and the business in force in various centres, particularly in the rural areas. Again, because of the poor data processing system, the operating offices are not able to obtain agent-wise, development officer-wise and branch-wise statistics of lapses and it is also not possible to get analysis of lapses according to plan of insurance or month of issue or other similar analysis. Non-availability of such statistics makes any effective, preventive or follow-up action in this important area extremely difficult. (Para 18.2)

84. A change over to a new data processing system as recommended by the Committee will naturally require careful planning and time for implementation. An immediate beginning must therefore be made in that direction. However, there is one area where immediate action is both imperative and fortunately possible as well. This is in the area of improving the data base for actuarial valuations and mortality investigations. . . . The Chief Actuaries of the LIC in their Valuation Reports have during the last ten years repeatedly been pointing out the large extent of inaccuracies in the Valuation Master Card Files which is affecting the credibility of the actuarial valuations. . . . The Committee recommends that the LIC should immediately examine the possibility of maintaining, purely a temporary measures, the valuation data at the Central Office on the Bombay computer. (Para 18.3)

85. Such a change over to a computerised data base for the basic valuation records would also enable the LIC to obtain various statistical statements required for management control purposes and also enable the Chief Actuary to experiment with different methods of valuation and analysis of surplus. The Committee recommends that the LIC should take immediate steps to effect a change over to computerised data base for the actuarial valuations and mortality investigations. (Para 18.4)

86. At present the financial controls within the LIC are not work-

ing at all satisfactorily in many areas. Though in many cases the unsatisfactory working of the financial controls can be attributed to limitations and the failures of the existing data processing system, the Committee feels that even under the present system it is both possible and essential to tighten up the existing controls. The Committee, therefore, recommends that the LIC should urgently undertake a detailed examination of the working of the existing financial controls based on a study of the Internal Audit Reports and take appropriate action for strengthening the existing controls. (Para 18.5)

87. The Committee is of the view that the Zonal Manager being the Chief Executive responsibile for exercising supervision over the working of all the offices in the Zone on behalf of the Central Office, should be the officer responsible for ensuring that corrective action is taken on the defects and irregularities pointed out in the International Audit Reports. Responsibility for all corrective action to be taken on the Internal Audit Reports should, therefore, be vested completely in the Zonal Manager. (Para 18.6)

88. The Committee further suggests that in each Zonal Office, an Audit Committee should be constituted consisting of the Zonal Manager and two Members of the Zonal Advisory Board which would go into all the Internal Audit/Inspection Reports of the various offices of the Zone and indicate the lines on which corrective action should be taken. (Para 18.7)

89. The Committee is of the view that for budgetary control to be really effective, it should start at the Branch level. The Committee, therefore, recommends that the LIC should urgently consider making the Branch office an accounting unit, so that formulation of financial budgets at the Branch level is facilitated. (Para 18.8)

90. The Committee also recommends that from the point of view of proper financial controls and planning, it is essential that the expenses which relate to the handling of investments, including investments in mortgages and buildings, are debited to the capital or interest or rent account as may be appropriate and not to the expenses of management so that a correct picture of the actual return on the investments of the LIC is obtained. (Para 18.9)

91. The Committee further suggests that rent at "market" rates should be charged on all properties (owned and occupied by the LIC), so that the costs incurred are correctly reflected in the revenue account of the LIC. (Para 18.9)

92. The Committee recommends that the LIC should consider in-

troduction of a detailed performance budgeting system covering all the important areas of the LIC's objectives and operations and also arrange for a continuous review to be made of the actual performance in relation to such budget. (Para 18.10)

Management of Human Resources

93. We have come to the conclusion that the LIC has not achieved much success in "involving all the people working in the Corporation to the best of their capability in furthering the interest of the insured public and providing efficient service with courtesy" and "promoting amongst all employees of the Corporation a sense of job satisfaction" which are the two corporate objectives of the LIC in the area of management or human resources. In the Committee's views this is a partly due to the general socio-economic environment in the country, partly a result of the continuing industrial unrest in the organisation and partly to a lack of any serious effort on the part of the management to understand and analyse the underlying problems and to develop personnel policies which could help in improving staff morale and attitudes. (Para 19.1)

94. The Committee is of the view that the present system under which responsibility for negotiations with its staff Unions is vested in the LIC while all decision-making authority involving even minor changes in any of the terms and conditions of service is vested in Government is inherently unsound. The Committee accepts the need for having a measure of uniformity in service conditions and wage structures amongst the different public sector institutions. However, in the Committee's view this can best be achieved by Government laying down guidelines in this matter to be followed by all public sector institutions. The guidelines should be in broad terms so that while ensuring basic uniformity in wage structure, levels or remuneration and other service benefits, they do not affect the freedom of the public sector management to evolve its own personnel policies. Once such guidelines are framed by the Government and issued as directions to all the concerned public sector institutions, the management of the institution should be left free to evolve their own personnel policies and also to conduct negotiations with their staff unions and arrive at specific decisions within the confines of the guidelines. This will ensure that a level of uniformity is maintained amongst the various public sector institutions and at the same time will still level enough freedom to the in-

stitutions to deal with the their own problems and evolve effective personnel policies. It would then to possible to evaluate objectively their performance in the area of management of human resources. (Para 19.2)

95. If the Government finds that it is not possible to lay down guidelines on the lines suggested by us, an alternative is to set up common Pay Commissions for all public sector institutions of similar type. The awards of such Commissions, with such modifications as the Government may consider necessary in the light of its general economic policies, would then be binding on the institutions and the institutions would not be required to conduct separate negotiations with their staff unions. (Para 19.3)

96. The Committee is convinced that for an institution of the size and importance of the LIC, which is required to work on business principles, it is essential to have some continuity in the post of the chief executive. The Committee, therefore, recommends that the post of the Chairman of the LIC should be treated as a tenure post with a fixed term of years . . . . What we have stated regarding the post of Chairman of LIC would apply equally to the posts of Chairman-cum-Managing Directors of the Zonal Corporations, if our recommendations of splitting up the LIC into five independent Zonal Corporations is accepted. (Para 19.4)

97. The Committee recommends that the LIC should review its policy regarding fixation of minimum and maximum periods for posting of Divisional Managers and other senior executives at a particular station and consider the desirability of avoiding frequent changes in these posts so as to ensure continuity in management. (Para 19.5)

98. An important area where a review of the existing procedure is necessary is the appraisal system and promotion policy for Class I officers. The present reporting system is not satisfactory. A General impression exists that there is a lack of objectivity in reporting and most of the confidential reports are colourless. The need for a thorough review of the existing system has, therefore, been recognised for a long time. (Para 19.6)

99. The Committee recommends that on the basis of the detailed suggestions made in the report as well as the studies which the LIC has itself undertaken in the past, it should take urgent steps for a thorough review of its existing appraisal system. (Para 19.8)

100. As regards promotion policy also, the Committee feels that there is an urgent need for a review. . . . An ideal promotion policy

should also provide for more rapid promotions for the few officers who have outstanding abilities. This alone will ensure that some outstanding officers can reach the top positions of the level of Zonal Managers and above at a reasonably young age. . . . We suggest that besides a study of the confidential reports, interview by the promotion Committee should be added as an additional factor, on the basis of which final decisions on promotions are taken. This will provide a corrective factor for any deficiency of the appraisal system as reflected in the confidential report. (Para 19.9)

101. The Committee also recommends that the LIC should evolve a properly planned management development programmes for its management personnel at all levels to that the existing management personnel are given adequate opportunities for development and future needs of the LIC in various areas are properly identified and steps taken to meet them. (Para 19.10)

102. An important part of a management development programme is an adequate training programme which would prepare the management personnel for changes in the organisations and in their own roles in the organisation. In our review we have indicated the three main areas where the existing facilities and programmes for training need to be strengthened. These are:

(i) Training of all employees promoted from Class III and Class II to Class I so as to enable them to fully appreciate the nature of the change in their roles in the organisation and effectively function in their new roles;

(ii) Training of all officers who are being posted as Branch Managers in-charge of Branches for the first time; and

(iii) Training of all officers who are being posted as Divisional Mangers in-charge of Divisions. (Para 19.11)

103. As far as the first two items of Para 19.11 are concerned, the Committee feels that the Officers' Training College with its present facilities is not equipped to handled these two assignment adequately. The Committee, therefore, recommends that the LIC should consider setting up of training centres at the Zonal headquarters also. (Para 19.12)

104. As regards the training of officers being posted as Divisional Mangers, the Committee understand that a new apex institution called the National Insurance Academy is being set up with the support of

both the LIC and the GIC with the specific responsibility of evolving senior management development programmes and this academy will be entrusted with the responsibility for organising training programmes for senior executives like Divisional Managers. The Committee recommends that the LIC and GIC should ensure that the academy states functioning effectively at a very early date, so that this urgent task can be taken up without any delay. (Para 19.13)

105. Apart from the general question of management development, it is necessary for the LIC to examine its existing man-power resources, it current and future needs of man-power with specialised knowledge and experience and draw up specific plans for proper utilisation of existing man-power and for meeting its current and future needs. (Para 19.14)

106. There is, however, one area where the actual availability of technically qualified man-power is likely to be substantially less than the present and future requirements of the LIC. This is in respect of actuarially qualified employees. The Committee recommends that the LIC should undertake an urgent study of this problem, prepare an estimate of the number of actuaries which should be required for its various offices in the coming two decades and draw up a specific plan and programme, which would enable it to meet these needs. (Para 19.16)

107. The most important problem in the area of management of human resources is how to improve the attitudes and motivation of staff at all levels. The Committee was informed that one of the major cause responsible for the feeling of a sense of frustration and lack of involvement is the absence of adequate promotional opportunities among Class III personnel in the LIC. The Committee feels that the ratio of officers to Class III staff is too low for a service organisation, and, therefore, recommends that the LIC should review its policies in the matter of relative strength of Officers and Class III staff with a view to providing additional promotional opportunities. (Para 19.17)

108. The Committee is of the view that splitting up the LIC into five independent Zonal Corporations as recommended in Chapter XX will by shortening the lines of communication help in creating a sense of identity and of belonging among employees of each of the Corporations. This would thus contribute to an improvement in staff motivation. (Para 19.19)

109. Further, the Committee's recommendations for complete decentralisation of policy-holders' servicing functions to Branch

Offices would also be a step in the direction of improving job satisfaction and staff motivation. (Para 19.19)

110. Generally, the Committee is of the view that if the LIC which has a large reservoir of trained and competent man-power takes steps to reorient its methods of organisation of work and evolve suitable man-power development programmes so that all the employees are given opportunities to utilise their qualifications, knowledge, experience and skills in their day to day work, and also given opportunities for self-development, it would go a long way in removing the feeling of frustration at present prevailing among the employees and improving the overall staff morale and staff productivity. (Para 19.21)

Organisational Structure

111. In spite of large growth in its business, efforts made for improving it service to policy-holders and achieving economy in management, the LIC has not been able to fulfil most of its primary objectives. The Committee is convinced that the present unitary structure has been a major factor in inhibiting progress. Some of the major considerations which have led the Committee to arrive at this conclusion are given below :

(i) The LIC Act had visualised autonomous Zonal Offices with only policy-making functions vested in the Central Office. In actual practice, however, there has always been a tendency to centralise both executive as will as policy-making functions at the Central Office, the Zonal Offices having only limited supervisory and co-ordinating functions. This development should not occasion any surprise because the tendency to concentrate power in its own hands a inherent in all apex bodies;

(ii) Practically all the Committees that had gone into the working of the LIC have felt that the present four tier set up is both wasteful and cumbersome. This Committee shares this view. The recommendation of the ARC and of the Morarka Committee to reduce one tier by abolition of the Zonal Offices has also not proved workable and after a brief experiment, the Government and the LIC found it necessary to restore the *status quo ante.*;

(iii) Because of overcentralisation of authority in the Central Office, which has endured not withstanding Shri Deshumkh's confident pronouncement to the contrary, the lines of communication have become tenous and there appears to be lack of identification and a sense of belonging in the management personnel at all levels. The Committee feels that with small Corporations it would be possible to build up a sense of belonging firstly because a smaller organisation does promote a feeling of belonging and secondly because shorter lines of communication between different levels give a feeling of participation; and

(iv) The Committee feels that if each Zone is made a separate legal entity with its own accounts and other published performance reports it is likely that greater efforts will be made by the management of the Zones to improve the performance. (Para 20.2)

112. In the light of the general considerations contained in Para 20.2 the Committee has come to the conclusion that it is desirable to split up the LIC into five separate Corporations. (Para 20.3)

113. The Committee recommends that the existing Zonal Offices should be set up as independent, non-competing Corporations with their jurisdiction restricted to their present areas. All these Zonal Corporations will be working on the basis of common premium rates and policy conditions. They will also have a common actuarial valuation and uniform bonus rates will be declared for all the Corruptions at least to start with. (Para 20.5)

114. The Committee recommends the following broad set up for the Zonal Corporations:

(i) The management of the Zonal Corporation will vest in a Board of Management with the Chairman-*cum*-Managing Director of the Zonal Corporation as full time executive Chairman. The Board should consist of the Chairman-*cum*-Managing Director, two or more full time Functional Director, a Central Government nominee and not more than 10 Directors selected on the basis of their expertise in related fields such as actuarial, accountancy, law, medicine, personnel management, etc.;

(ii) The Central Office of the Zonal Corporation will handle all the functions which are at present being handled by the Central and Zonal Offices of the LIC;

(iii) The two lower tiers of Divisional and Branch Offices will continue. However, with the complete decentralisation of servicing functions to the Branch offices, the role and functions of the Divisional Offices will undergo a change. The role of the Divisional Office will be supervision and control over the Branch Offices, planning for the development of business and organisation and technical guidance in the areas of underwriting and policy servicing; and

(iv) The bigger branch offices will perform all servicing functions directly with their own data processing systems based on micro-processors. The smaller Branch Offices will also render all essential services to the policy-holders but will depend upon the Divisional Office for certain mechanised services. The smaller Development-*cum*--Servicing centres will render limited services too policy-holders. (Para 20.6)

115. Though all the five Corporations will be working as independent Corporations reporting directly to the Government, in certain areas co-ordination will be essential. . . . For providing such common services and ensuring co-ordination of working between the different Corporations, the Committee recommends that a Central Body to be called the Life Insurance Board (LIB) should be set up. The role it visualises for the LIB is not that of an apex body controlling and supervising the working of the Zonal Corporations but only that of a co-ordinating body which will also be dealing with certain common functions. It will also provide a forum for discussion of common problems. The LIB will consist of a full time Chairman, three technical full time Directors dealing with the functions of investments actuarial and personnel and a Member representing the Central Government. The five Chairman-*cum*-Managing Directors of the Zonal Corporation will also be Members of the LIB. (Para 20.7)

116. The LIB will handle all investments in Government and approved securities as also all investments in the private corporate sector. All decisions regarding investments in the socially oriented State sector would be taken by the LIB but actual investments will be channelised through the Zonal Corporations so that the Zonal Corporations can remain in close touch with the respective State Governments in which such investments are being made. Investments in mortgages and house building activities would be handled completely by the Zonal Corporations but within the budgetary allocations approved by the

LIB. (Para 20.7)

117. The Committee would like to emphasize that the LIB would be only a co-ordinating body providing certain common services and not a controlling or a supervisory body so that the general tendency for centralisation which has been apparent in the LIC does not recur and each Zonal Corporation is able to function as a completely independent unit. Each Zonal Corporation will report directly to the Government and also be directly, responsible to the Government for the management of its affairs. (Para 20.8)

118. The recommendations made involving splitting up of the LIC and setting up of five independent non-competing Zonal Corporations will involve statutory changes and will take time to implement. However, if the Government takes a decision in principle accepting the recommendation, certain immediate steps can be taken within the existing statutory set-up in the direction visualised. The Committee recommends that in that event immediate steps should be taken to curtail many of the functions of the Central Office and decentralise the same to the Zonal Offices. (Para 20.9)

The overall effects of the interim steps suggested would be that the functions and staff of the LIC Central Office would be curtailed substantially and the Zonal Offices' functions and authorities would be correspondingly increased. (Para 20.10)

119. With the proposed increase in the functions and authority of the Zonal Office, it would be necessary to strengthen the Zonal Advisory Boards and review their functioning suitably so that their role is made more purposeful and effective. (Para 20.11)

120. As regards the statutory provisions relating to the Policyholders' Councils and Employees' and Agents' Relations Committees, the Committee is of the view that these provisions require to be reviewed.

The Committee would recommend the deletion of both these provisions. As regard the general question of employees' participation in management, the matter may be reviewed by the Government in the context of its general policy. (Para 20.12)

Other Related Matters

(Government's relationship with the LIC Role of the Controller of Insurance and Government's share of Valuation surplus).

121. The question of the relationship that should obtain between

the LIC and the Government has received the most careful consideration at the hands of every Committee that has gone into the working of the LIC. The Committee is in general agreement with the recommendation made by the Estimates Committee (1960-61). The Committee realise that a large measure of consultation between the Government and the LIC would be necessary and that it is also inevitable that such consultation would include a number of suggestions from the Government to the LIC. However, a clear distinction has to be drawn between a suggestion made for consideration by the LIC and a suggestions which is really in the nature of an instruction to be complied with. So far as the first category of suggestions is concerned, it would be open to the LIC to accept or not to accept the suggestion after considering is on merit in the light of its own interests. As regards suggestions which are in the nature of instructions, the Committee accepts that all of them need not be issued as directives. However, when such instructions are received, it would still be the duty of the LIC to consider each instruction in the light of its business interests and the practical problems involved in implementing them. If the LIC comes to the conclusion that implementation of the instruction would affect its working adversely, it should write to the Government giving reasons why it feels that it would not be in its interests to carry out the instruction. In such an event, if after giving due consideration to the LIC's observations, the Government comes to the conclusion that in the interest of public policy it is still necessary to direct the LIC to carry out the instruction, the Government should issue necessary directions under Sec. 21 of the LIC Act. The Committee recommends that the above procedure should be followed both by the Government and the LIC. The Committee trusts that all such suggestions, instructions of directions would relate to matters of policy or on any executive decisions which impinge on matters of public policy and not to matters relating purely to internal administration. (Para 21.9)

122. The Committee gathered the impression during the course of evidence that a convention appears to have developed that no proposal is passed by the Board of a Public Sector Undertaking unless there is specific concurrence of the Government representative on the Board, even on matters which do not impinge on public policy. If such a situation does really obtain in practice, the Committee feels that it would detract from the responsibility of the Board as a whole and the autonomy of the undertaking as well. The Committee is of the view that there should be a full discussion in the Board on the merits of

every proposal before it.

The Government nominee may point out to the other members, the implications of any particular proposal as far as it impinges on matters of public policy so that this aspect is given due consideration by the Board before arriving at a decision. Where any decision of the Board is not found acceptable to the Government, the Government has got the authority first to issue instructions and then if necessary a directive, as already discussed previously. The Committee recommends that guidelines should be issued in the matter of the role of the Government nominee on the Board of Public Sector Undertakings. (Para 21.11)

123. The Committee is given to understand that financial institutions such as LIC, GIC and Banks are outside the purview of the Bureau of Public Enterprises. However, the Committee was informed that in practice various circulars and instructions issued by the Bureau concerning many matters of general administration are being sent to the LIC through the controlling ministry. If these are meant as suggestions for consideration, the LIC should treat them accordingly and take a decision on the basis of whether acceptance of the suggestion would be in the interest of the LIC or not. However, if the circulars of the Bureau are meant to be instructions, the should be directly by the controlling ministry and not by the Bureau, and they should be dealt with in the same manner as other instructions emanating from the Government, as indicated earlier. (Para 21.12)

124. The Morarka Committee gave thought to the question of continuous scrutiny of the working of the LIC by the Controller of Insurance who is the statutory authority under the Insurance Act 1938. Their recommendations is given below:

> "It should be the duty of the Controller of Insurance to function as an evaluating officer who continuously studies the working of the LIC in all its aspects and assesses the economic efficiency of the undertaking and its achievements and failing in terms of the objectives of nationalisation. As the officer responsible for the vigilance and evaluation, he should be charged with the duty to draw the Government's attention to the kind of directives that the Corporation may need from time to time." (Para 21.15)

Although this recommendation was accepted by the Government, the position continued to remain the same. The Committee is in complete agreement with the recommendations made by the Morarka Committee.

125. The Committee recommends that to enable the Controller of Insurance to discharge his duties under the Act in the manner the Parliament intended him to do, it would be necessary to make the Office of the Controller of Insurance independent of any other wing of the Finance Ministry in regard to its functions as the statutory regulating authority. (Para 21.15)

126. At present the LIC is required to submit its Annual Accounts as well as the report of the Chief Actuary on the valuation of the assets and liabilities of the LIC, in the forms prescribed under the Insurance Act. The Committee recommends that the forms prescribed for submitting the Valuation Reports should be suitably reviewed so that the LIC is enabled to carry out its statutory actuarial valuation by the Bonus Reserve Method for submission to the Controller of Insurance of it so desires. (Para 21.16)

127. On the subject of actuarial valuation, the Committee would like to refer to the recommendations made by the Committee of Actuaries in their report that the LIC should accept the obligation to return in full the surplus contributed by a policy-holder at least when the policy result into a claim. The Committee is of the view that this principle should be accepted by the LIC, to ensure equity between different generations of policy-holders. The Controller of Insurance should be required to satisfy himself that this principle is being adhered to. (Para 21.18)

128. The Committee has noted that while the functions of the LIC are strictly defined by the LIC Act and regulated by the provisions of the LIC Act read with the Insurance Act, there is no such regulation of the life insurance business transacted by the State and Central Governments and by the Post Office Insurance Fund. The Committee, therefore, recommends that the provisions of the Insurance Act should be applied to the Insurance Schemes transacted by the Central and State Governments with suitable modifications, so as to ensure that the schemes are actuarially should and also that complete statistical information of the schemes is made available to the public. (Para 21.18)

129. The Committee recommends that the practice of publishing the Insurance Year Book should be resumed and the Year Book should contain the Controller's report on the working of LIC and GIC giving his detailed evaluation of their performance is terms of this objectives. The report should also give detailed statistics and information regard-

ing the working of various insurance schemes of the Central and State Governments. (Para 21.19)

130. The Committee recommends that reports of actuarial valuations of private pension funds and gratuity funds should be required to be submitted to the Controller of Insurance and the Controller should also prescribe forms in which the reports should be submitted. The Committee feels that this is necessary to ensure that these funds are run on scientific basis. (Para 21.20)

131. The Committee recommends that the Controller of Insurance should be vested with powers similar to those under Section 22 of the Insurance Act in respect of Valuation of Gratuity and Pension Funds also. This would be appropriate as the Controller is, in addition to his duties under the Insurance Act, also the Actuarial Adviser to the Government of India. (Para 21.21)

132. The Committee would like to emphasise that if the role of the Controller of Insurance is accepted as that of the Government Actuary, who is also responsible for regulation of the entire insurance industry in the country including the Central and State Government run insurance schemes, and evaluation and monitoring of the performance of the LIC and the GIC, it is essential that his office is strengthened by the posting of necessary complement of technically qualified staff. (Para 21.22)

133. The Committee has noted that even before nationalisation, leading insurance companies used to allocate more than 95 per cent of the valuation surplus to the policy-holders. The "Oriental" for instance, the largest life insurance company allocated 97.5 per cent to its policy-holders. The Committee has also noted that there were many mutual insurance companies in India and elsewhere where the policy-holders received benefit of the entire valuation surplus and that Section 6B of the Insurance Act enabled companies "limited by shares" to convert themselves into mutuals. The Committee is, therefore, of the view that there is no justification for the Government taking away such a large share of surplus as 5 per cent. (Para 21.24)

134. In the Light of the background given in Para 21.24 the Committee submits the following recommendations:

(i) As regards the ordinary life insurance fund, the share of surplus to be allocated to the policy-holders should be increased from 95 to 97.5 per cent;

(ii) Out of the 2.5 per cent share of the valuation surplus not more than Rs. 1 crore should be paid over to the Government which would give a 20 per cent return on the paid-up capital of the LIC provided by the Government. The balance should be set apart to constitute a reserve fund which will be utilised for such special schemes for the development of life insurance business for the benefit or rural areas and of economically weaker sections of the community, as may be approved by the Government; and

(iii) In the case of the special fund recommended by the Committee for policies which will not be eligible for income-tax relief, as these policies are meant for policy-holders from the low income group, the entire surplus should be reserved for and allocated to the policy-holders. (Para 21.25)

135. One scheme which would require a subsidy from the special fund referred to in sub-para (ii) of Para 21.25 is the proposal made by the Committee for opening a large number of development-*cum*-servicing offices in the rural areas. In the initial stages these offices will not be economically viable and would require some subsidy to ensure that the higher expenses do not reduce the benefits available to the policy-holders as a whole. The LIC should make a cost benefit study of the working of such offices and submit its proposals for a subsidy from this special fund for approval of the Government. (Para 21.26)

18

EXPERT COMMITTEE ON TAX MEASURES TO PROMOTE EMPLOYMENT, 1979 — REPORT[1]

Chairman Prof. V.M. Dandekar

Members Dr. A. Vaidyanathan; Dr. Anand P. Gupta; Shri L.C. Jain, Shri K. Narasimhan, Shri I.P. Gupta

M. Secy. Dr. A. Bagchi

Appointment

The Deputy Prime Minister and Finance Minister in his Budget speech in the Lok Sabha on 28th February, 1979 had announced the Governments intention to appoint an Expert Committee of economists and tax administrators to study the impact of tax concessions of the techniques of production used in industry and make recommendations for reform in order to encourage the adoption of labour-intensive methods and enlarge opportunities for employment. The Government of India, Ministry of Finance, Department of Revenue appointed an Expert Committee on Tax Measures to Promote Employment Vide its Resolution F. No. A-12026/26/79-Ad.I (Cen). dated May 30, 1979.

Terms of Reference

(i) To identify provisions in Central Tax laws which have an influence on the employment of labour in the economy;

---

1. New Delhi, Department of Revenue, Ministry of Finance, 1980. 131 p.

(ii) to examine the impact of these provisions on employment and the techniques of production in industry, agriculture and other areas of economic activity;

(iii) to suggest appropriate changes in Central tax laws so as to promote employment and adoption of labour intensive methods of production having due regard to administrative feasibility and other objectives of public policy such as economic growth and self-reliance; and

(iv) to make recommendations regarding any other related matter.

Contents

Introduction; The Context; Provisions in Central Direct Tax Laws Having Influence on Employment and Labour-intensive Techniques; Impact of Central Direct Tax Laws on Employment and Production Techniques; Indirect Taxes; Textile Industry; Other Industry Studies; Summary of Recommendations; Note of Dissent.

Recommendations

8.1 The employment potential of the village and small industries has been recognised beginning with the First Five Year Plan and strategies and programmes have been designed for the full exploitation of this potential which, in spite of rather unsatisfactory performance, have been continued from Plan to Plan right into the Revised Draft Sixth Five Year Plan 1978-83. Differential excise taxation has been recognised as an important instrument of policy to promote labour-intensive production though sufficient attention has not been paid to rationalise its structure. Provisions in direct taxation have also not been examined specifically from the point of view of their effect on employment. These constitute our main terms of reference. Other instruments of the policy to promote labour-intensive production have been physical regulation and direction of production and provision of necessary infrastructure for the supply of raw materials, credit, and technical assistance to the village and small industries and for marketing their output. Though these components are not specifically covered by our terms of reference, we wish to emphasise their importance. In the absence of such supporting infrastructure, tax incentives and disincentives by themselves will be not only not fully effective but their benefits and advantages may go to unintended quarters. (Para 2.21)

8.2 Our terms of reference require us (i) to identify provisions in Central tax laws which have an influence on employment, (ii) to examine their impact on employment and techniques of production, and (iii) to suggest appropriate changes in Central tax laws so as to promote employment and adoption of labour-intensive methods of production. First, we deal with direct taxes. (Para 3.1)

8.3 Since employment depends, among other factors, on the level of investment in the economy, it has been argued that an essential condition for growth of output and employment is to reduce the burden of taxation. This is clearly a debatable proposition. It also raises questions of the relative roles of public and private investment and the extent to which the country should depend upon private investment on its own terms. These are essentially political issues and, in our opinion, they are beyond the scope of an expert committee such as ours. Therefore, we have kept the question of level of taxation out of our consideration and confined our attention to those provisions in the tax system which are likely to influence decisions regarding choice of technology and scale of production. The most notable of such provisions in the Central direct tax laws are: (i) investment allowance for new plant and machinery, and (ii) tax holiday for new industrial undertakings. (Para 3.2)

8.4 A tax concession linked to the value of plant and machinery has a *prima facie* bias in favour of capital-intensive technology. Given the rising costs, direct and indirect, of employing labour, the preference for mechanisation is already strong. Even if fiscal measures may not succeed fully in neutralising the preference for capital-intensive technology, it would be inadvisable to strengthen these biases further. We therefore, recommend that the investment allowance be discontinued. (Paras 4.7 and 4.8)

8.5 The existing provisions for tax holiday, because they are not linked directly to investment in plant and machinery, may not have a capital-bias as acute as the investment allowance has. Nevertheless, because they are linked to capital employed, they also induce a certain capital-bias. Hence, we recommend that the tax holiday provisions should be delinked from capital employed and that, instead, an appropriate fraction of the profits of a new industrial undertaking should be given tax exemption during the period of tax holiday. As there will be no provision to carry forward any deficiency, we recommend that the tax holiday may be extended to seven years instead of five years as at present in the case of companies and to ten years instead of seven in the case of co-operatives. The separate provisions for tax holiday for new industrial undertakings set up in backward and rural areas (Sections 80 HH and 80 HHA) may be merged in the provisions for tax holiday by prescribing a higher percentage of profits of such undertakings for tax exemption during the period of tax holiday. (Paras 4.10 and 4.13)

8.6 The present provisions for tax holiday permit an existing concern setting up a new unit to set off losses in the new unit against the profits of the old units thereby reducing its tax liability immediately and claim tax holiday for the entire profits of the new unit in later years within the holiday period. This confers an unintended benefit in favour of existing concerns compared to new ones. In order to eliminate such differential advantage to existing concerns, we recommend that a clear option should be given to assesses setting up new units whereby one may avail of the benefit of tax holiday provided that the unabsorbed depreciation and losses of the new unit are carried forward and set off only against the profits of the new unit. In the alternative, it should be open to an assessee to set off/carry forward the unabsorbed depreciation and losses of a new unit against the profits of its existing units but in that case the benefit of tax holiday should not be available. (Para 4.14)

8.7 The tax holiday is at present granted to new industrial undertakings manufacturing products which do not fall within the non-priority items listed in the Eleventh Schedule to the Income-tax Act. It seems to us that, with the multiplicity of policy objectives, it is not easy to draw such a schedule and the schedule often becomes arbitrary. We, therefore, that a tax holiday in the form recommended above should be available to all new industrial undertakings irrespective of the products they manufacture. Where the manufacture of a product or its domestic use is to be discouraged, it would be desirable to rely on other instruments like licensing and excise taxation. (Paras 4.15 and 4.16)

8.8 The Central scheme of investment subsidy for backward areas introduced in 1971, linked as it is to fixed capital invested, may also appear to have a capital bias. Nevertheless, considering its primary object, namely, growth of industries in back-ward areas, we do not suggest any change in its formulation. (Para 4.17)

8.9 Recent provisions permitting carry forward and set off of accumulated losses and unabsorbed depreciation of a sick industrial unit in the hands of a company taking over the former under an approved scheme of merger (Section 72A) are intended to help revive and revitalise sick units and thereby utilise their fixed capital and protect employment in them. But there appears to be no adequate safeguards to ensure that the employment is in fact protected. We recommend that the concession under Section 72A of the Income-tax Act should carry an obligation on the part of the company taking over a sick unit to ensure employment according to the provisions of the merger scheme for a period of at least five years from the year in which the merger takes place. Failure to honour the obligation should entail proportionate withdrawal of the concession through a recapture provision in the Income-tax Act. (Para 4.18)

8.10 Exemption of the Khadi and Village Industries Commission and co-operatives of certain categories from income-taxation is intended to help the growth of tiny and cottage sectors which are in general labour-intensive in production. There are no reliable data regarding the cost of such exemptions and the benefits flowing from them. Consequently, no evaluation of these exemptions is possible. (Para 4.19)

8.11 We have considered suggestions to discourage excessive use of capital by levying a tax on plant and machinery. We do not think this is advisable as higher cost of capital may divert investment in directions relatively more profitable but of lower social priority and may also affect the small sector more adversely than the large sector. (Para 4.20)

8.12 We have also considered a suggestion for differential taxation of profits arising from capital-intensive and labour-intensive technologies. We think that this would be administratively too complicated. Differential taxation of different technologies may be administratively simpler and easier by discriminatory indirect taxation. (Para 4.21)

8.13 A measure to encourage employment of labour is a wage-subsidy which of course would be equivalent to a negative direct tax. We have carefully considered several alternatives. It seems to us that their revenue costs may become excessive and their employment benefits may turn out to be small and doubtful. We do not think that direct wage-subsidies will be practicable. (Paras 4.22 and 4.28)

8.14 Nevertheless, we recommend a limited use to wage-subsidy to protect and promote employment of women. One reason underlying the reluctance of employers to employ women is the additional cost entailed by maternity leave salaries and provision of creches for children, etc. To neutralise partly the extra cost of employing women, we recommend that (i) a weighted deduction of 150 per cent of the leave salary paid to women workers in respect of maternity leave (restricted to two occasions) should be allowed in the computation of business income of employers, and (ii) the initial depreciation on the cost of building creches, schools, and maternity homes should be raised from the existing 40 per cent to 50 per cent. (Para 4.29)

8.15 The indirect taxes levied by the Central Government consist mainly of excise and custom duties. In view of the problem of massive unemployment in the country, differential excise taxation of the mechanised and non-mechanised sectors as well as of the organised and decentralised sectors has been used to influence technological choices and thereby protect and promote employment. The main focus of the exemptions and concessions provided in excise duty has been to protect and encourage the growth of non-mechanised and small units vis-a-vis those in the organized sector. (Para 5.1)

8.16 While the non-mechanised and small units are given wide ranging exemptions and concessions in Central Excise, the units not paying excise duty on their products cannot naturally obtain any relief in respect of duty paid on their inputs. This may neutralise to some extent the duty advantage given to them. On a careful consideration, it seems to us that, in a majority of cases, there is ample justification for continuing the taxation of inputs. Hence, cases where such relief is justified will have to be identified after a detailed examination of each case. (Paras 5.19 and 5.20)

8.17 Where justified, such relief may be given either by exempting the specified inputs or by extending the facility of receiving dutiable goods from their manufacturers under bond subject to necessary licence and prescribed procedures. Where small units buy their inputs from the open market, and not directly from the manufacturers, similar relief may be provided by giving credit on a notional basis for duty paid on excisable inputs purchased from the market. (Paras 5.21 and 5.22)

8.18 One consequence of the preferential treatment of the small scale sector in the matter of excise duties has been the practice of farming out of production by large producers. Though this helps promote greater employment, the margin of profit realised by the large producers by marketing under their brand names appears in some cases to be disproportionately high. Nevertheless, because of the dependence of the small producers on the marketing organization of the large producers, it may not be advisable to levy excise duty on such products of the small producers when marketed by the large producers. (Paras 5.23 and 5.24)

8.19 Besides protecting and promoting non-mechanised and small units in different industries and thereby promote greater employment, excise duty exemptions and concessions may be used for promoting greater employment in specific processes, such as material handling and packaging of final product. We recommend that such processes should be identified industry by industry and appropriate rebate on excise duty leviable on their products should be allowed. (Para 5.25)

8.20 An important element in the structure of indirect taxation is the customs duties. Particular reference may be made to the duties on capital goods which are generally levied at the rate of 40 per cent *ad valorem*. To the extent plant and machinery imported from abroad are capital-intensive, high rates of import duty on capital goods serve to discourage excessive capital-intensive technology. On the other hand, high import duties on capital goods may be detrimental to growth of production in the country. Hence, it may be desirable to scale them down in certain cases. We agree with the recommendation made by the Jha Committee that scaling down of these duties should be both selective and phased. (Paras 5.26 and 5.27)

8.21 Besides the differential excise duties which the products of small-scale and labour-intensive technologies enjoy, sometimes direct assistance is given in the form of rebates on sale of their products and loans at subsidised rates. The policy has been in operation ever since the First Five Year Plan and in view of the difficult employment situation will have to continue for quite some time. It is, therefore, necessary to evolve norms and guidelines to judge the propriety and adequacy of a given level of assistance to a given technology. The following appear to us to be some of the relevant considerations. (Para 5.28)

8.22 It is generally recognized that enhancing employment by adoption of labour-intensive technology can only be a temporary and transitional solution to the problem of unemployment; that to the extent that it has to be supported by fiscal means it involves public cost and hence that the productive contribution of the employment must be sufficient to reduce substantially the burden of relief. But, beyond these general principles, there has been little concretisation and quantification of the several concepts involved. (Para 5.29)

8.23 The problem of viability of a labour-intensive technology arises from the fact that the value added per worker with such technology is very low so that it can offer only a low reward to the owner-operator, a low return on the capital, and a low wage to the wage-earner. When these are so low as to be unacceptable, the technology becomes non-viable. (Paras 5.30 and 5.34)

8.24 Besides the low value added by them per worker, the labour-intensive technology, being unorganized, also suffer from a number of other handicaps such as higher prices of raw materials, interest rates on loans, and lower prices for their products. The rationale of duty differentials is to place a handicap on the less labour-intensive technologies so that the more labour-intensive technologies, in spite of their several handicaps, may survive the competition. (Para 5.35)

8.25 As duty differentials do not involve any direct payments to any sector, they do not entail any explicit public cost. But there is an implicit public cost, an appropriate measure of which is the net additional revenue which could be collected if the entire production had taken place in the full duty-paying sector. Though it is essentially a hypothetical measure, without some such measure, it would be difficult to assess the propriety and adequacy of a given duty differential. (Paras 5.36 and 5.38)

8.26 Given a cost, its justification is to be judged by an assessment of the benefits flowing from it. The purposes of duty differentials is to protect the disadvantaged sector from competition and thus to protect the employment in it. Employment protected may be measured by two criteria. One is the number of workers employed. A large part of employment in labour-intensive industries is part-time. For a proper assessment of the quantum of employment protected, this must be converted into equivalent full-time employment. Moreover, it should be recognised that the less labour-intensive technology also provides some employment. Hence, the cost should be related, not to total employment in the labour-intensive sector, but to the additional employment that sector provides over and above the employment that the less labour-intensive sector would provide if the same output was produced in that sector. One could then work out the per worker cost of protecting such additional employment. (Para 5.39)

8.27 The other criterion is the level of wages at which the employment is protected. If we relate the cost to the total wage bill, that would indicate the extent to which the present wages were being protected or 'subsidised'. This presumes that the entire duty advantage is utilised to pay the workers a higher wage. This may not be true in most cases; much of the duty advantage might go to compensate the other handicaps of the sector such as higher prices of raw materials, high rates of interest on loans, and low prices for their products. In the circumstances, it would be wrong to interpret the entire duty advantage as a 'wage-subsidy'. To estimate the element of wage-subsidy, if any, one should find the productive contribution of labour, that is to say, the wages that the industry could pay and remain competitive with no duty advantage as also no handicaps other than low-productivity technology. The difference between the actual wage and such productive contribution, would indicate the element of wage-subsidy present. The balance of duty advantage and other direct assistance goes to the exploitative elements in the system. This happens because there has been no co-ordinated management of fiscal concessions on the one hand and development of institutional support on the other, to this sector. (Para 5.40)

8.28 The costs and benefits of prevailing differential excise duties and direct assistance through sale rebates and interest subsidies given to labour-intensive sector have not been systematically examined along these lines. Unfortunately, relevant datas are also wanting. We would like to underscore the paucity of even basic information relevant for decision-making in the first instance and its evaluation subsequently. (Para 5.41)

8.29 In Chapter VI we have examined the case of cotton textile industry in which the labour-intensive technology has an employment potential next only to that in agriculture. In Chapter VII, we have presented cases of a few other industries where apparently a choice of technology exists. They are: (i) sugar, (ii) match, (iii) soap, (iv) leather, and (v) mechanised agriculture. We should emphasise that we have gathered the data rather hurriedly and that it has not been possible for us, in all cases, to check the accuracy and reliability of these data. Our purpose in presenting them, nevertheless, is to indicate and illustrate the nature of monitoring that will be needed, case by case, before the data and analysis that will be needed for judging the propriety and adequacy of given duty concessions and direct subsidies from time to time.

8.30 Experience shows that duty differentials and direct assistance by themselves are not adequate to protect the labour-intensive technology from competition of the capital-intensive sector and that therefore a more positive policy of reservation of spheres of production is needed. We have not been able to examine the related question in depth. But several points emerged during our deliberations which we wish to place on record briefly. First, reservation is easy to administer if done by raw materials rather than by product. For instance, the entire silk could be reserved for weaving on handloom. Second, when an entire sphere of production is reserved for labour-intensive production, protection by duty differentials and direct fiscal assistance becomes irrelevant. The product should carry a duty which the consumer can bear. For instance, if silk is reserved for handlooms, there is no reason to exempt either silk or silk textiles from excise duty. The present exemptions of such items constitute at least in part a subsidy to the rich consumer. Finally, it should be recognised that the burden of protecting low productivity employment ultimately falls on the consumer of the product. Hence, items of elite and rich consumption should be identified for reservation for labour-intensive production.

8.31 Before concluding, we wish to emphasise once again that it is mostly the traditional village and cottage industries which use labour-intensive technology. These industries being unorganised are at present in the clutches of merchant capital. Unless this is replaced by a non-exploitative institutional infrastructure, the policy to protect and promote employment in these industries, while it protects and promotes low productivity and low paid employment, also helps perpetuate exploitation by merchant capital through the trader-money-lender nexus it creates. This is a pre-capitalist form of exploitation and less amenable to regulation and control than is the capitalist form of exploitation.

RAILWAY ACCIDENT INVESTIGATION REPORT ON THE DERAILMENT OF 26 DOWN PASSENGER TRAIN AT KM 146/3-5 AT NEW BONGAIGAON STATION ON BONGAIGAON-ALIPURDUAR JN. M.G. SECTION OF ALIPURDUAR DIVISION OF NORTHEAST FRONTIER RAILWAY OF ABOUT 05.45 HOURS ON JUNE 11 1979 – REPORT[1]

One Man Commission Shri A.A. Rego

Appointment

The Commission was constituted under Ministry of Tourism and Civil Aviation (Commission of Railway Safety) in accordance with Rule 4 of the Statutory Investigation into Railway Accidents Rules 1973 Vide Notification No. RS. 13-T(8)/71 dated April 19, 1973 on June 11, 1979.

Terms of Reference

To enquire into the Derailment of 26 Down Passenger Train at Km 146/3-5 at New Bongaigaon Station on Bongaigaon-Alipurduar Jn. M.G. Section of Alipurduar Division of Northeast Frontier Railway at about 05.45 hours on June 11, 1979.

Contents

Summary; Inspection of Site and Inquiry; Relief Measures; The Train; Local Conditions; Summary of Evidence; Tests and Observations; Discussion; Conclusion; Remarks and Recommendations; Annexures;

1. Delhi, Controller of Publications, 1983, 30 p.

Railway Board's Comments on various paras of the Report.

Conclusion

Cause

(a) On full consideration of the factual, material and circumstantial evidence, I have come to the conclusion that the derailment of 26 Down Passenger train in New Bongaigaon Station (between Km 146/3-5) on Bongaigaon-Alipurduar Junction M.G. Section of Alipurduar Division of Northeast Frontier Railway at about 05.45 hours on 11-6-1979 was primarily due to the left leading wheel of the trailing bogie of ICF Coach No. NE GS-7191, 4th from the locomotive, mounting and taking a wrong route near the broken tip of the left tongue rail of the facing point of Cross Over No. 20 in New Bongaigaon station yard.

(b) The wheel mounted on account of its type having a sharp flange and a knife-edge as a result of "biased wear" in the rear trolley of the coach.

Responsibility

Primary responsibility rests with:

(a) Shri Saurindra Narayan Ghosh HTXR Gauhati, who carried out the last pit examination of the rake of 26 Down Passenger at Gauhati C&W pit line on 10-6-79; and

(b) Shri Prafulla Carriage Fitter Gr. I Gauhati, who assisted his HTXR Gauhati in this examination and who specifically examined wheel No. 4 of ICF Coach No. GS-7191.

They failed to detect the sharp flange and knife edge in the flange of wheel No. 4 of ICF Coach No. GS-7191 and gave an incorrect "fit-to-run" certificate for this coach. They both violated Rules 3-2-2, 4.2 and 'S' 4.22.1, PLATE 51 SHARP FLANGES and PLATE 53 of the Conference Rules Part IV, Chapter III and Chapter IV Rejections (reproduced in Annexure IX).

Relief Measures

I am satisfied that the medical aid and relief measures were prompt and adequate.

Recommendations

9.1 ICF Coach No. 7191 belonged to N.E. Railway.

According to their current Rake Link No. 16, in force from 1-4-1979, this coach was allotted to Lucknow Jn. as a "Mail and Express spare coach". No marking to this effect was stencilled on the coach. In fact it had an incorrect marking "Base Agra Fort 17 Up/18Dn." painted on its end on 11-6-1979. This coach had undergone its last POH in Gorakhpur workshops on 13-8-1978. Yet the correct marking as per allotment current at that time was not stencilled on the coach. Even Lucknow Jn. failed to correct the old painted mark when it started from Lucknow junction by 16 Dn on 20-4-1979 for Gauhati. This coach never came back to N.E. Railway thereafter and was worked by N.F. Railway on 24 Dn./23 Up, which forms a part of 26 Dn./25 Up ex-Gauhati to New Jalpaiguri till the date of the accident, i.e., 11-6-1979. The importance from the safety angle, of correct stencilling of the rake link and base station and periodical drives by Railways to return all coaches to their base stations cannot be over emphasized. This gives all concerned a correct indication of its base station and will also ensure proper and better attention to the coach. In fact, after Agra Fort Stencilled Dash Pot Oiling (DPO) done on 6-2-1979, nobody bothered to check and stencil the date if at all the DPO was done as it should be monthly thereafter till the date of the accident, i.e., 11-6-1979. It is, therefore, suggested that at periodical intervals, say once in 3 months, all Railways should undertake a drive to return all coaches not belonging to them and on wrong links to their parent Railway and within the Railway too to their base stations. Further, at the time of P.O.H. and every time a rake link is published, the stencilling done on the coach should be checked and corrected as necessary.

9.2 A second hand tongue rail was used to replace a defective tongue rail on 19-9-1978. It was slightly chipped but serviceable on 8-12-1978. After the accident the tip was found broken for a length of 140 mms and the top non-gauge face found serrated for a further length of 160 cms. Never-the-less incorrect/vague remarks like "good" have been recorded by the PWI Gr. III and "fair" by the PWI Gr. I and the AEN Rangiya in the points and Crossings Register during their subsequent inspection of this turnout between 19-9-1978 to 10-6-1979. The face that it was in a chipped condition on 8-12-1978 and no broken pieces were found near the tongue rail leads to the conclusion that it was chipped as seen after the accident much earlier to 11-6-1979 and should not have been allowed to remain at this important location in this condition. The AEN Rangiya Shri A.K. Goel, PWI Gr. I Bongaigaon Shri A.C. Das and PWI Gr. III New Bongaigaon Shri Santi Ranjan were therefore, careless in allowing this tongue rail to remain in an important cross over in New Bongaigaon Yard in this condition. It should also be impressed on all AENs and PWIs that remarks of defects should be specified and incorrect/vague remarks should be avoided when recording the results of their inspections in their Points and Crossings Register. Suitable instructions may be issued by the Chief Engineer in the matter.

9.3 Manuscript Brake Power Certificates are still being issued to Guards and Drivers by Train Examiners on N.F. Railway from make shift booklets as printed forms have not yet been supplied to the Depots in terms of CMEs IMPORTANT LETTER No. 5/C&W/2 circulated under Headquarters letter No. M-32/2/P1(M), dated 16-11-1978 (reproduced in Annexure VIII). There is no mention in the circular that the forms under print will be machine numbered in 3 foils. This is considered necessary to exercise a check on the correct issue of such certificates. It is also the practice to print these forms in booklets and machine number such Brake Power Certificates on Northern Railway. The N.F. Railway may consider doing likewise.

9.4 According to the N.F. Railway's booklet No. 5 showing rake links and stations responsible for maintenance of rakes in force from 1st April 1979, 23 Up/24 Down which constitutes rake link No. 6 has its primary maintenance done at New Jalpaiguri and secondary maintenance at Gauhati vide pages 12 and 13. Likewise 26 Down/25 Up which constitutes rake link No. 11 has its primary maintenance done at Gauhati and secondary maintenance at Dhubri vide pages 18 and 19 of the same booklet. Since the two rakes form a combined train between Gauhati and Fakiragram, the Railway Administration may consider allotting the primary maintenance of the entire rake to Gauhati and the secondary maintenance of 24 Down/23 Up portion to New Jalpaiguri to avoid any confusion or dilution of responsibility in the maintenance of the different coaches attached to 26 Down at Gauhati.

9.5 TXRs on N.F. Railway and on other Railways may be alerted on the propensity or biased wear on the wheel tyre flanges of M.G. ICF Coaches especially on the M.G. and asked to check this when doing the primary examination of ICF coaches hereafter. My impression after my

Inquiry was that TXRs on N.F. Railway are not aware of the dangers posed by such biased wear on M.G. ICF Coaches.

9.6 It appears necessary to check whether the method of rectification of alignment defects on bogie frame of MG Coaches built by ICF as recommended in ICF's Technical Pamphlet circulated by ICF to all Railways in reference to Board's letter No. 64/M(C) 142/80, dated 4-6-1965 is yielding the expected results or this method of rectification is creating a more dangerous safety hazard, i.e., "biased wear" concentrated on one wheel instead of being distributed on adjacent wheels as was the Railways' past experience. A study through the Research Designs and Standards Organisation is suggested.

Railway Board's Comments on Various Paras of the Report

Para 9.1: Necessary action has been taken by the Railway Administration in compliance with this recommendation. Suitable instructions on the subject have been issued to all the Zonal Railways. (Para 9.1)

Para 9.2: Necessary instruction have been issued by the Railway Administration to all concerned to give specific remarks about the defects and to avoid incorrect/vague remarks, while recording the results of their inspections. It is seen that the Chief Commissioner of Railway Safety has noted the action taken by the Railway.

Para 9.3: The recommendation to print these forms in booklets and machine number the brake-power certificates has been accepted by the Railway who is taking necessary action in the matter. The Chief Commissioner of Railway Safety has noted the action taken by the Railway.

Para 9.4: The possibility of undertaking primary maintenance of 23 Up/24 Down at Gauhati, as suggested by the CRS, has been examined by the Railway but not found feasible as the present capacity at Gauhati does not permit undertaking any more workload of primary maintenance. There is no difficulty in maintaining rakes of 23 Up/24 Down at New Jalpaiguri.

Para 9.5: Instruction have been issued by the Railway to C&W Depots for checking the propensity for "biased wear" on the wheel tyre flanges of MG ICF coaches at the time of primary examination. Instructions in this regard have also been issued to all the Railways.

Para 9.6: Manufacture of MG coaches was started by ICF in 1964. A number of Railways had experienced problem of unusually heavy tare flange biased wear on these coaches. Based on the investigations conducted, it was concluded that the biased wear was attributable to alignment defects in the bogie frame and accordingly. Railways were instructed vide letter No. 64/M(C)/142/80, dated 4-6-1965 for rectification of the bogies, ICF also issued a rectification procedure for these bogies. Simultaneously, action was also taken by ICF to rectify bogies manufactured by them before fitment on coaches that are being turned out.

In all, 507 bogies had shown evidence of biased flange wear and all these were rectified in accordance with Board's instructions and ICF's rectification procedure. The performance of the rectified bogies was also monitored and only 4 of these showed evidence of continued flange wear and these were rectified again. Subsequently, no further reports have been received regarding excessive wear or biased wear or wheel sets fitted on to the MG bogies, i.e., after 1967.

The view that rectification of the bogies is responsible for the biased wear is not thus borne out by the facts. It is quite possible that rectification of the bogies was not done properly by the Railways. It is also possible that the alignment got distorted during service in some bogies. These cases will result in continued biased wear of the wheel sets as noted by CRS. Railways have been alerted to watch out for such cases and rectify the bogie alignment in case it is found to be incorrect. RDSO is also being directed to keep a watch on the performance of all MG bogies and should the problem continue to exist, work out improvements/modifications to the rectification procedure for implementation by the Railways.

COMMITTEE ON EXPORT STRATEGY 1980's — REPORT[1]

Chairman	Prakash Tandon, Director General National Council of Applied Economic Research, New Delhi
Members	G.V.K. Rao; K.S. Krishnaswamy; Mantosh Sondhi; Romesh Bhandari; Rahul Bajaj; D.K. Rangnekar; Amit Bhaduri; Mahendra G. Mehta; N.C.B. Nath; Brij Nehru; A. Hafeezur-Rehman (resigned Dec. 1980)
M. Secy.	Vijay L. Kelkar
Alterations	V.P. Punj; R.K. Singh; Montek Singh Ahluwalia; Rear Admiral Krishnan Dev

Appointment

This Committee was constituted by Government of India, Ministry of Commerce, Civil Supplies and Cooperation (Department of Commerce) vide Resolution No. 4(23)79-EPL dated 20th June, 1979.

Terms of Reference

(i) To work out scenarios for the developments in the world economy over the next decade;

(ii) To formulate export strategy including identification of dynamic export markets and commodities;

(iii) To recommend a suitable framework of national policies and steps required for creating an adequate production base and surplus for export in both manufacturing and agricultural sectors;

(iv) To recommend measures for developing the required institutional and physical infrastructure for effective export promotion and

---

1. Ministry of Commerce, Government of India, New Delhi, 1980, p. 321, Volumes/Parts.

international marketing;

(v) To recommend measures for strengthening the role of public sector in country's export drive; and

(vi) To review the Export Policy Resolution and to suggest amendments thereto.

The Committee may consider, if necessary, any other aspect related to the above terms of reference.

The Committee will submit its report within a period of twelve months.

Contents

The Committee – Membership and Terms of Reference; Recommendations, Appendices from I to IV.

Recomendations

Our recommendations are of three kinds.

(1) A few, the first to the fourth, are called from the Export Policy Resolution 1970, because they are equally relevant and congent today; infact Government's recent announcements on Export Policy underline them.

(2) Some recommendations are general in nature; their acceptance would help to reorient policy, and action would follow later.

(3) Other recommendations, if they are acceptable would lead to now.

It is not easy to separate the second from the third; perhaps we might illustrate the distinction with reference to technology policy. While our recommendation for free import of technology for export production is meant for action now, the recommended reappraisal of what is appropriate technology is meant for policy consideration and its reorientation.

1. *Export Production Capacity (Interim Report)*

A steady increase in export earnings in dependent on the continuous development and expansion of export-oriented production.

(i) Our industrial policy will consequently be guided not only by internal requirements but also by the rising demand for our industrial products in overseas markets. Recent changes in industrial licensing policy provide facilities for fostering the creation of new export capacity. In implementing it, the aim will be to generate expanding surpluses of industrial products; and

(ii) The main responsibility, for the task of further improving their (Indian industries) competitive ability naturally rests with producing units. Government will, however, provide the necessary assistance to build up efficient production.

2. *Exporters' Access to Materials* (Chapter 4)

It is essential to ensure that exporters have adequate access to raw materials and components of acceptable quality of international prices. Import control and the resulting non-availability or the high cost and poor quality of domestically available substitutes, puts exporters at a disadvantage in the highly competitive international markets. The present import policy falls short of this objective. There is scope for further extending some aspects of the present liberal policy for exporters, especially as far as the coverage and procedures of the duty exemption scheme are concerned and also the access to banned items and capital goods. Furthermore, the policy must be kept under continuous review to insure that any changes in the overall import policy implemented for Balance of Payments reasons do not lead to a deterioration in the position of exporters.

3. *Exports Profitability* (Chapter 4)

It is indeed essential to recognise that even if we create the technical and institutional conditions in which exportable goods of the required quality can be produced, exports will not take place if exports are less profitable than domestic sales. Export profitability is lowered by (a) undue bias towards import substitution in trade policy (b) higher relative rates of inflation compared to inflation abroad and (c) an inappropriate exchange rate. An effective export strategy must counter all these biases. It must ensure that over time the bias towards import substitution is progressively reduced and in the interim these disadvantages must be compensated. Macro-economic policy should insure that aggregate demand pressures are contained within the potential for supply so that inflation rates are held down. Finally the exchange rate facing exporters must not be allowed to become unfavourable.

4. *100 per cent Export-oriented Units* (Chapter 4)

The export strategy for the eighties should not be based on the principle of limiting concessions offered only to 100 per cent export-oriented units. There scope for these units and we endorse the concept of extending to them privileges normally available only in Free Trade Zones. However, entrepreneurs cannot be expected to build up an export trade on the basis of exclusive reliance upon the export market. The system of incentives should extend to units in which exports are only a part of total activity.

5. *"Stop-go" Exports* (Chapter 6)

"Stop-go" exports are considered abroad as causing much avoidable damage to the Indian export effort one which can be avoided through:

- A careful planning on supplies – where possible through buffer stocks – in the case of a new product and some sacrifice by domestic consumer in an unforeseen shortage; and
- A permissiveness towards the importers with valid contracts for fortuitous gains.

6. *Delivery and Quality* (Chapter 6)

(i) A reputable exporter, with an established record, should be allowed self-inspection, while others should compulsorily obtain a bank guarantee or give a financial bond to the concerned Export Promotion Council. In case of default the punishment should be exemplary and the party should be removed from the category of self-inspection.

(ii) Consideration should be given of cash incentive say an additional 10 per cent to the normal assistance, to be handed over when the contract is complete, and the exporter submits an acceptance from the importer, a no-claim statement that the delivery and quality were according to the contract terms, no extension of LC. At the present level of cash assistance of Rs. 300 crores, an additional 10 per cent, Rs. 30 crores should be an incentive worth trying. At the same time existing penalty rules should be enforced vigorously.

> A point of view was placed in the Committee that an incentive may have a negative implication of rewarding for something which in any case is the fundamental duty, moral or legal, of an exporter. On the other hand, as quality enforcement has not worked successfully and complaints are prevalent everywhere; at least on an experimental basis; the Committee's recommendation may be tried to see if a nutritive instead of punitive measure, will produce better results.

7. *Packaging* (Chapter 6)

We should invite some competent packaging materials firms, from India and abroad, to develop and modernise appropriate packaging of international standards in quality, strength and cost.

8. *Claims* (Chapter 6)

(i) For small claims it should be enough to receive a declaration from the importer and exporters; for large amount some supporting evidence from our mission or a public agency, or some institution abroad, such as chamber of commerce, a superintending agency or public analysts. For claims of large magnitude we could quickly agree with the exporter and the Export Promotion Council concerned on a procedure to suit the case. The essence of the new system should be to expedite claims, with a record maintained of the incidence nature, time taken, and to separate the grain from the chaff; and

(ii) Reserve Bank should also examine its own procedures to ascertain whether they in any way hamper a prompt and equitable settlement of claims.

9. *Procedures and Regulations* (Chapter 6)

A small group may be appointed to continually monitor and to simplify and streamline procedures, and offer exporters help to solve their procedural problems, especially of the small exporters.

10. *Selectivity* (Chapter 6)

A practical solution to a problem that has remained unsolved for long, despite complete agreement, would be to harmonise through some franchising system, the national exporters' interests and the small exporters' who have their production and enterprise, by linking them with larger exports, who possess the requisite technical and export marketing skill. This is elaborated later under a recommendation on franchising.

11. *Export Production and Industry* (Interim Report)

(i) *Exportable Surpluses:* Exportable surpluses do not always arise automatically. Sometimes when there is a shortfall in production or indigenous production on an adequate scale is yet to be developed, there tends to be a temporary conflict between domestic consumption and export. Since export markets once lost can hardly be regained, a part of the production must always be made available to earn needed foreign exchange through, if necessary, temporary restraints on home consumption.

(ii) *Export Investment:* In order to encourage export orientation of production, the investor must have the assurance that export policies shall be reasonably stable and that production for exports would be advantageous to the producer. To this end, export policies should enjoy a degree of stability of at least over the period of the next plan.

(iii) *Export Infrastructure:* There are of late growing inadequacies of the existing infrastructure of shipping facilities, railways, air freight, cargo complexes power, an export-import bank (now accepted) dry ports, bonded warehouses, free zones. All these have been the subject of much discussion and enough data and suggested solutions exist, which can be examined and implemented.

Production for Exports

(i) Prior Government approval for the unit to produce more for exports should not be necessary and it would be sufficient for the unit to only notify government.

(ii) Although it has been accepted that there should be no constraints on an industrial undertaking to produce more for export, irrespective of the licensed capacity, this has not been translated into an appropriate amendment to the Industries (Development and Regulation) Act. On 15th February, 1975, government announced that the facility of recognition of export performance and capability should be made available to licensed undertakings and such undertakings were permitted to come up for recognition of enhanced capacity on the basis of additional production established in the past or claimed prospectively. This was a clear indication of government's readiness to recognise export capability and to have it endorsed on the industrial licence; and it is recommended that government should extend this facility.

(iii) In respect of FERA companies and large houses, a special procedure will have to be followed by making an application to the administrative Ministry, who will consider the proposal in a Task Force and then place it before the relevant Approval Committee. If, however, the undertaking happens to be dominant according to the current definition, an order under the MRTP Act will have to be passed.

(iv) In order to facilitate this, the application made to the administrative Ministry should be deemed to be an application under the MRTP Act and the procedure for issuing a notice, etc., should be dispensed with under the powers available under Section 5(5) of the Rules.

(v) A special, favourable view should be taken about industries located within metropolitan limits and standard urban area limits that are in a position to produce for export.

Definition of a 'New Article' in the Industries R&D Act

(i) Once an industrial undertaking is licensed for a product under a generic description, any variation of the product arising from a change in the composition or otherwise should also be deemed to be covered under the licence.

(ii) As long as the generic description covers the variations in the products, it should be sufficient that the same industrial licence should permit manufacture of the product under different names. The entries in the First Schedule to the I (R&D) Act, if necessary, may be so broadened that against each item, any other item(s) belonging to the same class are, by the large, covered.

Public Agencies

(i) State trading agencies monopoly functions should be reconsidered, with some natural or created competition by having:

- more than one agency in the same area.
- perhaps a joint sector in export marketing, representing, say, 40 per cent Central Government, 20 per cent State Governments, 20 per cent export houses in private sector, and 20 per cent perhaps to public.
- third country and offshore linkages.

(ii) This does not preclude a role for public agencies, as pacesetters and catalysts; in fact we would wish to strengthen it, particularly in new products and new areas where they can play an important development role, whose multiplier effect would be much more than in straight forward monopoly importing and exporting.

(iii) Each public enterprise with an export potential should prepare its own export plan. These plans should be put together sectorally and totally to make an export plan for the public sector.

(iv) Linkages between trading and manufacturing, and between manufacturing firms, should be planned to ensure that there is a common effort that avoids duplication of the public agencies appearing competitively in the same area.

(v) We should seriously review the role of public sector trading infrastructure of STC, MMTC, PEC, HHEC and others to take some basic decisions on whether international trading can operate effectively in an administrative culture of multi-tiered accountability, audit and control, where eight or nine agencies, may subject the organisation repeatedly to the same checks and questions and on the same issues, over many years?

(vi) Specific export targets of public sector enterprises should be fixed by the administrative Ministries concerned in consultation with the Ministry of Commerce and Bureau of Public Sector Enterprises and the enterprises should be made responsible for fulfilling them as a part of production and corporate planning.

(vii) An export division may be set up in the Ministry of Commerce for monitoring and evaluation of exports by public sector undertakings.

(viii) Public sector enterprises should be permitted to enter into technical collaboration and increase in capacity, even if it involves further investment, in order to diversify its operations for increasing their export earnings.

(ix) Greater autonomy should be given to industrial enterprises in the public sector in investment decisions, for the purpose of increasing export earnings, additional investment upto Rs. 10 crores should be allowed to be made by such enterprises without approval by the Public Investment Board.

12. *Industrial Exports* [Appendix 2(ii)]

(i) Since February 1973, a total of 807 items were reserved for production in small scale sector. The reservation policy should not be applicable to the export-oriented units. In theory, the present policy is supposed to be flexible. However, the experience has shown that in actual implementation, there have been inordinate delays. The delays have already affected exports and have been a contributory factor in poor quality standards. Hence, it is necessary to have an expeditious system of permitting capacities in the items even if these are in the medium sector or large scale sector as long as these capacities are aimed at enlarging export production. Notwithstanding reservations for small scale sector, additional capacity should be licensed on the basis of 100 per cent export of production, arising from such capacity.

(ii) Since September 1975, a list of 15 industries was allowed automatic expansion in registered or licensed capacity to the extent of 5 per cent annum or 25 per cent in a Five Year Plan period. The list should be enlarged so as to cover all exporting units which export more than 10 per cent of their production except in the case of MRTP and FERA Companies which should be subject to task force discipline.

Engineering Goods

(i) Exports and the possibility of foreign demand should be an integral parameter for the creation of additional industrial capacity. This approach is of equal relevance to investment and project planning in public enterprises.

(ii) Export production should be encouraged in industrial undertaking, including MRTP Companies, notwithstanding the restriction in terms of licensed capacity; the licensed capacity restriction should be applicable only in relation to domestic production and distribution. The Industrial Policy Statement of July 23, 1980 has recognised the need for expansion of the existing units exclusively for export and for allowing higher production for exploiting fully the emerging export opportunities. Follow-up action to implement this, decision should be expedited.

(iii) The present facility of allowing separate endorsement for export production and capability has not been adequately publicised. This should be done and even the MRTP Companies should be allowed to avail of the facility and necessary amendments to the MRTP Act be brought about.

(iv) While determining the dominance of undertakings, production for export should be kept out, and for this purpose appropriate revision of the definition in the MRTP Act should be made.

(v) The Industrial Policy Statement of July 23, 1980 envisages that where a larger production base would increase the competitiveness of Indian industry abroad, Government will consider favourably the introduction of advanced technology and will permit creation of capacity large enough to make it competitive in world markets provided substantial exports are likely. As this involves value judgement and may be difficult to implement, more liberal treatment for the import of latest technology should be extended to all exporting industries. Import of latest technology should be freely allowed for export industries wherever it is without foreign equity participation. In other words, in such cases involving no foreign equity, technology imports should be on Open General Licence.

(vi) As projects exports are going to become important for engineering exports in the 1980s, and as such exports require large financial resources, some special financing arrangements will have to be considered. Such arrangements will have to be considered. Such arrangements could avail of the Euro-dollar markets where India enjoys high creditability. The proposed EXIM Bank should be equipped to meet the financial requirements of projects and service exporters adequately.

(vii) At present on all bought out items required for project exports, excise duty has to be paid for which refund can be claimed later on. This is not only a time-consuming process, but also adds to the total cost of the export project. As such, it acts as serious constraints. Sub-Group is strongly of the view that in the case of bought out items also, the same procedure should be followed as in the case of manufacture exports wherein a bond furnished by the manufacturer exporter is accepted and payment of excise duty is to be waived.

(viii) Since our main thrust in the 1980s will have to be on project exports, we will have to ensure quick and smooth transportation arrangements. Higher priority should be given in the allocation of wagons including special type of wagons required for project exports.

(ix) Urgent action should be taken to explore new markets, particularly for project exports in Africa and Asia. Our technology and experience is particularly relevant to some of the developing countries in Africa. Oil rich countries in the Middle East have thrown up unlimited opportunities in the field of construction activities and our achievements in this regard have been only marginal so far. India's participation should be both directly as well as indirectly through reputed companies of the developed countries.

(x) Public sector undertakings, including railways, producing engineering products should pay urgent attention to increase their marketing abroad particularly of heavy equipment, consultancy, turnkey jobs and construction on the basis of pooling their experience and resources.

(xi) One of the important prerequisites for encouraging exports of engineering projects and services in an up-to-date information system. While TDA, FIEO and EEPC can continue to collect information relevant to their activities, it would be necessary to make use of organisations like MECON, EPI, NIDC, Railways, FCI and BHEL to collect the specialised data and information for heavy engineering exports, consultancy, turnkey projects, joint ventures, etc. The expenses on this account could be met from MDF.

(xii) Following the pattern of developed countries, we should encourage our consultants to take up preliminary studies free of cost to the recipient countries which are considered potentially rewarding. India consultancy organisations, where they feel it necessary, should be encouraged to establish links with similar organisations in advanced countries.

(xiii) Our capabilities in the field of design, consultancy and engineering should be publicised abroad by preparing a roster of top level experts and specialists, both public and private sectors, and by publishing a brochure on consultancy services obtainable in the country, with detailed reference to work done by them in India and abroad.

(xiv) Considering the comparatively small requirement of power by engineering industry, the power cuts as applicable to them should be less severe and should be applied by stipulating a ceiling on maximum demand for energy. Export oriented engineering units who wish to set up their own generating sets should be allowed to do so, with a subsidy, and they should be assured of adequate supply of diesel oil, for the operation of the generation sets for which the allocation should be made by the Central Government on the same analogy as the allocation of furnace oil for DGTD industries. This procedure could be further extended for essential inputs like coal, coke and pig iron required by exporters.

(xv) The restrictions on setting up of industrial units in the vicinity of urban areas for a population of more than 5 lakhs should be relaxed for export-oriented industries, exporting more than 10 per cent of their production. Such units should be accorded special facilities in respect of availability of inputs, finance, etc. The Industrial Policy Statement of July 23, 1980 has recognised that it would not be in public interest to permit licensing procedures or a rigid location policy to stand in the way of maximising production.

(xvi) Industrial units which export more than 25 per cent of their production continuously over a period of three years should be allowed to import duty-free capital goods. In the case of 100 per cent export-oriented industrial units all imports requirements, including capital goods, raw materials and fuels, should be allowed to imported duty free under bond, as in the case of Free Trade zones. All licensing formalities in case of all such units should be streamlined and Ministry of Commerce should be made responsible for clearing all the licensing for these units.

(xvii) In order to enable engineering industry to launch an aggressive export drive, entrepreneurs should be encouraged through financial and other assistance for participation in exhibitions, delegations, study teams and other promotional activities. It is also necessary to ensure that all displays in the exhibitions held in foreign countries should project a total image of our manufacturing capabilities and therefore in all cases include sophisticated and high-technology items. To ensure this Ministry of Commerce might consider some assistance from Marketing Development Assistance or through similar agencies. The Sub-Group was also informed that items of display when they are reimported into this country from abroad are subjected to different levels of countervailing duties. This should be done away with.

(xviii) As new capacity for export-oriented industrial projects is hampered by rising investment costs, the Committee recommends the following fiscal concessions for encouraging investment in export production units.

– Prior to March 31, 1970, tax credit was allowed to the extent of increase in export earnings in corporate sector. This should be revived.

- In the Finance Act, 1976, the scheme of development rebate and additional depreciation allowance was replaced by a scheme of investment allowance @ 25 per cent of the cost of new plant and machinery. According to the modification effected in 1977, investment allowance in respect of machinery and plant is allowed to all small scale industrial undertakings. However, in the case of other industrial undertakings it is available only in such cases where the machinery and plant installed for the purpose of construction, manufacture or production of any article except certain articles of low priorities listed in Appendix I. The appendix contains a number of articles like tobacco, electronic goods, aerated water, electric fans, furniture, sanitary-wares, glasswares, detergents, pigments and colours, etc., which have a high export potential. New units in all such industries, which are important from the point of view of exports should be deleted from the appendix and made eligible for investment allowance.
- The Jha Committee has brought out the seriousness of cascading effects of excise duties on raw materials and intermediates on the finished products. Some methods should be devised to rationalise the indirect tax structure on the export-oriented units so that they are exempted from the incidence of excise duties on raw-materials and intermediates.
- To encourage joint ventures abroad, taxation of dividends received in India by Indian participants should be exempted from income tax. To take care of escalation of investment costs the Group is of the view that the current limit of allowing equity participation of Rs. 2 million in joint ventures should be raised to Rs. 5 million.

Electronics

(i) A large part of the export target for electronics will have to be fulfilled by the Santa Cruz Electronics Export Processing Zone. The facilities available at the Zone are far below the facilities offered by other similar zones in the neighbouring countries. The major areas in which incentives and facilities need to be upgraded are on-the-spot delegation and centralisation of decision-making authority on all matters pertaining to setting up of units such as imports production and exports. The Zonal Authority should be competent to give all clearance on-the-spot including central customs and excise matters.

As SEEPZ units have little or no domestic markets in the hinterland, where profits are high, and also the fact that the exports from the Zone do not qualify for cash compensatory support, it is necessary to extend more incentives should be in form of tax holiday, accelerated depreciation provision of at least 30 per cent each year, abolition of service charges, exemption from levies other than Central Customs Excise Duties such as Central and State Sales Tax, Octroi and electricity duty, etc. In several other directions like export credit finance, market development grants for export promotion, travel and publicity, etc., the zonal units should at least be treated on par with exporting units in the hinterland. Similarly, in procurement of supplies of domestic raw materials such as cement, steel communications, etc., facilities should be provided to the zonal units without delay.

(ii) For increasing the exports of consumer items such as radio receivers, tape recorders, cassette players, TV and public address systems, design changes should be encouraged, adequate production and testing facilities provided, and quality and technology be upgraded all along the line.

(iii) There is a large scope for promoting joint ventures in the developing countries in electronics with or without cooperation from Third Countries in the developed world. The system of clearance of joint ventures in the electronics should be entrusted to a separate board. This is necessary because of the need to have an integrated organisational approach to the growth of electronics industry, which differs from other industries in many respects.

(iv) As regards the hinterland units, although some incentives and facilities like import replenishment of components, cash compensatory support, duty drawback, packing credit are available, incentives and facilities to hinterland units should be augmented through raising of the cash compensatory support, liberal duty drawback rates, simplification of duty, free imports for committed exports, flexibility in import replenishment and additional facilities for market development and packing credit.

(v) Special arrangements should be made to ensure standardisation and quality control in the exports of electronics items. This should be done through pooling of the existing testing facilities available in the country and by making available to the industry codified reprints of standards and specifications.

(vi) For a concentrated export drive in electronics, which offers tremendous scope, there should be a distinct and separate export promotion council, consisting inter alia of representatives of the Ministry of Commerce and the Department of Electronics.

Leather and Leather Goods

(i) There should be optimal utilisation of domestic hides and skins and liberal imports should be allowed to improve availability of raw materials.

(ii) The import of latest machines, chemicals and technology for leather should be encouraged to achieve higher unit value realisation and a quantitative shift for production of superior grade of finished leather.

(iii) An accelerated thrust should be made to explore new markets by continuous process of identification of fast changing fashions and designs.

(iv) In order to supplement the supply of finished leather to exporting units, the sale made by finished leather units to export-oriented units of leather manufactures should be set off against the export obligation of the former.

(v) Liberal and concessional finance should be made available to the industry for stimulating the conversion of the industry for production of high value leather manufactures.

(vi) In view of the demand and prices of reptile skin and crocodile skin in Italy and other international markets, export of non-reptile skins in processed from may be allowed on a limited basis.

(vii) The reservation of manufacture of footwear by small scale sector should not be applicable to large exporting units and export obligation may be introduced in a phased manner so as to allow such units to come up to full capacity.

(viii) Export of sophisticated products like fashion shoes, leather garments, leather woollen garments, jackets, overcoats and fashion textile garments, etc., should be encouraged through foreign technical collaboration and marketing arrangements. The emphasis on higher unit value items of export is necessary to circumvent the present restrictive measures which are aimed at restricting quantities.

(i) *Gem and Jewellery*

Alternative Sources for Raw Material *Availability* – Liberal treatment in imports should also be extended for import of machinery, testing apparatuses, synthetic stones, etc., required for export production.

(ii) *Market Surveys and Research*

Specific market surveys on a continuous basis should be conducted to identify market potentials for different gem and jewellery products in carefully selected markets. Some of the important markets which need to be surveyed by the professionals are the USA, Canada, Japan, Western Europe, Eastern Europe, Middle East, Hongkong, Singapore, Taiwan, Korea, Brazil, Egypt and Argentina. This should be supplemented by market research to be conducted by the professionals within the country of the production and quantity available of different products for export markets. Market orientation teams consisting of professionals and small as well as medium exporters should be sent to important overseas markets.

(iii) *Organising Exhibitions and Participation in Trade Fairs*

India should organise Jewellery exhibitions in important world markets atleast once in every three years as they have become effective instruments to project the technological development and higher standards of manufacturing achieved. The major regions suggested for such exhibitions are: the USA and Canada, Japan, West and East Europe, Middle East, South East Asia, North Africa, Latin America, Australia and New Zealand. Similarly India should annually participate in important international jewellery trade fairs.

(iv) *Design Development Centre*

Design Development Centres should be established to study the fashion trends prevailing in foreign countries and creating oriental designs to suit foreign buyers. A centre for development of international trading and marketing should also be set up. Jewellery Market Research and Monitoring Centres should be set up at London, New York, Tokyo and Kuwait. A National Design and Technology Institute should also be set up at Bombay or Delhi.

(v) *Training Programmes*

Training programmes for artisans should be organised to apprise them with the latest techniques and designs of manufacture. The ultimate aim of such a training programme should be to set up a 'Ratnalaya' in every district of the country. Such training programme should be started at five levels:

- Massive training programme for Artisans of Lapidary Crafts (Diamonds, precious stones and semi-precious stones).
- Jewellery manufacturers' training programme.
- Training in gemmology.
- Apprenticeship training.
- Upgradation of skills.

Development of a senior technical cadre is also essential to modernise the industry. No trained technical cadres are available at present. Sending 100 persons or more abroad for training in various fields of diamond cutting and polishing, pearls, precious, semi-precious stones, designing, gold jewellery, etc., for a year or more would prove to be very helpful. They can, on return, change the face of the future industry and impart training to many more within the country.

(vi) *Hall-marking, Gem Testing and Diamond Grading*

With a view to standardise the product and to give proper boost to gold jewellery exports in particular, hall-marking institutions should be set up at Bombay, Jaipur, Delhi, Madras and Calcutta. Such hall-marking institutions should be modelled after the hall marking institutions working in England and other European countries. Machinery and expertise for this purpose should be imported from these countries with the assistance of ITC/SIDA, etc., while special techniques should be developed for Indian enamelled gold jewellery.

Gem testing laboratories on the lines of Delhi and Jaipur should be set up at various important supply centres of the country. Similarly for certification of bigger diamonds and their classification diamond grading laboratories should be set up at Bombay and Surat. Equipments and expertise for this purpose could be imported with the assistance of ITC/SIDA.

(vii) *Schemes for Gold and Silver Jewellery Exports*

Suitable schemes should be revived for exports of gold and silver jewellery with minimum value added stipulation and provisions for import of gold. Provision for covering the order with gold at the reigning price should be made and export should be allowed on that basis. Fluctuations in the price of raw-gold should not be an impediment for jewellery exports and the policies followed by the leading jewellery exporting countries like Italy, Spain, Hongkong, etc., should be studied in depth for implementation in India. Tremendous potential exists in metal jewellery exports with a low added value of 15 to 20 per cent including articles, particularly for the West Asian and South East Asian markets, which should be suitably reimbursed by quantity or value whichever is higher.

Government of India Mint should evolve various modern alloys such as white gold, coloured gold and other purities (Karat contents) of gold as required by the jewellery fabrication industry.

(viii) *Co-ordination Amongst Principal Agencies*

Presently there are a number of Government agencies such as the Gem and Jewellery Export Promotion Council, All India Handicrafts Board, Handloom and Handicrafts Export Corporation and the State Trading Corporation which handle the export of gem and jewellery. There is an urgent need for the demarcation of their respective areas of activity. There activities should, however, be coordinated by one single committee of agency to put every thing in proper perspective.

(ix) *Product Diversification*

Incentives should be provided to the entrepreneurs for diversifying their production so as to encourage them to make use of expensive and better quality of diamonds. In case of precious and semi-precious stones calibrated production with the help of latest technique and machinery should be encouraged. Cultured pearl farming should be undertaken within the country and if necessary foreign assistance should be sought in this respect. Alloy and plating technology should be developed with respect to pure metal jewellery. For giving export orientation to our jewellery products modern equipped factories on a pilot basis should be set up.

(x) *Exporting Artwares*

Items such as utensils, plateware, silverware, cutlery gold, and silver chains for ornamental purpose, watch straps and other ornamental articles have a tremendous potential in export markets which need to be exploited. There is also a large potential for export of synthetic stones, imitation jewellery and costume jewellery to the overseas markets.

(xi) *Data Bank*

A Data Bank should be set up for the trade and industry which should be like a Central Pool of information regarding raw material availability at mining countries competing countries' capability and monitoring research and developments the world over, designs, etc.

(xii) *Foreign Exchange Accounts*

Fluctuations in exchange rates have been detrimental to exports of gem and jewellery because of high input content. This could be avoided if exporters are permitted to have foreign currency accounts.

(xiii) *Import Licensing*

Replenishment import licences are presently being issued on the basis of Bank certificates as produced by the exporters of their foreign exchange earned of the exported products. Procedural delays could be minimised and such issue of REP licences can be made sooner if the Bank certificate format could be redrafted and the Bank remittance received certificates in itself be made valid as an Import Licence for import remittance and customs import formalities.

(xiv) Bombay is becoming an important international procuring centre for gems and jewellery and diamonds in the Eastern Hemisphere even over Hong Kong.

Antwerp is the Western Hemisphere as the international trading centre has a turnover of $ 6 bn. annually with a large infrastructural base.

The next decade should visualise the development of International Trading Centre and Internal Market base at Bombay, buyers from world over coming to Bombay and growth of a Fem Exchange in the Eastern Hemisphere.

Chemical and Chemical Products

(i) There is a large potential for increasing exports of chemicals and drugs to developing countries in Asia, Africa and South America provided more attention is paid to research and development of natural products. As regards dye stuffs and intermediates, highly developed countries such as Japan, USA and Western European countries are vacating the manufacture of these items because of labour shortage and problem of pollution. The industry is labour intensive and its exports to developed countries can be pushed up on a selective basis particularly in respect of varnishes and dye intermediates.

(ii) In regards to perfumes, cosmetics and toiletries, their exports can also increase appreciably by improvement and diversification of products and research and development.

(iii) A number of items particularly rubber manufactured products (including footwear), wooden furniture and plywood, fireworks, cement tiles, refractories material and books and publications offer excellent scope for rapid expansion in exports within a short span of time provided basic raw materials are made available at international prices, improvement of quality, augmentation of infrastructural facilities and modernisation of production units.

(iv) In the case of paints and varnishes, large manufacturing units with foreign collaboration and idle capacity could be persuaded to take active interest in the development of exports, at also in the case of drugs and pharmaceutical units.

(v) In view of the large export possibilities, publishing should be declared as an industry without qualifications, trade discount should be liberalised and air cargo rates on exports of books and publications rationalised.

(vi) Items like spectacle, frames, fountain pens, plastic electrical accessories, helmets, etc., and linoleum have good export potential but they are suffering mainly because of high cost and low quality.

Textiles

(i) There is a virtual ceiling on weaving capacity in the organised sector o the industry. The creation of additional capacity and specific export targets may be considered. Public sector NTC mills should be geared to play a more important role in promoting exports of textiles as the rising prices of synthetic fibres in the wake of hike in all prices has tilted the balance of advantage in favour of natural fibres, specially cotton.

(ii) Imports of wide width looms, terry looms and other sophisticated processing machinery of width between 60" and 100" for production of such varieties are canvas terry towels, pillow covers, bed sheets and other made ups and fabrics for which there is a very large demand in the inter-national market, should be allowed exclusively for the purpose of export.

(iii) Import duty on raw wool should be abolished or reduced to encourage the export of woollen textiles and woollen carpets.

(iv) Adequate yarn at reasonable prices and of right quality should be made available to handlooms which export more then 10 per cent of their production either in the form of cloth or made-ups.

(v) The ban on creation of additional powerloom capacity and recognition of existing powerloom should be removed provided they export more than 10 per cent of their production.

(vi) Recent market surveys of the Textile Committee show that there is a large potential for increase in exports of blended fabrics which are fast replacing the use of pure cotton fabrics in the international market. Given the supply of raw materials at international prices, export of blended fabrics can increase annually at the rate of 16 per cent. The supply of man-made fabrics to handloom and powerlooms at reasonable prices for export production should be improved and beginning may be made for the introduction of polyester khadi for export.

(vii) The development of export based silk textiles industry should be encouraged by augmenting supplies of silk through increase in domestic production, import of silk and blending of silk with artificial fibres.

(viii) There are five Export Promotion Councils for the promotion of exports of textiles – Apparel EPC, Cotton Textile EPC and Handloom EPC. In addition export effort in the field of silk and silk products and hand knitted carpets are supplemented by Central Silk Board and All India Handicrafts Board. The need to reduce multiplicity of the agencies should be examined, as also the need for better coordination of their export activity. The formation of an apex body, with subsidiary agencies should be considered.

Sports Goods

(i) The production base of the industry is organised and strengthened by modern large scale production with due attention to quality.

(ii) Supply of all the necessary raw materials to the industry and improvement of marketing arrangements.

(iii) Arrangement of specialised displays, exhibitions and publicity abroad.

Fabricated Mica

(i) Exports can increase appreciably if quality of processed and fabricated mica could be improved according to international requirements with high value-added items. A Committee was set up in July, 1980 by the Department of Mines to consider the problems of mica industry. The Committee should particularly look into the steps that should be taken to improve the equality and value of mica exports.

(ii) Apart from the export possibilities of manufactured goods mentioned above, the two other areas which hold large promise for exports are the handicrafts and processed food industries. Training programmes, improvement in technology, wider publicity and intensive market services can result in large increase in export earnings of these labour intensive industries which do not require large capital.

Locational Policy

(i) Industrial Policy Statement of December 1977 has pronounced certain decisions regarding location of industries in metropolitan areas, standard urban limits and municipal areas limits. These decisions are sound and need to be implemented; but an outright rejection on the ground of location may be counter-productive, such as the following which need careful consideration.

- Certain sick units wishing to expand or take up a new line of production for the sake of their survival.
- A unit wishing to increase the shift for the purpose of viability.
- Diversification for a new product or a line of manufacture within the existing infrastructural facilities.
- Induction of new technology which would increase production and upgrade the technological level of production.
- Diversification or even allowing marginal investment in machinery or addition to employment without serious pollution problems.
- The economy of expansion compared with setting of a new unit elsewhere.
- The strategic location of the ancillary industries catering to

the mother industries located in the forbidden limits.

– Where licensed capacity is expressed in monetary terms and increase is necessitated on account of cost escalation.

Quality Control

(i) The concept of self-certification should be accepted and its scope gradually enlarged depending upon performance of each unit and the systems which have been established for in-house inspection and quality control. Therc should, however, be no question of any further export inspection where the product carries ISI certification. Small scale sector should also be rendered necessary assistance in quality control through consortia approach or other mechanisms like transfer of technology and common testing facilities. In this respect, the Sub-Group suggests that the proposed Franchising corporation for small industries have an important role to play.

Market Intelligence

(i) Concerted efforts are required to improve our market intelligence abroad through improvement in quality and magnitude of our representation abroad and dissemination of necessary information to exporters, particularly in selected countries where greater export potential exists.

Export Obligation

(i) Export obligations, although considerably diluted over the past three years, are still cumber some and in certain cases the exports have been effected at uneconomic prices because of obligation. Since exports is a specialised activity, more emphasis should be laid on basic policy incentives to lay a more solid foundation for a satisfactory rate of growth.

Complementarity of Production

(i) A stage has now also been reached where greater complementarity of production between the developing countries using their national resources endowment should be attempted. A good illustration of this would be the proposal which is now under consideration whereby pallets produced in India based on our large iron ore reserves would be converted into aponge iron in Indonesia using their natural gas to be used both in India and Indonesia for the growth and development of their steel industries. This in fact, if implemented would provide a tripartite arrangement where the natural resource endowments of two countries would be used to their mutual advantage using sophisticated technology from a developed country. Regional coopera-tion of this type amongst the developing countries must grow rapidly as the Brandit Commission puts it in this context, there is a vast potential for special economic relations, exchange of know-how and reduction of dependence (between the developing countries). In fact a stage has now been reached when exchange of complete technology packages including know-how, training facilities, supply of equipment, consultancy as well as project management and after sales service would become a regular feature of trade among developing countries.

(ii) Developing countries must also now gradually shift from the export of raw materials to their value added derivatives. Kudremukh was a good example of this, as a concept though this project has now run into difficulties which no body could have foreseen when this project was first conceived. A better and more recent example of this is the aluminium plant to be set up in Orissa based on our large east coast bauxite deposits with French technical and financial assistance. This fully integrated aluminium plant with a capacity of 800,000 tonnes of alumina and 218,000 tonnes of aluminium will be set up with French assistance with a comprehensive financial package based on Government credits on preferential terms as well as bank loans. The total investment in this project will be Rs. 1,400 crores to be financed mostly through the export of alumina. This adds a new dimension to our strategy for resources mobilisation to be paid for through exports, in this arrangement financing of local costs is also taken care of at least partially. We should think of many more of such projects which are based on mutually on interests between a developing country and a highly developed country. Recent discussions with Kuwait and some other countries at the highest level augur well for this type of economic cooperation.

(iii) We should also try to export our know-how on the exploration and development of mineral resources to other developing countries, in this we are very well placed with the G.S.I. which has a tradition which goes back to 125 years. A systematic and determined approach in this area is necessary so that the burden of non-oil producing developing countries due to high energy costs in the years to come can at least be partly alleviated through the development of mineral resource base; this may help them to artially muffle the blow.

Duty Drawback Scheme

(i) It is essential to streamline and simplify the procedures and practices relating to the fixation of drawback rates and also to simplify the settlement of drawback claims of the field level. There should be a mechanism to ensure automatic and expeditious adjustment in the rates of drawback on the basis of changes in customs, excise duty and prices of imported components.

12. *Small Manufacturers/Exporters* (Chapter 7)

(i) Their capital needs, both for the fixed and working, to be specially met, to avoid their recourse to high cost private borrowings and help them expand their production and export business. In view of this, it is recommended:

- A window should be opened for small scale sectors for medium term finances in the new EXIM Bank, while for short term lending the Bank can offer refinancing facilities through exporters' commercial bank.
- EXIM Bank may have a special scheme for helping small scale sector to give an access to international short-term capital market.
- We have recommended elsewhere a franchising scheme, under which large exporters may also help with financing of production which they buy from small exporters.
- Credit to small exporters may be considered on softer terms.

Books and Periodicals

(i) Indian publishing industry and trade have made much progress of late, and their exports now amount to Rs. 8 crores. World imports of printed matter have been going to 16 per cent annually, reaching $ 5bn in 1978. India currently is the third largest English books producing country, accounting for 16,000 titles out of a total 591,000. Given suitable encouragement with incentives, simple procedures, visits of study and sales team, through the help of the State Trading Corporation, the Trade Development and the Trade Fair Authorities, and our missions abroad, Indian books could gain an important position abroad, especially in the neighbouring South Asia and African countries. In due course this position could be enlarged from English language books to printing books in other languages, offering our advantages of general skills and cheaper costs. General development, financing and training facilities through the formation of a National Book Development Board may be considered.

13. *Banking* [Appendix 2(iii)]

(i) Necessary steps should be taken to make the banks interested in export financing, so that no worthwhile export proposals suffer for want of adequate credit facilities.

(ii) Exporters may be allowed, on a selective basis, to raise finance abroad.

(iii) The periods for concessional pre-shipment credit allowed at present may be reviewed in the light of the prevailing situation.

(iv) Provide direct finance, in collaboration with commercial banks, in respect of medium and long-term exports, both at pre-shipment and post-shipment stages.

(v) Provide refinance facilities to commercial banks in respect of medium and long term export credits.

(vi) Provide investment finance for export oriented projects and export promotion, e.g., for product development, setting up quality control measures or upgrading technology.

(vii) Provide term credit to finance overseas equity investments by Indian promoters in their joint ventures abroad.

(viii) Provide overseas Buyers Credit. The financial aid provided by India to various developing countries may also be routed through the Export-Import Bank.

(ix) Issue bid bonds and guarantees for supply of goods.

(xix) The Reserve Bank of India (Exchange Control Department may examine the possibility of devising a suitable scheme for exporters on a selected basis to book forward contracts for lump sum amounts with discretion regarding currencies and timing of deliveries of foreign exchange under the contracts, with necessary safeguards and penalties for transgression.

(xx) Progressively, the extent of cover, presently between 2 per cent to 35 per cent may be increased and the rate of premium may be reduced from the present 40 paise per Rs. 100 per annum.

(xxi) The existing Blanket Permits may be issued on the basis of annual budgets submitted by the the exporters.

(xxii) The establishment of overseas offices to provide consumer advice, after-sales service, and off-the-shelf delivery of engineering and non-traditional goods should also be encouraged to stimulate export growth.

(xxiii) The present system of pre-shipment inspection by the agencies of the Government of India should be reviewed as it has not been able to effectively settle the problem of complaints by overseas buyers about the inferior quality of goods being shipped. Perhaps, a time has come to formulate a new approach and of which two important aspects may be self-inspection and the bank guarantee covering the prompt payment of claims with exemplary punishment in cases of default. For late shipments which may be due to delays in manufacture, as a result of shortage of essential inputs, the Committee believes that at least some of the constraints on the availability of inputs could be solved through constant monitoring at Government level with the assistance of the various Export Promotion Councils and Commodity Boards.

(xxiv) Exporters may be allowed to meet their commitments made before the imposition of an embargo on exports.

(xxv) Apart from avoiding claims in lieu of specific performance, such a concession will avoid damage to goodwill between exporters and importers, if necessary, outstanding contracts could be registered within brief specified period with an approved government body.

(xxvi) The Reserve Bank of India may undertake a study which may look into the present procedures to ascertain whether they are in any way hampering the growth of merchanting trade.

(xxvii) The rates of commission and the relevant procedures for payment thereof may be reviewed periodically in the light of the prevailing circumstances.

(xxviii) The simplification and standardisation of documents should cover not only shipping documents but also documents that exporters are required to submit to banks, customs authorities, Reserve Bank of India (Exchange Control Department), etc.

(xxix) A Working Group may be constituted to examine the desirability of adoption of the set of documents as finalised by the

IIFT, to standardise documentation practices of commercial banks, and to review the customs documentation.

14. *Export Processing Zones* (Chapter 11)

The Kaul Committee made a number of recommendations, of which we notably feature the following:

(i) Unless some safety clause is provided, 100 per cent export obligation would mean performing of a "circus act without the essential safety net" and would continue to deter the new units from coming to the Zone. One such safety net is to, permit these units to sell a part of their production in domestic market, of course on payment of duty. Such a measure would remove a great psychological block preventing new entrepreneurs from coming to Kandla Free Trade Zone.

(ii) The Kandla Zone should be declared a Custom House, and the customs appraisers and examiners, incharge of clearing the import consignments, should be placed under the administrative control of the Development Commissioner.

(iii) To avoid second checking of the export consignment at Bombay Port, containerised truck service should be introduced between Bombay and Kandla.

(iv) The Development Commissioner Kandla may be authorised to recommend waiver of bank guarantee up to 100 per cent at the time of movement of imported goods between Bombay and Calcutta.

(v) A general notification to grant exemption from central excise duty on goods brought into the Kandla for production of goods or for use by or on behalf of the importer in connection with the production of goods meant for exports should be issued.

(vi) Kandla units should be permitted by the Development Commissioner to make semi-finished products out of the zone for processing, and bring them into the zone without, submitting each case to the Kandla Board for approval.

(vii) Air service to Kandla is an important facility for the development of Zone, together with an air cargo.

(viii) The policy with regard to import of capital goods, raw materials, etc., under the Open General Licence Scheme in Free Trade Zone, should be on a permanent footing so that there is not uncertainty on this score.

15. *Export Houses* (Chapter 14)

Two of the major recommendations of the Jain Working Group on Export Houses are reiterated.

(i) Setting up of a High Powered Committee or Board consisting among others, Chief Controller of Imports and Exports, Export Commissioner; Development Commissioner (Small Scale Industries), Representatives of FIEO etc. to oversee the entire scheme of Export Houses and lay down the minimum requirements to be fulfilled by an Export House before it qualifies for renewal of its Export House Certificate.

(ii) The Export Houses which are identified as being highly satisfactory by the above body should be given liberal support for their expansion plan, including long-term capital from Market Development Grants and other special facilities and recognition at the national level.

16. *Trading Houses* (Chapter 14)

(i) There should be created a new category, the Trading Houses, which should combine the franchising function of the Franchising Corporation, recommended elsewhere, and a highly specialised export marketing capability. Export Houses, Franchising Corporation, and Trading Houses are all an upgrading of our export instruments, to keep up with the growing demands of world trade, in our peculiarly large and mixed exporting community. A three-tired system would therefore be specially advantageous under our diverse conditions.

(ii) The facilities extended to Trading Houses, to the extent they are relevant, should also be made available on a selective basis to manufacturing exporters whose export performance justifies this.

17. *Compensatory Support* (Chapter 16)

(i) In the interest of simplification of affectiveness of cash assistance to exporters, and to obviate external objections, different elements of cash assistance may be merged/augmented with other components of compensatory support to exporters as suggested below.

– Cash compensatory support is provided on exports of specific products, primarily with a view to compensating the exporter for the unrefunded taxes, imports and levies which he has paid on the exported goods and on the inputs in manufacture of such goods. This becomes necessary because under the Duty Drawback Scheme exporters are allowed a refund a part of the indirect taxes, namely custom duties and central excise on materials — comprising raw materials, components used and packing materials — used in the manufacture and packing of export products.

The Jha Committee on indirect taxes has pointed out the cascading effects of excise duties and sales tax at various stages of production which lead to a multiplicity of taxes. There are a number of indirect taxes at the Central State and Municipal levels, including that on energy and transport, which have a cascading effect on the end product. The need for cash assistance in case of residuary indirect taxes will disappear if the Duty Drawback Scheme provides for a comprehensive refund of all the indirect taxes through a revised and enlarged scheme. The revised scheme may be designated as Tax Remission Scheme for exporters.

(ii) In regards to compensation for freight and other cost differentials, exporters should be made eligible for concessions at the source. In the case of compensation for differentials in interest rates, the interest rate on working capital needs of exporters should be brought in line with the international interest rates –, e.g., Euro-dollar market, an average of interest rates prevailing in principal financial markets of its world. The interest rates on working capital for exports should not be related to the interest rate structure in the domestic market. Similarly freight disadvantage for exports from distant places in the country should be provided for by concessional rates on freights charged at the source, thus eliminating the need for a separate provision under this head under 'Cash Assistance'.

(iii) The Marketing Development Assistance at present provides for grants-in-aid to Export Promotion Councils and other Export Promotion organisations for the development of exports, for meeting the expenditure on export promotion councils, and for projects for development of foreign markets for Indian products and commodities. The scope for this fund should be enlarged so that expenditure on 'Initial promotional expenditure for new products and in developing new markets', which at present is being financed through cash assistance, is met through the Marketing Development Assistance. The

Fund should provide for all types of Export Development Services on a continuing basis.

(iv) The existing fiscal relief to exporters in the form of direct taxes is cumbersome and inadequate to meet the exporters' handicaps, specially small exporters in marketing and tendering in competitive export markets. Prior to March 1970, tax credit was allowed to the extent to increase in export earnings in corporate sector. It is recommended that exporters should be allowed a relief in direct taxes on income or profit in proportion to the income or profit derived on export sales as a percentage of total income/profit. A suitable scheme should be devised on these lines to afford direct tax concessions to all types of exporters.

(v) To the extent that subsidies are meant to compensate for the higher costs, it would be better for the exporter to be rebated as each cost element is incurred, in relation to some international price norm, rather than to be paid a lump sum at the end – and that after delay. The exporter would then not be subsidised, strictly speaking but charged a lower price for the inputs comparable with his export counterparts abroad pay. It would have the merit of its realisticness, especially abroad, where a subsidy has always the appearance of a "bonus", which infact some small exporters share with the importers through price cutting usually undercutting other exporters. In any case the importers abroad can work out our prices form the subsidies available.

18. *Agricultural Products* [Appendix 2(i)]

(i) It would be desirable to create a revolving fund through control budgetary support or other means at the level of the National Bank for Agricultural and Rural Development (NABARD) to provide soft loans to export-oriental crops. A separate Wing for agricultural and rural development to exclusively attend to export-oriented crops in all respects should be set up in the new NABARD.

(ii) There is need for setting up of a Spices Board to plan production and take an integrated view of demand and supply to push up exports.

(iii) Separate Corporations should be set up for development of plantations crops, particularly tea and coffee, in North Eastern States. The entire equity capital for the corporations may be provided by the Central and the re-finance assistance by the ARDC/ NABARD.

(iv) In regard to plantation corporations in other States, equity capital may be shared between the Centre and the States on 50:50 basis and refinance assistance up to 90 per cent may be provided by the banks.

(v) Regular surveys of the Persian Gulf and Middle-Eastern countries should be undertaken, and effort should be made to meet the entire demand of agricultural goods of these countries, particularly foodgrains, poultry, mutton, etc.

(vi) Import policy and procedure for imports of seeds and other agricultural imports should be liberalised and simplified.

(vii) The development of animal production should be properly organised. It may be desirable to set up a Meat Board for regulating domestic production, marketing and export of meat.

19. *Tea* (Appendix 3)

The following issues concerning tea should be carefully examined.

(i) The comparative benefits of foreign exchange earnings from tea against the internal tax revenue it produces.

(ii) Examine the comparative tea price structure of India and Kenya, our most important and growing competitor to see:

– What is Indian Tea Industry's competitive strength abroad; and
– Its capacity to generate the required surpluses for replanting and new growth.

(iii) As still the world leader, tea's annual research spend at about Rs. 2 crores on a Rs. 800 crores turnover is woefully inadequate, especially as it is spread over two research centres, in the north and the south, both working more or less independently and therefore duplicating its effort, at least in part.

(iv) As a result, although our agronomic research has made considerable headway, we still provide little international leadership. Moreover, in product research and formulation, we have played virtually no role – instant tea, tea bags, tea drinks have all been developed abroad by the consuming countries. Infact tea chemistry is a subject that our research has barely touched.

(v) The story of jute is repeating itself in tea; but we hope not with the same consequences.

(vi) We should therefore, consider an apex autonomous research body, independently funded, under the aegis of Tea Board and associating itself with CSIR, tea industry and its two R&D centres at Tocklai (North) and Cinchona (South).

(vii) Tea research should be extended from agronomic and product to market and consumer research, combined with economics, statistics and a data bank for the industry.

(viii) A Plantation Board or Corporation may be formed to foster, coordinate, plan and prepare projects, and priorities the plantation crops' interests of research and development both agro-economic, processing, packaging and marketing at home and abroad; identifying new areas and their allocation, planting, inplanting and replanting; production and exports of tea, coffee, cardamom, spices, rubber, cashew, cocoa, etc. The large added financing, which in total over the next decade, would amount to over Rs. 1,000 crores, would draw for equity upon the Centre, States and the industries concerned, for grants needs of expansion and replanting upon the financial institutions like Agriculture Refinance and Development Corporation (ARDC) and National Bank for Agricultural and Rural Development (NABARD), while the working capital needs would continue to be met by the commercial banks. There may be parallel boards and corporations in the States, as at present.

20. *Marine Infrastructure* [Appendix 2 (iv)]

(i) Our infrastructure facilities need urgently to be improved and strengthened to meet the requirements of the growing new types of the trade and its handling, taking into account the new technology that is emerging for transportation of cargo at sea. It will require large investments by port trusts to introduce structural and organisational, and also the many corresponding changes, to ensure that Indian merchant marine keeps pace with international trade needs, both qualitatively and quantitatively. For instance:

- Our ports will need to be modernised in all aspects – sheds, equipment, administration, and most importantly, productivity;
- We must provide facilities for inter-model form of transport;
- We should improve container handling facilities both at ports and in the interior; and

Customs and ports procedures and regulations should be updated to fit in a more practical manner with today's cargo handling requirements.

(ii) One of the joint ventures in which India can participate in shipping. The country has developed adequate 'shipping' management skills/knowledge in all its facets whether relating to carriage of general cargo, tramping, bulk cargo (both liquid and dry). S.C.I. for example has a joint venture with Iran – called Irano-Hind and is working fairly successfully. Similarly it has lent personnel to foreign shipping and companies like Libya's Tanker Co. With the advancement of technology, greater movement of cargo in containers, which necessitates consortium approach, increasing spread of multi-model transport concept, etc., are pointers in this direction. India should therefore, fully exploit this situation, enter into more joint ventures, provide greater manpower to man foreignships and explore the possibilities of fully exploiting multi-model concept by institutionalising loose arrangements.

(iii) It may be mentioned that where National Shipping Lines are required to provide a promotional service, and adequate cargo is not initially available, some compensation should be provided to the shipping line concerned so that the export trade of the country does not suffer for want of shipping.

21. *Tourism* (Appendix 4)

(i) The Tourist Industry, public and private, may be asked to prepare a 10-year Plan for 1980-1990, showing the costs and earnings, in rupees and foreign exchange; and if the tourist industry can make the substantial contribution it feels it can, it should be given such assistance and incentives as would help achieve the targets.

(ii) Tourism has an obvious commercial viability but Government may, through the Ministry of Tourism examine the benefits of foreign exchange earnings together with the domestic cost-benefit.

(iii) Tourism should be given the status of industry to enable it to qualify for such benefits, fiscal and others, as are granted from time to time to domestic and exporting industries.

22. *Transnationalisation* (Chapter II)

(i) We should begin to look ahead with our own new transnationals and plan their contribution to our exports and foreign exchange earnings. They are concentrating so far mainly on the neighbouring countries of South East Asia and Africa, where we have excellent scope for inter-developing countries trade, but they are also beginning to look further afield, and especially at the developed world. While in the next decade a substantial part of our exports would continue to come from our own enterprises from public and private sector, we also recognise that in selected products and markets transnationals in India can contribute to our export expansion, provided our policies are carefully framed. Their world-wide connections and international marketing culture should be utilised to our export advantage, especially in sophisticated sectors, and where they have developed new technology and products, for both owned and bought-out products. It would be useful to invite some to prepare a Five-Year Plan for the best they can do in exports, especially in new directions, and the circumstances in which they could do it. If the terms involved cost less than the potential benefit, on cost-benefit consideration alone, we should consider their proposals.

(ii) *Manpower*

- Selection and training of skilled workers and craftsmen may be undertaken to meet the varied and changing demand;
- Suitable agreements should be negotiated in the interests of the expatriates and host country, in regard to regulations and restrictions; and
- Reasonable and attractive facilities should be given to encourage them to save and remit, as also for the personal purchases they bring home out of their savings rather than encourage them to spend abroad.

23. *Export Management* (Chapter 13)

Exports have been directed instead of managed, and wherever there is slippage there is at best a management by crisis rather than a long-term planning, implementation and monitoring. The following frame is suggested for consideration.

(i) An export management department in the Ministry of Commerce should be formed with ten divisions, each responsible for a generic group of export industries, offering a single point treatment.

- Plantations, tea, coffee, cashew, cardamom, spices, coir, etc.;
- Steel, metals, engineering and machinery;

- Services, advice, consulting education and science;
- Food products, agricultural dairy and horticultural produce;
- Textiles and fibres;
- Handicrafts, garments, leather, gem and jewellery;
- Chemicals, pharmaceuticals and drugs;
- Tourism;
- Shipping, ports and air; and
- Miscellaneous.

The Divisions and their respective industries will work closely together in a five step exercise:

I. Certain basic policies will be developed and announced, derived from the long- and short-term compulsions and within social and economic parameters, to which government will stand committed normally – to some for a period of three years and others for one year. These policies will relate to both basic and operational issues, so that the exporting community will know where it stands on matters that are outside its own decision-making.

II. Each Division will prepare, in conjunction with industry, and its units accounting for 80-90 per cent exports in that area, in the manner of an ABC analysis, a detailed three year base plan, phased down to a one year period, stating the objectives constraints, assistance needed, and casting it into an agreed annual plan, with budgeted financial and other resources employment and the targeted performance. The group sectors plans will be consolidated into a total exports plan, which will be placed before an inter-ministerial seniors committee and finally be approved by a Cabinet Exports Committee.

III. As backup support to the Export Plan, there will be careful planning of production capacities required to create the needed export surpluses, and if inputs of raw materials and services to ensure the planned exports.

IV. Monitoring of implementations is most important and the desks and their industries will prepare a quarterly progress report, which the two committees, the seniors and the Cabinet's will receive and review. The report will state progress, compare it with the annual plan, examine and explain any deviations and shortfalls, suggest remedies, make mid-course corrections, re-estimate performance, and thus generally help to keep the original plan on an even keel.

V. The Division desks will meet industries' representatives quarterly to review progress and help solve problems.

The National Export Plan will also:

(i) Relate domestic production and supply possibilities of product groups to a market segment in the world, South-East Asia, Middle East, Latin America, South and West Africa, etc.

(ii) Specify the national cost of net earning of foreign exchange in each group in terms of subsidies and cost of incentives, and cost of imports of inputs and technology.

(iii) Starting with the current position, move to a five-year forecast, whose linkages can be changed with altered circumstances and developments.

(iv) Assign priorities for assistance on the basis of likely earnings of foreign exchange and outgo with a view taken on the long-term prospects.

24. *State Governments* (Chapter 15)

(i) State Governments should assist in the export effort by forming an Export Promotion Board or Corporation, acting directly and in liaison with other State Corporations in agriculture and industry. The Corporation will help small exporters in areas where they are handicapped.

(ii) Lack of understanding of export trade and attitudes, which continue to be aligned with internal trade in a seller's market.

(iii) An inability to cope with sophistications of export trading abroad and the multifarious procedures and regulations at home.

(iv) Ready access to inputs at the right time, quality and prices.

It would offer the following facilities.

- Identify expanding and exportable surpluses and accessible markets abroad.
- Disseminate information to producers and industrial and agricultural associations and corporations.
- Assist producers with infrastructure inputs – power, transport, raw materials, finance, warehousing, subsidies, drawbacks, etc., so that the small producers are assured the requisite inputs at the right time, quality and price.

21

IMPORT SUBSTITUTION COMMITTEE, 1979 — REPORT[1]

Chairman Shri S.M. Agarwal

Members Shri Lavraj Kumar; Shri C. Venkataraman; Shri K.N. Ramaswami; Shri Rahul Bajaj; Shri P.S. Deodhar; Shri R.N. Malhotra; Shri Ram K. Vepa; Shri K.V. Swaminathan; Shri S. Varadarajan; Shri F.A. Mehta; Shri M. Satyapal; Mrs. Usha Dar (replaced Shri N.K. Das after 31-1-1980).

M. Secy. Shri R.N. Basu

Appointment

Government have been pursuing various policies and programmes with a view to reduce the dependence of the country on import of capital goods, technology and know-how, processed and semi- processed components, industrial raw materials, etc., and simultaneously to promote the rapid growth of the indigenous industry for meeting internal demand and for exports. It has been felt that a review of the working of various measures initiated during the last few years in this regard should be made for devising suitable strategies to ensure that the indigenous industry becomes as far as possible, self-supporting and that the country's dependence on imported items is reduced to the minimum. So the Government of India in the Ministry of Industry (Department of Industrial Development) Constituted a Import Substitution Committee Vide their Memorandum No. 16(130)/LP/79 dated June 26, 1979.

Terms of Reference

(i) To review technical economic and fiscal policies for the

1. New Delhi, Ministry of Industry, 1980, 177 p.

promotion of import substitution and to recommend suitable policies for greater self-reliance in the industrial sector;

(ii) To review the progress of import substitution in important manufacturing facilities, including the capital goods industry, and to suggest suitable measures for further indigenisation;

(iii) To examine the effect of the liberalisation of industrial licensing policy, and import and export policies, on the programmes of import substitution, and to recommend measures for the development of indigenous technology and manufacturing capability within a time-bound programme; and

(iv) Any other issues which the committee considers relevant in relation to promotion of import substitution and self-reliance, in technological and industrial development.

Contents

Introduction; Historical Perspective; Survey of Imports; Policy Framework; Important Areas; Infrastructure; Supporting Measures; Monitoring and Coordination; Recommendations; Some Conclusions; Appendices; Acknowledgements.

Recommendations

9.1. **Policy Framework**

9.1.1. *Industrial Licensing Aspects*

(1) *Total Capacity to be Authorised*

The total industrial capacity to be licensed for an item should take into account the estimated aggregate domestic demand and the export potential on the one hand, and a reasonable gestation period in the setting up of the particular industry, including the possibilities of slippages in establishing the licensed capacity and in achieving efficient levels of operation of the installed capacity on the other. (Para 4.1.17)

(2) *Utilisation of Licensed Capacity*

(i) To encourage establishment of new capacities, and utilisation of capacity up to the licensed level within the specified period,

Government may announce as a matter of policy, that units which achieve efficient operation of the capacities licensed will give clear preference in participating in future industrial growth. (Para 4.1.13)

(ii) To promote speedier setting up of licensed capacity, particularly in areas of heavy imports, entrepreneurs who clearly guarantee earlier completion of projects be permitted to import requisite plant and equipment, if such early completion is found to be of definite advantage to the economy. (Para 4.1.14)

(3) *Failure to instal licensed capacity*

(i) In case of manifest failure on the part of an entrepreneur in installing the capacity, or in operating the plant steadily at the approved capacity, the licensed capacity be suitably reduced to the actual level so that more capacity to be licensed does not get pre-empted (Para 4.1.15)

(ii) To assist entrepreneurs who have not been able to instal full licensed capacity, expert groups be appointed to study and report on the causes for under-utilisation, and the possible remedial measures in the light of which the entrepreneur may be required to take appropriate action to rectify the situation. (Para 4.1.16)

(4) *Regularisation of capacity installed*

To accelerate industrial growth and import substitution the concession announced recently in the new Industrial Policy regarding regularisation of actual productive capacity established in excess of the capacity licensed, in certain selected industries which are important from the point of view of national economy or mass consumption, be extended also to other important industries where large imports are taking place and are expected to continue, or where shortages are apprehended, particularly if the excess production has been due to factors like high productivity, use of improved techniques, technological improvements and innovations, modernisation and replacement of old and obsolete equipment and plant, etc. (Para 4.1.18)

(5) *Optimal/viable economic size of units*

Capacities to be authorised in future licensing, particularly in capital intensive and high technology areas, should be for units of optimal/viable economic sizes, the existing units also being enabled to enhance their capacities to the economic level where necessary, by replacement and/or modernisation of installed plants. (Para 4.1.19)

(6) *Expansion Through Marginal Investment*

In capital intensive areas in which large and sustained imports are taking place, or where the total domestic production only marginally meets the existing demand, and in which expansion of existing units at marginal costs is attainable with minimum additional costs, permission for increase of capacity through expansion be authorised readily. (Para 4.1.20)

(7) *Modernisation*

(i) Detailed techno-economic plans be prepared and implemented for the modernisation of important industries needing heavy investment, where imports are taking place or which have a significant export potential. (Para 4.1.22)

(ii) Future investment plans in these industries should provide for compulsory funding for modernisation including penalties for units not adequately funding for the purpose. (Para 4.1.23)

(8) *Automatic Growth*

The facility of automatic growth of capacity to the extent of 5 per cent per year (25% for five years) which was being permitted to 15 selected industries, and which has now been allowed to 19 additional industries included in Appendix I of Press Note of 1973, be extended also to other important industries in which large and sustained imports are taking place and are expected to continue. (Para 4.1.24)

(9) *More than one Unit*

Even where the demand of an item is not large enough to justify establishment of more than one manufacturing unit on economic considerations, if the item is critical or of strategic importance, and serves as input to other industries in the country, setting up of a second unit, to avoid a monopolistic situation, may be given consideration. (Para 4.1.25)

(10) *Investment Limit for De-licensing*

In the context of continuing increases in the cost of plants, equipment, materials, etc., the exemption limit of Rs. 3 crores for de-licensing, as also the foreign exchange limits for import of raw materials, components, etc., applicable to such undertakings, be reviewed periodically. (Para 4.1.26)

(11) *Relaxation of the Provisions of I(D&R) Act in Respect of Specific Industries*

To stimulate investment in the priority sectors and to ensure fuller utilisation of the installed capacities, the list of 24 industries which had been exempted from industrial licensing requirements and the list of 29 industries which had been permitted to utilise their capacities without limit in 1975, be reviewed and enlarged by adding industries in which import substitution is of special importance. (Para 4.1.27)

(12) *Schedule 'A' of IPR, 1956*

Consideration be given to allowing manufacture of certain items, included in schedule 'A' of Industrial Policy Resolution, 1956, which are being imported in substantial quantities on a sustained basis, and which do not have strategic angles, in the private sector also, if necessary on an interim basis, if the capacity in the public sector cannot be augmented adequately. (Para 4.1.28)

(13) *Production in Excess of Capacity for Exports*

Existing units, which produce more than the licensed quantity and export the excess production, should not be restricted in regard to capacity operation under the provisions of the I(D&R) Act to compulsorily apply for an industrial licence for the enhanced production, provided they sell in the domestic market only up to the licensed capacity. (Para 4.1.32)

(14) *Export obligation being less than 100 per cent*

If a unit in the organised sector wants to manufacture primarily for export an item, including one reserved for exclusive manufacture by the small scale sector, for which a 100 per cent compulsory export obligation is at present imposed, it may be permitted to sell a small percentage of the production (with an upper limit of 10%), in the domestic market, mainly to enable it to test the product in terms of quality, design, performance, etc., the sale in the domestic market not to exceed 1/3rd of the total consumption, the export obligation being only for the remaining quantity. (Para 4.1.33)

(15) *Small Scale Sector*

(i) *Technical guidance, marketing support and testing facilities*: A special action programme be prepared and implemented for providing marketing support, technical guidance and testing facilities to units in the small scale sector, if possible, by creating a specific organisation for the purpose and also by enlisting the assistance of selected organised sector units, especially those in the public sector. (Para 4.1.36)

(ii) *Ancillaries*: Large units in the private sector and public sector undertakings should be encouraged to make special efforts to set up small scale units as ancillaries to their undertakings and the programme of setting up of ancillaries be monitored. (Para 4.1.37)

(iii) *Reservation of items*: In reserving items for exclusive production in the small scale sector and during the review of the list, important aspects such as social-cost-benefits to the community as a whole, the effect on overall industrial growth, etc., may also be kept in view. (Para 4.1.35)

(iv) *Capital investment limit*: The capital investment limits recently enhanced for small scale sector units and ancillaries need to be periodically reviewed and enhanced every five years, based on one or other published economic indicators. (Para 4.1.38)

(v) *Growth and performance data*: Statistical techniques to choose a manageable sample be adopted to collect data about the growth, production and performance of the small scale sector. (Para 4.1.39)

(16) *MRTP and FERA Companies*

(i) Recommendations No. 2, 3, 4, 5, 6, 7, 8, 12, 13 and 14 above may be appropriately applied to MRTP and FERA companies also, subject to the particular approvals required under the relevant Acts. (Para 4.1.40)

(ii) Consideration might be given to the periodic review of items included in Appendix I of the Industrial Policy Notification of 1973 to cover industries in which sustained and large imports are taking place, and are likely to continue. (Para 4.1.41)

(17) *Public Sector*

Government may consider instituting schemes for the periodical assessment of performance and expert scrutiny of public sector projects by the concerned Ministries. (Para 4.1.46)

(18) *Encouragement for Proven Performance in the Context of Import Substitution*

Proven performance of industrial units in the context of industrial growth and import substitution like achievement of significant successes in substituting imported materials and processes by indigenous ones, successful innovation of technology, reduction in consumption of energy, minimisation of pollution, horizontal transfer of technology, maintenance of approved levels of quality, etc., may be taken into account when considering further licensing. (Para 4.1.47)

(19) *Balanced and Integrated Approach*

The overall policies be directed to encourage each sector to develop those industries in specific areas in which they can be most cost-effective as also to ensure that unintended restrictions are not placed on some sectors, particularly where there are shortages, and substantial imports are taking place. (Para 4.1.8)

(20) *Simplification of Procedures for Approvals*

The steps taken so far to simplify, streamline, and rationalise existing procedures for dealing with applications for licensing, import of technology, regularisation of capacity, expansion, import of capital goods and raw materials, etc., should be reviewed periodically so that further improvements are introduced. (Para 4.1.48)

(21) *Continuing Review of the Performance of Regulatory Mechanisms*

In the context of the changing industrial needs, continuing review of the performance of the regulatory review of the performance of the regulatory mechanisms by Government at all levels, is required so that the objectives of rapid industrial growth, import substitution, and export promotion are successfully attained. (Para 4.1.49)

9.1.2 *Technology Aspects*

(1) *Industrial R&D in large units*

The setting up of industrial R&D in large units, particularly in the large establishments in the public and private sectors within a reasonable time must be ensured through ear-marking of funds for R&D and having time-bound R&D plans and programmes which are monitored. (Para 4.2.2.)

(2) *Task force approach for technology development in selected areas*

An institutional or a task force approach be adopted in selected areas for developing suitable technologies, industrial processes and know-how, as a joint effort of Government and industry, for appropriate utilisation of India's large resource of technical manpower to achieve greater self-reliance and technological independence, and to promote exports. (Para 4.2.3)

(3) *Import may be allowed unless complete technology available*

Import of technology be allowed unless the concerned technology is readily available and an entrepreneur wishing to take up manufacture of an item could be guided by an authorised Governmental agency about the source(s) from where the appropriate technology in full (process know-how, advice and guidance on plant and equipment and raw material requirements, etc.) could be procured by him against payment of a reasonable technology transfer fee, and satisfactory arrangements for transfer could be worked out. (Para 4.2.6)

(4) *Guidance at the time of issue of letter of intent itself*

For expeditious clearance of proposals for import of technology, entrepreneurs be guided at the time of issue of the letter of intent about the source(s) in the country from where the entrepreneur could buy the technology package in the manner indicated at (3) above. (Para 4.2.7)

(5) *Review of 'illustrative list'*

The 'Illustrative List of Industries' indicating the industries where no foreign collaboration is considered necessary be reviewed, in the light of the criteria enunciated at (3) above. (Para 4.2.8)

(6) *In-house R&D as complementary to imported technology*

Every unit importing technology should arrange suitable in-house R&D activity, as an effort complementary to the utilisation of the imported technology for absorbing it and for developing it further, to evolve processes more suited to the Indian conditions and to effect substitution of imported raw materials by indigenous ones. (Para 4.2.9)

(7) *Repetitive import of technology*

With a view to reduce the incidence of repetitive imports and/or multiple purchase of technology for the same item by a number of units, a consultancy and engineering design organisation be associated wherever possible with one or more of the industrial units buying technology, and a suitable R&D unit with adequate facilities identified for absorbing the technology and further developing it for diffusion which the country, and for export. (Para 4.2.10)

(8) *Horizontal transfer of technology*

To facilitate the horizontal transfer of a full technology package from one unit to another wanting to set up manufacture of the item, on suitable payment terms, a consultancy and engineering design organisation be associated with the task; persuasion from Financial Institutions who have provided the funds and possible imposition of restrictions on expansion or further licensing might also considered. (Para 4.2.11)

(9) *Sponsored research and development by national laboratories, etc.*

It may be arranged that industry adequately funds, or undertakes jointly, sponsored time-bound research and development projects with selected National Laboratories, R&D organisations, and Universities for developing appropriate technology for domestic use, and also potentially for export to third world countries; such projects also covering specific import substitution areas with the objective of (a) replacement of existing imported production processes by some suitable locally developed processes, and (b) substitution of imported raw materials by indigenously available ones. (Para 4.2.12)

(10) *Funding of R&D in capable organisations*

Support be given to development of industrial technology, including funding, in any research or academic institution in the public or private sector whose R&D capability for undertaking the task has been well established and proven. (Para 4.2.13)

(11) *Preparation of technology packages*

For preparation of optimised and full technology packages for transfer of technology from one plant to another, support including funding be extended by Government organisations such as CSIR and NRDC, to R&D organisations, consultancy and engineering design organisations, and even manufacturers where necessary; the small foreign exchange that may be needed for optimising the existing technology package being readily provided. (Para 4.2.15)

(12) *Transfer of data for improving efficiency of plants*

Arrangements be made to obtain data from efficiently operated plants on the improvements in technology and operating techniques adopted by them for suitably transferring the same to less efficient plants on mutually beneficial terms through the intermediacy of suitable consultancy and engineering design organisations. (Para 4.2.16)

(13) *Annual publication of 'technology status and availability'*

To assist and guide existing and new entrepreneurs, both in the organised and the small scale sectors, an annual publication on 'Technology Status and Availability' be published by Government which might also include immediate and futuristic technological developments and trends, in selected fields of relevance to the Indian Industrial scene. (Para 4.2.17)

9.1.3 *Policy for regulation of imports*

(1) *Import of banned finished products in CKD condition*

Consideration might be given to the enlargement of the list of 'restricted' items to include components, parts, sub-assemblies, covers, etc., of finished products whose import is banned, but which can be imported in full at present, broken in parts in CKD condition, under O.G.L. (Para 4.3.4)

(2) *Review of lists of banned, restricted, and canalised items*

The list of 'banned', 'restricted' and 'canalised' items might be periodically reviewed. (Para 4.3.5)

9.1.4 *Customs and Excise Duty Aspects*

(1) *Rationalisation of duty on raw materials, components and finished products*

The rate of duty on finished products ought to be higher as compared to the duty on intermediates and components, and duty on raw materials ought to be the lowest. (Paras 4.4.1 and 4.4.2)

(2) *Removal of anomalies in duty structure on individual items*

The customs and excise duty structure of individual items be reviewed and rationalised to remove anamolies and to reduce imports. (Para 4.4.3)

9.2. **Important Areas**

9.2.1 *Petroleum Crude and Petroleum Products*

(1) *Increasing production*

A special 10 year plan be prepared and implemented vigorously for intensified oil prospecting, exploration, and production, using the most appropriate technology; and for simultaneously increasing refining capacity. (Paras 5.1.1 to 5.1.5)

(2) *Reducing consumption*

Special emphasis be given for formulation and adoption of short-term and long-term measures for reducing consumption of oil through modernisation of plants, standardisation of oil using equipment, improved designs for engines and pump sets, furnaces, diesel and petrol engines, and cooking devices. (Para 5.16)

(3) *Growth to be less dependent on oil*

The level of oil consumption for future has to be reduced by planning a pattern of growth which is less dependent on oil. (Para 5.1.7)

9.2.2 *Oil Exploration and Production Equipment*

A special task force be set up urgently for assessing the immediate and future requirements of equipment for oil exploration and production, and for initiating necessary steps, in association with appropriate engineering and machinery manufacturing units in India, for indigenous development and production of the important items, especially offshore equipment under a time-bound programme. (Para 5.2.)

9.2.3 *Nine Capital Intensive Key Industrial Areas*

(1) *Short-term and long-term perspective plans*

Government may initiate urgent action to subject the nine capital intensive industrial areas, namely, iron and steel, fertilisers, chemicals (organic, inorganic and resins), textiles – man-made, drugs and pharmaceuticals, cement, paper, aluminium, and electrical machinery and power generating equipment, to detailed optimal investment planning studies leading to the preparation of short-term and long-term perspective plans through groups of official experts, or specialised outside agencies, and including representative of Financial Institutions. (Paras 5.3.1 to 5.3.4)

(2) *The scope of the plans*

The plans based on such studies should cover different time horizons of 5, 10 or possibly 15 years, and should indicate whether production be established to meet the demand in full or whether deliberate gaps be left between demand and production to be met by imports. (Paras 5.3.5. to 5.3.8)

(3) *Action programme*

The perspective plans when completed should be published to generate full discussion, and based on the final decisions, detailed action programmes be prepared and announced. (Para 5.3.9)

(4) *Coordination Committees*

The progress of the action programmes in each of these industrial areas be closely monitored by specially constituted Co-ordination Committees including professional experts under the chairmenship of the Ministers of the administrative Ministries concerned. (Para 5.3.10)

9.2.4 *Electronics and Data Processing Equipment*

(1) *Production of components in bulk*

Government may urgently get a detailed time-bound programme prepared for establishing an adequate electronic components base for production of components in large bulk, in viable economic level plants, for professional as well as the entertainment fields, through liberal licensing, import of required technology where necessary, and the offer of a special package of financial concessions. (Paras 5.4.1 to 5.4.4)

(2) *Computer and data processing equipment*

Urgent action is necessary for promoting the development of indigenous industry for the manufacture of mini-computers, microprocessor based systems, small and medium size computers, computer peripherals, as also for the development of software for meeting indigenous needs and exports, under a well planned time bound programme. (Paras 5.4.5. to 5.4.8)

(3) *Small scale sector and ancillaries*

Small scale sector and ancillaries be given special support in the manufacture of equipment and devices in the electronics area, which involve labour intensive assembly operations. (Para 5.4.9)

(4) *Coordinated R&D base*

As the rate of obsolescence of R&D in electronics is rapid, and as the employment potential is large, special measures be instituted for continuous updating and development of technology by setting up a coordinated R&D base in electronics in the country, through pooling the efforts in industry, National Laboratories, academic institutions, and other R&D organisations. (Para 5.4.10)

(5) *Export potential*

Government may urgently set up a special task force consisting of official and non-official experts to go into the entire area of electronics exports, its potential and strategies, including development of exclusive export processing zones (like SEEPZ at Bombay) and prepare a time-bound programme for early implementation. (Para 5.4.11)

(6) *Appropriate technology for equipment and devices*

Existing as well as new entrepreneurs engaged in the manufacture of electronic equipment and devices as also components may be permitted to import appropriate technology where necessary on a liberal basis to improve the quality, durability, reliability and export-worthiness of Indian manufactured electronic items. (Para 5.4.12)

(7) *Large growth potential*

To tap the very large potential for growth in the electronics industry, perhaps the largest for any industrial sector in the country, Government may adopt very special and deliberate measures in this area. (Para 5.4.13)

(8) *Speeding up of procedures*

The procedures for dealing with applications for licensing, expansion, collaboration, and import of technology and equipment in the area of electronics should be streamlined and speeded up so as to reduce the time for decision-making and approvals. (Para 5.4.14)

9.2.5 *Telecommunications*

(1) *Production Plans for self-reliance*

A Committee of Specialists be set up urgently for assessing the present and the future demand, the existing production facilities, etc in the field of Telecommunications and for preparing a detailed plan for indigenous production in the public and private (mainly for components, etc.) sectors, using appropriate technology, for minimising imports and for making the country substantially self-reliant over a 5-10 year period. (Paras 5.5.1 to 5.5.8)

(2) *Coordinated development and modernisation*

A Coordinating Body be set up in the Ministry of Communications for handling the growth and modernisation of all telecommunication services and facilities including meeting the capital needs of specialised users such as Defence, Railways, Police, Electricity Boards, Airlines, etc., on a homogeneous and coordinated basis, and for providing adequate and reliable national and international telephone, telex and data link facilities in the country, including the backward and the rural areas. (Paras 5.5.9 to 5.5.10)

9.2.6 *Instrumentation*

(1) *Reduction of variety through standardisation*

Special programmes may be initiated in each area of instrumentation such as electronics, electrical, scientific, mechanical, telecommunication, etc., for reducing the type and variety of instruments through standardisation and rationalisation of specifications as a pre-requisite for increased indigenous manufacture. (Paras 5.6.1 to 5.6.3)

(2) *Import of professional grade components*

Import of the professional grade and high quality components – mechanical, electrical, electronics, etc., needed for the instruments industry may be liberally permitted till these become indigenously available, to reduce the need for import of the costly finished products. (Para 5.6.4)

(3) *Standard procedures for testing*

To assure high quality of the products, standard procedures may be evolved for testing of instruments in coordination with National Laboratories, academic institutions and research organisations. (Para 5.6.5)

(4) *Increased production and export*

Detailed time-bound programmes for increased production of instruments in each important area of instrumentation be prepared and implemented, for meeting the domestic demand and also for generating exports. (Para 5.6.6 and 5.6.7)

9.2.7 *Commercial Vehicles and Automobile Parts and Components*

(1) *Increased production*

A special scheme may be drawn up early, and implementation initiated, for increasing the annual production of road transport vehicles of different haulage capacities. (Para 5.7.1)

(2) *Improvement in quality and design*

Government may initiate in close association with industry, design work for improving the quality of the different vehicles in general as also for evolving suitable and more efficient designs for the petrol and diesel engines in line with sophisticated designs available internationally. (Paras 5.7.2 and 5.7.3)

(3) *Automobile parts and components*

A Task Force may go urgently into the various aspects of the automobile parts and components industry with a view to standardisation, establishment of viable capacities for manufacture, and stepping up of production and reduction of imports. (Para 5.7.4)

9.2.8 *Edible Oils*

(1) *Specialists' Group*

Government may set up a Specialists' Group on Edible Oils on an urgent basis consisting of agricultural, economic and technical experts to take stock of all aspects of the production and supply of edible oils and to suggest the policy and action programme to be adopted for increasing domestic production and minimising imports over the next 5 to 10 years. (Paras 5.8.1 to 5.8.3)

(2) *Increased production*

To increase production of oilseeds, Government may like to consider announcing a package of incentives for motivating farmers and cultivators, including fixing of domestic support prices accompanied with schemes for procurement and storage of oil and oil seeds as appropriate. (Para 5.8.4)

(3) *Improving designs of village Ghanis*

Government may initiate a special project for improving the designs of village oil extracting equipment such as Ghanis, manufacture of the redesigned equipment in the States, and for providing financial assistance to small extractors for the adoption of the new designs. (Para 5.8.5)

(4) *Other measures in the area of edible oils*

It is necessary to adopt other supplementary measures for intensifying production of non-traditional oils and to minimise the use of edible oil for non-edible purposes. (Para 5.8.6)

9.2.9 *Photographic Materials and Equipment, etc.*

Action needs to be taken for increasing the capacity for the manufacture of photographic paper and films including colour films, and setting up production of sophisticated photographic equipment, including cameras, lenses, etc. (Paras 5.9.1 to 5.9.2)

9.2.10 *Manufacture of Spare Parts for Special Equipment and Devices*

(1) *Support for development of components and parts*

Entrepreneurs engaged in development and import substitution of spare parts and components, etc., required by various Government Departments, public sector organisations, and public utilities particularly in Ministries of Defence, Railways, Communications, Transport and Shipping, etc., may be given special financial support and concessions in the form of development expenditure for manufacture, testing and trial of proto-types, etc. (Paras 5.10.1 to 5.10.2)

(2) *Continuancy of orders*

The successful entrepreneur(s) may be assured to continuous orders at appropriate process over a reasonable period, if the need continues, provision also being made for making advance payment of part value of the order, if necessary. (Para 5.10.3)

(3) *Industrial licence not to be obligatory*

The entrepreneurs on whom specific orders for the development and manufacture of such items are placed by organisations like the Ministry of Defence, may not be asked to compulsorily obtain industrial licences for such manufacture (Para 5.10.4)

9.2.11 *Joint Ventures Abroad on a Co-sharing Basis*

A special programme be prepared for setting up joint ventures abroad on a co-sharing basis, particularly in the areas of minerals, essential raw materials, and intermediates not adequately available in India, as also of products requiring large energy inputs for processing, using Indian know-how, equipment, etc., wherever possible; suitable schemes may be evolved for the funding of such ventures in association with Financial Institutions. (Paras 5.11.1 and 5.11.2)

9.2.12 *Fabrication of Components and Parts for Imported Plant and Machinery*

To avoid continuing Imports of components and parts, for imported plant and machinery, the units which have built up capability to manufacture these items for use in their own plants be permitted to supply these to other units needing such items, but meeting their requirements through imports. (Para 5.12)

9.3 **Infrastructure**

9.3.1 *Power*

(1) *Time-bound programme for increasing capacity and improving efficiency*

Special time-bound programmes be drawn up for installing additional capacity in all sectors – thermal, hydroelectric and nuclear – and for correcting the factors responsible for power shortage on an urgent basis; the latter, if necessary, by using the services of competent engineering design and consultancy organisations. (Paras 6.2.2.1 and 6.2.2.3)

(2) *Support for hydroelectric and other sources*

Greater support for power generation be given through development of hydroelectric (including low-head) and other sources of power. (Para 6.2.2.4)

9.3.2 *Coal*

(1) *Time-bound strategies for increasing coal supplies*

Well thought out production and transportation strategies on a tight time-schedule be adopted on an urgent basis to increase coal supplies. (Paras 6.2.3.1 to 6.2.3.3)

(2) *Plan for demand management*

A detailed plan for demand management of coal in consultation with major users be evolved and implemented on a continuing basis. (Para 6.2.3.4)

9.3.3. *Oil*

As mentioned earlier, urgent action needs to be taken under a time-bound programme for increasing the indigenous production of oil and refining capacity, and for initiating and implementing measures for conservation in its use. (Paras 6.2.4.1 and 6.2.4.2)

9.3.4 *Rail Transport*

(1) *Special programme for increasing wagon and loco fleets*

A special programme be drawn up for increasing the wagon and loco fleets to handle the present and future traffic on an urgent basis, and implemented within a time-bound schedule. (Para 6.3.3.1 and 6.3.3.2)

(2) *Movement of wagons and freight trains to be computerised*

The movement of wagons and freight trains be speeded up, by resorting to computerisation of the operations, and through adoption of operations research and other modern techniques. (Para 6.3.3.3)

9.3.5 *Ports and Cargo Handling Equipment*

Modernisation of port facilities including cargo handling equipment be undertaken on an urgent basis, and schemes using operations research techniques for optimum utilisation of the facilities be worked out and implemented. (Paras 6.3.5.1 to 6.3.5.4)

9.3.6 *Monitoring of Infrastructure*

(1) *Each Ministry to have an expert body for monitoring*

To closely monitor the progress of the implementation of the plans to prevent slippages, each Ministry/Department/Agency, dealing with any of the vital infrastructural sectors such as power, coal, oil, railways, road transport, shipping, ports, inland water transport, telecommunications, etc., may set up an expert body under the chairmanship of the

Minister concerned. (Paras 6.5.1 to 6.5.3)

(2) *Operations research system for monitoring*

For monitoring the inadequacies and operational bottlenecks of the infrastructure at the national as well as the regional and sub-regional levels, use may be made of cybernetic operations research systems. (Para 6.5.4)

(3) *Cabinet Committee on Infrastructure*

In view of the significant importance of coordination of all aspects of infrastructural activities as a whole which could result in effective correction and prevention of adverse effects on industrial growth due to sectoral failures, consideration might be given to the continuance of the recently constituted Cabinet Committee on Infrastructure until the situation becomes satisfactory. (Para 6.5.5)

9.4 **Supporting Measures**

9.4.1 *Standardisation of Designs of Selected Items*

(1) *Institutional approach of preparation of standardised designs*

Government may take initiative in adopting an institutional approach with adequate funding, preferably under the aegis of DGTD, with the associations of appropriate research, development, consultancy and manufacturing organisations for the preparation of updated, economic and standardised manufacturing designs of selected items such as engines and pump sets, electric motors, switchgear, switches, contractors, automobile components and spares, various domestic and other appliances, etc., by pooling together technology available in the country, and if necessary supplementing it with technology from abroad. (Paras 7.1.1 to 7.1.3)

(2) *Designs to be available off the shelf*

The designs which could be in the form of blue-prints, showing detailed drawings and dimensions of parts, detailed specifications of materials used, as also of special processes involved, may be made available at nominal cost, off the shelf, primarily for guiding existing small scale sector and other producers of the items. (Para 7.1.4)

(3) *Certification of products*

Entrepreneurs taking up manufacture according to these designs and getting their products tested and certified by appropriate Government agencies such as ISI, Export Inspection Councils, National Laboratories, etc., may be permitted to stamp their products with the standard design numbers on which they are based. (Para 7.1.5)

9.4.2. *Quality Certification*

(1) *Testing, calibration ad standardisation*

Activities such as testing, calibration and standardisation be recognised as important technical activities is national interest. (Para 7.2.1. to 7.2.2.)

(2) *Laboratories and technical institutions to function as testing organisations*

Existing laboratories, academic institutions and similar establishments with adequate testing facilities be recognised by Government to function as testing organisations for specific, selected products, and for issuing Quality Certificates. (Para 7.2.3)

9.4.3. *Quality Evaluation of Consumer Products*

Private, non-profit, voluntary consumer organisations and societies be encouraged by Government and industry, through appropriate funding where necessary, to evaluate, and to bring out periodic publications giving comparative evaluation of the quality of selected consumer products manufactured by different producers, for the benefit of consumers as also of manufacturers. (Para 7.3.1 to 7.3.3)

9.4.4. *Stock-piling of Raw Materials*

A programme of stock-piling of selected raw materials taking into account the critical and strategic nature of the item, its supply position, etc. be drawn up and the work entrusted to either one or more of the existing Government Trading Agencies such as the STC, MMTC, etc., or to a special organisation to be set up for the purpose. (Para 7.4.1 to 7.4.2)

9.4.5 *Specialised Construction and Erection Equipment*

To facilitate rapid completion of erection of projects, consultancy and engineering design organisations, and public sector undertakings such as NIDC, EIL, BEML, etc., be permitted to procure specialised construction and erection equipment from overseas (and simultaneously the fabrication of such equipment in the country be activity promoted). (Paras 7.5.1 and 7.5.2)

9.4.6 *Import of Used Machinery*

The areas in which, and the practical guidelines under which, the import of second-hand plant and machinery is likely to be permitted, may be clearly announced and the administrative clearances for imports of such machinery simplified and speeded up by handling the work through a suitably constituted Committee, with a time-bound programme. (Paras 7.6.1 to 7.6.2)

9.4.7 *Anti-Dumping Measures*

Action be initiated for promulgating 'anti-dumping' measures on lines of similar laws existing in other countries to ensure that plans and goods are not 'dumped' by foreign manufacturers into the country, adversely affecting industries contributing to the substitution of imports. (Para 7.7)

9.4.8 *Energy Conservation Group*

An Energy Conservation Group be set up to devise strategies and prepare detailed short- and long-term plans and action programmes for reducing the consumption of energy in the industrial sector through use of up-dated and improved technology, modernisation of plants and equipment, improvement in designs of oil using equipments, diesel and petrol engines, etc., based on the study of consumption of energy in existing industrial plants and devices, and the action plans might be implemented under time-bound programmes. (Paras 7.8.1 to 7.8.10)

9.4.9 *Pollution Abatement*

Industrial units need to evaluate the correction needed to bring their pollution effects within the specified norms, and to prepare and implement phased time-bound programmes for adopting pollution abatement measures to achieve this. (Paras 7.9.1 to 7.9.2)

9.4.10 *Import Data*

(1) *Import data to be disaggregated*

The items of import in important industries be urgently re-classified in a sufficiently disaggregated, preferably computerised, form to enable proper assessment of the imports of important items. (Paras 7.10.1 to 7.10.2)

(2) *Publication through Trade or Industry Association*

To speed up publication of such computerised disaggregated import data, an Industry or Trade Association be invited, if necessary, to undertake the work. (Para 7.10.3)

9.4.11 *Data about Industries*

(1) *'Guidelines for Industries' to be published early*

The 'Guidelines for Industries' containing information up to the previous financial year be published within 3 months of the commencement of the year like other annual Government publications. (Paras 7.11.1 to 7.11.2)

(2) *Information to be more comprehensive*

The information published be made more comprehensive by including data about future demand profiles, viable economic size of plants, availability of technology, broad investment patterns, imports, international scene, exports, export potential, etc., by using the facilities and expertise available with the Indian Investment Centre, and where necessary, by commissioning expert assistance to prepare specific chapters for separate industries. (Para 7.11.3)

9.4.12 *Development Councils*

(1) *Assistance in determining targets and achieving faster growth*

Development Councils, strengthened with adequate full time staff, where necessary, and the association of professional experts to an increasing extent, may reorganise their programme of work for assisting Government in fixing the targets of growth, coordinating the production programmes in each area of industry, and suggesting the strategies to be adopted for faster industrial growth, import substitution and exports in important industrial areas. (Paras 7.12.1 to 7.12.4)

(2) *Expert studies*

These Councils should acquire funds for arranging expert techno-economic studies in selected industrial areas on commission basis where required, and also plan to obtain, and publish, up-to-date and comprehensive data about important individual industries in India and abroad. (Para 7.12.5)

9.4.13 *Consultancy and Engineering Design Organisations (CEDOs)*

(1) *Encouragement to CEDOs*

Government may encourage as a policy, suitable domestic consultancy and engineering design organisations (CEDOs) in different industrial sectors, as also specially support professional engineering and allied bodies which have expertise in selected areas to develop CEDOs (Paras 7.13.1 to 7.13.2)

(2) *Domestic CEDCs as prime contractors*

Only domestic CEDOs should be selected as prime engineering design contractors as far as possible. (Para 7.13.3)

(3) *Independent consultancy units by foreign companies*

Foreign design companies may not be allowed to set up independent units within the country and only collaboration-cum-purchase of specialised services be permitted, where necessary, without substantial foreign equity investment. (Para 7.13.4)

(4) *Role of CEDOs in setting up industrial plants*

Domestic CEDOs be permitted to acquire imported process technology in selected areas (generally those in which equipment design is of special importance), through suitable licence agreements, which can enable them to assist in setting up industrial plants for a number of entrepreneurs and this in enlarging the domestic manufacture of suitable equipment. (Para 7.13.5)

(5) *Co-ordination with industry*

Domestic CEDOs be specially encouraged for–

(i) coordinating with industry and R&D institutions to assist in the selection of the most appropriate technology to be imported, and absorption and further development of the technology imported for the purpose of (a) evolving indigenous processes and substituting imported raw materials by indigenous ones; and (b) horizontal transfer of imported technology and know-how to other units;
(ii) building expertise in the areas of commissioning, operating and maintaining plants, and handling turn-key jobs in India;
(iii) establishing links with R&D institutions and industry for coordinating the successful transfer of indigenously developed technology to the industry;
(iv) building expertise for exporting Indian consultancy services and for taking up turn-key jobs abroad;
(v) exporting Indian technology and know-how to other countries, particularly to the developing countries; and
(vi) establishing links and working in close cooperation with Financial Institutions to assist in the preparation of feasibility reports needed for taking planning and investment decisions. (Para 7.13.6)

(6) *Centralised purchase of technology and the CEDOs*

Suitable domestic CEDOs be involved as agencies for the centralised purchase of technology where such a course of action seems feasible and many prove to be more attractive. (Para 7.13.7)

(7) *Promotion of consultancy services*

A Coordinating Council be set up for assisting in development of consultancy and engineering design organisations to cover all sectors of industrial activity. (Para 7.13.8)

9.4.14 *Consultancy Organisations in Special Fields*

To provide consultancy and other services to industrial units in problems pertaining to specialised maintenance, corrosion prevention, pollution abatement, energy conservation, etc., for fuller utilisation of industrial capacity and achieving efficiency in the use of scarce materials and capital equipment, it is suggested that specialised organisations in these areas be promoted. (Para 7.14)

9.4.15 *Improvement of Technical Training*

To greatly improve and orient training in Technological Institutions, Polytechnics and Industrial Training Institutes to meet the changing needs of industry, the courses in these institutions need to be reviewed carefully and much closer coordination established between such institutions and industrial enterprises, specially in their vicinity. (Paras 7.15.1 and 7.15.2)

9.5 Monitoring and Coordination

9.5.1 *Expert Groups for Monitoring*

Expert Groups with adequate financial, economic and industrial expertise may be set up on an urgent basis with the officers dealing with important industries in each Administrative Ministry/Department as focal points for monitoring of implementation of the programmes of development of each particular industry. (Para 8.1.4)

9.5.2. *Cabinet Committee on Industry*

Government may consider constituting a Cabinet Committee on Industry as early as possible for coordinating the growth of industry as a whole. (Paras 8.1.6 and 8.1.7)

9.5.3 *Economic Cells in each Ministry/Department*

Adequately staffed Economic Cells may be set up in every Ministry/Department dealing with Industrial or infrastructural growth (where such cells do not exist at present). (Para 8.1.8)

9.5.4 *Advisory Committee on Import Substitution*

Government may consider the early setting up of an Advisory Committee on Import Substitution to be located in the Ministry of Industry, (Para 8.2.1), to –

(a) periodically review the programmes of import substitution in the country and advise Government about the special measures to be adopted in specific areas to avoid large imports in the immediate future, (8.2.2);
(b) review on a continuing basis the various fiscal and regulatory measures in the area of industrial licensing and allied policies to ensure that they do not inhibit import substitution efforts, (Para 8.2.3); and
(c) assist in bringing out annual reports indicating the role of import substitution, the efforts made, the extent of import substitution achieved, the economic and social costs and benefits of the strategy, the future efforts needed, etc. (Para 8.2.4)

Conclusions

10.1 The Committee has reviewed the technical, economic and fiscal policies for the promotion of import substitution in accordance with its Terms of Reference. It has also reviewed the progress achieved in the substitution of imports in important manufacturing facilities, and has examined the effect of the liberalisation of industrial licensing, import, and export policies on the programme of import substitution.

10.2 In undertaking these reviews and examinations, the Committee obtained expert advice from Heads of Government Departments, Chairmen of Public Sector Undertakings, and a number of Industry and Trade Associations, Chambers of Commerce, etc. The

Committee studied the published literature on import substitution, Five Year Plan documents of the Planning Commission, Annual Reports of various Ministries and Departments and Public Sector Undertakings as also the reports of various Working Groups constituted by the Planning Commission. Advice was also obtained from experts and knowledgeable persons. The Committee held over a dozen meetings and undertook consultations in depth.

10.3 As a result of these reviews and examinations, the Committee has come to the conclusion that the problem has to be viewed in a broad perspective. It is neither feasible nor desirable to deal with import substitution as an exercise in isolation. Industrial growth is fundamental to the progress of import substitution and export promotion. It is obvious that rapid import substitution can be achieved only through faster industrial growth. Special efforts have no doubt to be directed towards import substitution of major individual key products; but these have to be identified after careful study of both the resource base of the country and the comparative costs of production. Unless a particular item is to strategic nature, the approach has to be to select an item whose indigenous production will have comparative cost advantage.

10.4 The balance of trade position is becoming increasingly adverse due to the rising quantum and value of imports, and the relatively slow growth in exports. This gap was as high as Rs. 2,232 crores in 1979-80, imports being Rs. 8,579 crores and exports Rs. 6,347 crores. As matters stand, this gap is expected to grow further. Apart from accelerating the promotion of exports, adoption of more effective import substitution strategies is crucial for bridging this gap.

10.5 With this in view, the Committee has recommended a number of measures in the area of industrial licensing, technology, import regulations, and customs and excise policies. The major thrust of these measures is rapid, coordinated and integrated industrial growth leading in turn to accelerated import substitution, increased self-reliance and improved export performance.

10.6 In the area of industrial licensing policies and procedures, the Committee has considered the maximisation of capacity utilisation as one of the most important factors in the rapid increase of production leading to reduction in imports, in the shortest possible time. It has recommended special support to units which build up the required capacity quickly, and which operate the licensed capacity efficiently. Units which fail to utilise their licensed capacity for long periods are not to be allowed to pre-empt capacity. Another important recommendation of the Committee is that the production for exports be not reckoned against the licensed capacity. For cost effective production, the Committee has suggested setting up units of optimal viable economic sizes. New plants as well as existing plants have to be brought up to such viable capacity levels. The Committee has proposed appropriate encouragement to those entrepreneurs who set up effective R&D facilities and who exhibit capability in reducing the import content significantly by using indigenous materials and adopting indigenously developed processes, who make notable contribution to horizontal transfer of technology, who get their products quality certified, who adopt pollution abatement measures and whose schemes are based on the minimum use of energy.

10.7 In regard to technology, the Committee has suggested that every unit which imports technology must set up adequate in-house R&D facilities within a reasonable period. All industries, particularly the large industries, should compulsorily set up R&D facilities on an urgent basis. For promoting development of indigenous technology, sponsored research and development with adequate funding from Government and industry in National Laboratories, R&D organisations and Universities has been suggested. In the view of the Committee, import of technology can be reduced by developing full packages of technology on the basis of which an entrepreneur could set up indigenous production. The Committee has emphasised the need and the large potential for horizontal transfer of technology through the medium of consultancy and engineering design organisations. Considerable emphasis has been laid by the Committee on the role of such organisations. These should function as prime engineering design consultants. They could also build up competence for assisting domestic manufacture of equipment. These organisations could be involved in the centralised purchase of technology whenever it is found possible and attractive, building up to expertise for exporting Indian consultancy services, and for taking turn-key jobs abroad.

10.8 In the area of import, customs and excise policies, the Committee is of the view that the Open General Licence should not be allowed to be used for import of banned finished products in CKD form as components since such imports affect the growth of indigenous industries. The restricted list needs to be suitably enlarged for this purpose. The Committee has also suggested the removal of anomalies in respect of customs and excise duties for items whose demand is met partly by imports and partly by indigenous production with a view to minimise imports.

10.9 The Committee has also suggested that in the context of the changing industrial needs, Government at all levels, continue to review the performance of the regulatory mechanisms, so that the objectives of rapid industrial growth, import substitution and export promotion are successfully attained.

10.10 In the main areas of import, special recommendations have been made by the Committee in respect of nine capital intensive key industrial areas which at present account for about 30 per cent of total imports of the country. These are iron and steel, fertilisers, chemicals (organic, inorganic and resins), textiles – man made, drugs and pharmaceuticals, cement, paper, aluminium and electrical machinery and power generating equipment. Though manufacture has been well established in these areas, the production is inadequate; wide and fluctuating gaps between production and demand have been leading to sustained imports. In some of these areas, such as steel, cement and aluminium, India's comparative advantage and cost effectiveness in such that in the past significant quantities of these items had actually been exported. These industries provide excellent opportunities for immediate and cost effective import substitution. They have to be handled under closely monitored action programmes which have to be prepared on the basis of short- and long-term perspective plans based on rigorous investment planning studies for determining the most optimal size, location, technology, investment, time-phasing and other strategies.

10.11 The Committee has recommended special treatment for high technology industrial sectors like telecommunications, electronics and data processing equipment, instrumentation, etc. These are labour intensive industries in which India has substantial advantage, but in which large imports are taking place. Development of these industries has to be handled under time-bound programmes. Special emphasis has to be laid on technology development in these areas on a coordinated basis. These industries have high export potential as demonstrated by developing countries like Taiwan, Singapore, Hong-Kong, Mexico, South Korea, which have developed very large exports in these areas during the last decade.

10.12 The Committee has taken note of the two important areas of petroleum and edible oils, which are accounting for a high percentage of total imports. In both these areas, special action programmes have to be formulated and pursued to increase domestic production and conserve use. In the area of edible oils, the Committee has suggested setting up of a Specialists' Group for devising strategies for increased production of oil seeds, improvement of oil extraction equipment, development of non-traditional edible oils, etc. In the area of petroleum, the Committee's recommendations are for increased production, and refining capacity, adoption of special conservation measures, and greater emphasis on the production of oil exploration equipment.

10.13 The Committee has suggested special financial and administrative support to entrepreneurs for taking up development and manufacture of critical components and spare parts of a variety of special equipments and devices imported by Ministries of Defence, Railways, Communications and other organisations to keep the large quantum of sophisticated imported equipment in operation.

10.14 The Committee has laid considerable emphasis on quality control, quality certification and standardisation, as these will result in manufacture of equipment and devices which use less materials and consume less energy. In the area of standardisation and standardised designs, the Committee has suggested an institutional approach for evolving blue-prints of design of selected items like engines and pump-sets, electric motors, switch-gears, switches, contractors, automobile components and various domestic and other appliances. Designs in the form of blue-prints for these items should be available off-the-shelf at nominal cost.

10.15 The Committee has stressed the importance of stock-piling critical and strategic raw materials, if necessary by creating a special organisation to handle the work, so that in times of scarcity there would be no shortage of strategic materials, and industrial progress will not be hampered.

10.16 The Committee has suggested special action for setting up joint ventures abroad on a co-sharing basis with part Indian and part foreign equity in areas of scarce materials, intermediates and energy intensive products in which India is likely to continue to be deficient.

10.17 The Committee has suggested setting up of an Energy Conservation Group for studying the consumption of energy in existing industrial plants, and for preparing special programmes for improvements in designs of oil using equipment, engines, etc., and modernisation of equipment for promoting energy conservation. Special emphasis has also been laid on the adoption of appropriate measures for pollution abatement in industry.

10.18 The Committee has left that for an effective exercise in import substitution, the data base for imports should be more comprehensive and up-to-date. Special recommendations for speedy publication of up-to-date import data have been made by the Committee. Suggestions have also been made for speedy publication of current information about industries for the guidance of entrepreneurs. The information has to be more comprehensive and include investment patterns, international scene, export potential, etc. The Committee has also high-lighted the possible role of Development Councils in determining the targets for growth and coordinating the production programmes in each area of industry, and suggesting strategies for faster industrial growth and import substitution. These Councils could also assist in the preparation of expert techno-economic studies.

10.19 The Committee has emphasised the special role of the public sector and the need for monitoring its performance so that slippages are corrected in time.

10.20 The Committee has suggested that the small scale sector which is making a significant contribution to the industrial growth of the country should be specially supported in the matter of technical guidance and marketing. An institutional approach has to be adopted and special policies and programmes evolved for this purpose.

10.21 The Committee has laid emphasis on balanced and integrated growth highlighting the role of all the sectors and categories of industries in the country. This has been suggested so that restrictions in policy may not inadvertently inhibit growth. For avoiding substantial and sustained imports, the Committee has suggested in this context that the industrial licensing measures recommended such as capacity utilisation, viable size plants, and export production being excluded from licensed capacity, should be made applicable to MRTP and FERA companies also, subject to approvals under the relevant Acts governing the operation of such companies.

10.22 The Committee has suggested increased use of computerisation in speeding up movement of railway wagons and operation of ports. It has also suggested use of operational research systems for monitoring the development and utilisation of infrastructure.

10.23 The Committee has laid considerable stress on various aspects of monitoring and coordination. It has suggested creation of economic cells in every Ministry and Department dealing with industrial growth. The Committee has also suggested the setting up of expert Groups, with the officers directly concerned with important industries in each Ministry and Department as focal points, for monitoring of implementation of the programmes. The Committee has further suggested that Ministries/Departments/Agencies dealing with any of the vital infrastructural sectors like power, coal, oil, railways, road transport, shipping, ports, inland water transport, telecommunications, etc., should set up expert coordinating bodies at the apex level under the chairmanship of the Minister concerned to avoid slippages. The Committee has also suggested that the recently constituted Cabinet Committee on Infrastructure may be continued until a steady satisfactory situation is achieved. For coordinating the growth of industry as a whole, the Committee has suggested the constitution of a Cabinet Committee on Industry.

10.24 Setting up of an Advisory Committee on Import Substitution has been suggested to function more or less as a Standing Body to deal with import substitution strategies. The Advisory Committee could review the programmes of import substitution and advise Government about special measures to be adopted in specific areas to avoid large imports. It could also review on a continuing basis the various fiscal and regulatory measures in the area of industrial licensing and allied policies in the context of import substitution and assist in bringing out annual reports indicating the import substitution achieved, and future efforts needed.

22

STUDY GROUP ON FILM TECHNOLOGY, 1979 — REPORT[1]

Chairman Dr. K.S. Karanth

Members Shri Adoor Gopalakrishnan; Shri Basu Bhattacharya; Shri M. Bhaktavatsala; Shri Ramanand Sagar; Shri P. Neelakantan; Shri Shyam Benegal; Smt. Vijaya Mulay

M. Secy. Shri S.L. Kapur

Appointment

Of all the arts cinema has perhaps the most sophisticated technological base. Advances in film technology not only change the technical qualities of cinema but also help to enlarge its language, sharpen its grammar and alter its content. This is not to say that with the availability of sophisticated technology the quality of cinema automatically improves but merely to emphasise the correlation between technology and the potential for improvement in the quality of this medium.

In view of the above and further in view of its specific terms of reference which cover the whole range of film technology, the Working Group on National Film Policy in its preliminary meetings held at Bombay resolved to set up a Study Group on July 21, 1979.

Terms of Reference

"To enquire into all aspects of technology of film industry including hardware, software, processing and raw materials".

1. New Delhi, Ministry of Information and Broadcasting, 1980, pp. 121 to 153 (Bound with the Report of Working Group on National Film Policy)

Contents

Introduction; Production Facilities and Production Equipment; Processing Facilities and Equipment; Projection Equipment, Sub-Titling and Dubbing Technology; Raw Stock and Hindustan Photo Films; Assessment of Available Technical Knowhow; Strategy for Future Development of Technology; Research Development and Training; Annexures from I to V.

Methodology of Study

The Study Group adopted the following approach for its investigation:

(i) On-the-spot study of the various public and private sector establishments which the directly involved in various aspects of film technology such as manufacture of equipment, development of technological infrastructure for film production, processing and exhibition;

(ii) Visit to research institution or research-cum-production institutions engaged in areas not directly connected with film technology but whose potential could be utilised for development of film technology;

(iii) Examination of various memoranda on film technology received by the Working Group from various Associations of the film industry;

(iv) Discussions with film technicians directly engaged in film making;

(v) Discussions with Government representatives dealing with the subject of cinema; and

(vi) Discussions with scientists in the Department of Science and Technology responsible for formulation and execution of science policy.

Research, Development and Training

8.1 The survey contained in the previous chapters highlights the following significant points:

(i) Despite the long history of film making in India, there continues to remain heavy dependence upon imported technology;

(ii) There has been no sustained or coordinated effort either on the part of the film industry or the Government to either directly undertake or to assist the indigenous development of film technology;

(iii) The development work done so far shows a lot of promise and potential. However, this has been done almost entirely by small scale technician-entrepreneurs who have undertaken it entirely at personal risk which makes them vulnerable to exploitation by established manufacturers who buy parts from these small entrepreneurs at low prices; and

(iv) There are several Research and Development organisation or Research-cum-Production organisations which have the know-how and the potential which can be used for development at work in film technology. This is, however, not being utilised in the area of film technology for want of information exchange and lack of coordination between the research institutions and entrepreneurs engaged in development of film technology

8.2 There is a range of sophisticated film equipment such as cameras, studio sound recording equipment, etc., the demand for which is limited and the development cost extremely high and, therefore, these would continue to be imported for the present. At the same time there is a whole range of equipment and types of raw stock, the manufacture of which can be indigenised with suitable R&D back up. A list of items being currently manufactured in the country as also a list of items which can be taken up for manufacture are placed at Annexures III and IV. Both these lists are merely illustrative, without being exhaustive, of the major types of equipment which are being manufactured and which can be taken up for development and manufacture.

8.3 Research and Development is part of the charter of the Film and Television Institute, Pune, as also the Institute of Film Technology, Adyar, Madras. However, both these Institutes have primarily become training institutes and have not been able to devote attention to research work in the area of film technology. Even otherwise the training requirements in various disciplines of film technology by themselves are so large and so specialised that the institutional framework for training needs to be separated from research and development work in film technology.

Centre for Research and Development in Film Technology

8.4 The Group in its visits has become aware of capabilities in diverse fields which would be eminently handy in application for the purpose of developing cinema technology. Secondly achievement of any specific objective will follow the course of any technological development, i.e., (a) Product development including design, (b) Manufacture of prototype, (c) Pre-production Planning, and (d) Actual manufacture. This is clearly impossible without an agency specially manned and equipped for the purpose.

8.5 The Study Group, therefore, recommends that two separate Centres for Research and Development in Film Technology should be established and located in two of the most prolific film making regions of the country. The Advisory Boards of these Centres should consist of nominees of Central and the State Governments undertakings concerned with analogous technologies representing specific disciplines such as optics, instrument technology, electronics, mechanical and electrical engineering, etc. The Centres should be manned by persons with technological background in relevant disciplines. It is suggested that the Centres be jointly financed by the Central Government and the State Government where these are located.

8.6 The activities of these Centres will be as follows:

(i) *Product Development* : Product development will many concern itself with indigenisation;

(ii) *Development of need based technology* : Removal of bottlenecks in technology which may be holding up progress in wide areas, e.g., the development of 16 mm projector with intermittent sprocket and Xenon or Halogen lamp which is holding up the spread of 16 mm technology in the country;

(iii) *Application of technology* : Emanating from the work areas calling for application of technology to working methods followed in the film industry;

(iv) *Manufacture of Proto-type together with preparation of production pre-planning documents* : The products thus evolved will be covered to manufacturing models to be made available to any intending manufacturer through the development of a proto-type as well as complete break-down information on material sources and application of production technology;

(v) *Maintenance and Maintenance Training* : Development of maintenance knowledge for equipment already being used in the country and training of Maintenance Engineers for the purpose;

(vi) *Refresher Courses* : Training in methods of operating refresher courses for projectionists for persons to be deputed from each State; and

(vii) *Attitude oriented technology* : Co-relating aptitudes to skills required in unfamiliar operations. An example is manufacture of lenses, loud-speaker cones and programme wiring.

8.7 From the point of view of concentration of capacities in electronics, machine tools instrument technology, the ideal place of location of these Centres are Madras, Bangalore and Bombay, it is considered that a close proximity of a centre of film making activity is absolutely essential to facilitate the functioning of these Centres.

8.8 We may clarify here that the Research and Development Centres which we have suggested will not require very high investment. What are basically envisage are Centres in the nature of all purpose workshops with tooling and machineship facilities. These Centres will not undertake any fundamental research in film technology, as the basis research in the areas of optics, electronics, etc., which go into film technology will have to be undertaken by highly specialised institutions. In fact, as we have mentioned earlier, considerable research work in such basic areas is being already undertaken by different research organizations, primarily in the context of defence requirements. The main purpose of these Centres would be to integrate the advances achieved in different fields for designing equipment and technology for the needs of the film industry and to generally assist small scale entrepreneurs functioning in the field of film technology by providing tool room and machine shop facilities.

8.9 Considering that the field of film technology is continuously expanding and research in the major areas such as optics, electronics, computers is already being undertaken by various specialised research institutions, there is need to monitor the technological requirements of Indian film industry and assess the extent to which these can be met by making use of R&D available in specialised institutions. The Group is of the view that India has sufficient expertise in undertaking research and development work for evolving appropriate film technology. During our discussion with Dr. P.K. Katti, Project Manager of the

Department of Science and Technology and the Managing Director of the National Instruments Ltd., Ghaziabad, it was clearly indicated that these agencies would be willing to undertake research on problems of film technology to be identified by an appropriate body on behalf of the film industry and the Ministry of Information and Broadcasting. During discussions with Dr. P.K. Katti, the idea of a Film Technology Monitoring Cell to be set up under the Ministry of Information and Broadcasting for monitoring the technological requirements of film industry and for assigning specific projects to existing institutions, was accepted. A note prepared by Dr. P.K. Katti and approved by the Secretary, Department of Science and Technology, spelling out this proposal is placed at Annexure V. Such a Monitoring Cell should consist of the representatives of the Ministry of Information and Broadcasting, Department of Science and Technology, Ministry of Industry, NFDC, film technicians and film makers.

8.10 To sum up, we propose the following three tier structure for promoting research and development in the area of film technology:

(i) A Film Technology Monitoring Cell to be set up consisting of the representatives of various interests as mentioned above to identify problems of film technology, locate the groups, institutions and individuals who could work on these problems and recommend adequate grants for these jobs. Funds for this Monitoring Cell should partly be provided by the Department of Science and Technology through its Instrument Development Programme and partly by the Ministry of Information and Broadcasting and NFDC;

(ii) Two Institutes of Film Technology to be set up in the nature of all purpose workshops which will work on smaller projects not requiring high technology inputs and which will provide workshop and tooling facilities to small entrepreneurs and give them information and advice on the latest technological developments; and

(iii) Financial and technological support to individual entrepreneurs who are struggling to indigenise specific items of film equipment. This support should be provided by the Monitoring Cell, the Institute of Film Technology and the NFDC.

8.11 While recommending the above mentioned three pronged approach towards a major attempt for indigenisation and development of an appropriate film technology, the Group would hasten to add that this should not result in immediate cessation of import of equipment. The Group is aware of the fact that quite often once a licence for indigenous manufacture of any items is given, it becomes an immediate reason for stopping import even before the indigenously manufactured item has been marketed and field tested. Such a policy results in providing protection to inefficient and obsolete technology. It is, therefore, important that in view of the continuously expanding nature of film technology, import of the latest film equipment should continue to be permitted until the locally produced technology comes up to international standards.

Annual Cinema Equipment Exhibition

8.12 The field of cinema equipment and technology is a highly developing and innovative field wherein new equipment and technology as also improvement in the existing equipment are being introduced almost every year. India, which is the largest user of cinema equipment, should keep abreast of the latest development. This can be achieved if along with India's International Film Festival an International Cinema Equipment Exhibition is organised every year particularly with focus on the needs of developing world. Such an annual exhibition will vastly assist the continuous and consistent growth indigenous technology for the following reasons:

(i) Direct input of the latest technology will force the indigenous industry out of its partly self-imposed technological obsolescence. The home consumer would naturally want better development activities in the manufacture of equipment;

(ii) Apart from highly sophisticated equipment such as a movie camera, there are a large number of smaller gadgets and aids to production which on exhibition are certain to trigger off interest among small entrepreneurs engaged in manufacture of cinema equipment; and

(iii) An exhibition of this kind will make everyone connected with cinema technology and particularly the technicians conscious of developments in technology. If such exhibitions are held coinciding with International Film Festivals, the advantage of widening the ambit of the Festival is obvious.

8.13 While the main responsibility for organising the annual cinema equipment exhibition should rest with the same organisation which organises the International Film Festival, it should be useful to collaborate in this area with the Trade Fair Authority which has considerable experience in organising International Industries' Fair in India. It is not unrealistic to hope that such expositions may also encourage exports of Indian film equipment by making particularly the third world countries aware of the kind of film equipment being manufactured in India.

Training Facilities

8.14 Our survey has revealed serious gaps in the training of personnel who are engaged in various aspects of film activity particularly in the processing and the exhibition sectors. The Cine Laboratories Association in its memorandum has itself underscored the need for proper training to the workers employed by the laboratories particularly in view of the technological advance and the use of sophisticated machines.

8.15 As far as training in laboratory processing is concerned, we recommend that FTII should expand its curriculum to introduce a course in this area. As the demand for this field will not be very large, it may be met by setting up appropriate facilities at the FTII. Similarly the repairs and maintenance training for camera, editing and sound recording equipment should be built into the existing courses in FTII for editors, cameramen and sound recordists.

8.16 As far as training for projectionists is concerned, the number for parsons required to be trained is very large but the level of training required is not very sophisticated. It would not, therefore, be possible for FTII to provide training in this area. However, as has been suggested earlier in para 4.14, training facilities in this area should be set up at the local level by the film industry either independently or in collaboration with the State Governments. The proposed Centres for Film Technology will be able to provide training only for teacher-trainees who will run the training courses for projectionists at the local level.

23

RAILWAY ACCIDENT INVESTIGATION REPORT ON THE REAR-END COLLISION BETWEEN NO. 1 DOWN BOMBAY-HOWRAH MAIL AND NO. Y-10 DOWN GOODS TRAIN AT KM-806/4-5 BETWEEN BORKHEDI AND BUTIBORI STATIONS ON WARDHA-NAGPUR B-G SECTION OF CENTRAL RAILWAY ON AUGUST 4, 1979 — REPORT[1]

One Man Commission Shri B.P. Sastry

Appointment

The Commission was constituted under Ministry of Tourism and Civil Aviation (Commission of Railway Safety) in accordance with Rule 4 of Statutory Investigation into Railway Accidents Rules 1973 Vide Notification No. RS. 13-8(T)/71 dated April 19, 1973 on August 4, 1979.

Terms of Reference

To enquire into the Rear-end collision between No. 1 Down Bombay-Howrah Mail and No. Y-10 Down Goods Train at KM-806/4-5 between Borkhedi and Butibori Stations on Wardha-Nagpur B-G Section of Central Railway on August 4, 1979.

Contents

Summary; Inspection and Inquiry; Relief Measures, The Trains; Local Conditions; Summary of Evidence; Observation and Tests; Discussion; Conclusions; Remarks and Recommendations; Railway Board's Com-

1. Delhi, Controller of Publications, 1983, 15 p.

ments on Various Paras of the Report.

Conclusions

Cause

Having carefully considered the factual, material and circumstantial evidence at my disposal, I have come to the conclusion that the collision between No. 1 Down 'Bombay-Howrah Mail' and No. Y-10 Down Goods train at Km. 806/4-5 between Borkhedi and Butibori stations on Wardha-Nagpur Double line Board Gauge section of Central Railway on the 4th August 1979 was caused on account of (i) the speed of the Goods train not having been regulated as required in S.R. 339-2(4) while approaching the curve leading to the location where the Mail train was standing in mid-section; and (ii) the Mail train not having been protected in rear when held up in mid-section at an Engineering banner flag on account of floods in the nearby river at Bridge No. 807/1 at Km. 807/5-6.

Responsibility

Shri R.P. Shukla, Driver of No. Y-10 Down Goods train is held responsible for violation of Subsidiary Rule 339-2(4) inasmuch as he failed to regulate the speed of his train while approaching the curve in Km. 805-806 where visibility was severely restricted.

Shri Shukla who is of 52 years of age, was first appointed to Railway service in 1947 as Yard Khalasi Cleaner. At the time of the accident he was working as a Diesel locomotive Driver in Grade-C.

He had no accidents to his credit earlier and the accident index is accordingly computed as zero.

Shri A.D. Patil, Guard of No. 1 Down Mail train, is held responsible for violation of S.R. 339-2(8) inasmuch as he failed to protect his train in the rear when it was stopped at a banner flag in mid-section for over 25 minutes.

Shri A.D. Patil, who is 57 years of age, was first appointed to Railway service in 1942 as Trains Clerk. At the time of the accident he was designated as Guard, Grade-A working Mail/Express trains. So far, he was twice warned for detention and once censured for negligence of duty and careless working.

Relief Measures

I am satisfied that medical aid was made available to the injured as expeditiously as could be expected in such circumstances.

Recommendations

9.1 Coach No. SE SLR 4753, the last one on No. 1 Down Mail was of BEML design with luggage portion at either end and with the passengers and Guard's compartments in the middle. Both the end portions got badly crushed but casualties on this coach were few because the end portions happened to be luggage portions. This would indicate that the crash-worthiness of a BEML coach cannot be relied upon and should not be treated on par with ICF Anti-telescopic coaches for Marshalling purposes. This has been pointed out by this Commission on a number of occasions and accident investigation reports and has also been taken up separately vide letter No. RS. 25-T(26)/77 dated 23-24/9/1977. Railway Board have also accepted this view point vide their letter No. 78/Safety (A&R)/1/1 dated 24-2-1979, but have so far not modified their earlier directives regarding marshalling of coaches on Mail and Express trains. They may be requested to look into this deficiency and take appropriate action.

9.2 The Accident Relief Medical Van stationed at Wardha was ordered to be moved to the accident site 12-08 hours but it did not leave the station before 13-00 hours thus taking 52 minutes against 25 minutes prescribed in Rules. Although the Van was not utilised and its late movement made no difference to the situation, it is all the same necessary to take notice of the abnormal delay in its turning out in spite of instructions contained in Railway Board's No. 77/Safety (A&R)/29/30 dated 6-7-1978. Central Railway Administration may be directed to seriously look into the factors causing such delays in turning out Medical Vans with a view to avoid similar situations in future.

9.3 It come to notice during the inquiry that the Guard of the Goods train did not have with him his Vacuum Gauge nor any of the Rule Books. Although lack of sufficient brake power was not an issue in the present case, it is all the same deplorable that Goods train should be worked without vacuum gauges on the Guard's Brake Vans. Central Railway Administration may be directed to take steps to ensure that such deficiencies are not allowed to occur.

Annexure I

Extracts of Rules

(1) S.R. 131-1: Engine Whistle

Whistle Code

S.No.	Code of Engine Whistle	Indication
x	x	x x x x
5.	0000	(a) Train cannot proceed on account of accident, failures obstruction or other exceptional cause. (b) Protect train in rear.
x	x	x x x x

Note—the signals above are illustrated by '0' for a short whistle and "............" for a long whistle

(2) *S.R. 339-2*:—Rules and Regulations for running of trains on double line sections during total interruption of communications: –

(1) x x x x x
(2) x x x x x
(3) (a) x x x x

(b) A caution order restricting the speed to 25 kilometres per hour over the straight and to 8 kilometres per hour when approaching or passing any portion of the line where the view ahead is not clear due to curve, obstruction, rain, fog, or other cause;

(c) x x x x

(4) In the event of Driver approaching of passing any portion of the line where the view ahead is not clear, a Railway employee with Hand signals must be sent in advance to guide the further movement of the train. A sharp look-out ahead should be kept and the engine whistle freely used.

(8) The Guard shall keep a sharp look-out in the rear and be prepared to exhibit a danger signal to present the approach of a train rom the rear and to protect it if necessary as per extant rules. Before entering a section where there are tunnels, he

shall also light the side and tail lamps.

Railway Board's Comments on Various Paras of the Report

Para 9.1: As already advised, ICF and BEML coaches have anti-telescopic features and are designed to withstand the same test loads given in RDSO's specifications. The specifications include capability to withstand certain loads applied at the ends of the body. While the crash-worthiness cannot be directly related to these end loads, they do provide an indication of the capabilities of the coaches to withstand collision conditions.

While BEML Coaches have been found to be not as crash worthy as ICF Coaches, they do have anti-telescopic features and cannot be classified as non-anti-telescopic. Besides it will be almost impossible to run train services if BEML coaches are not permitted next to engine or as last vehicle on the grounds that their crash-worthiness is not at par with ICF Coaches, and because a large number of coaches on Indian Railways particularly SLR Coaches are manufactured by BEML.

Further, steps have already been taken to improve the crash-worthiness of BEML Coaches so as to bring them at par with ICF BG Coaches by strengthening the end structure. A prototype coach with strengthened end structure has already been built and it is to be subjected to tests in a rig being developed by RDSO. Pending test and further modifications that may arise out of such testing, BEML has already been instructed in October 1979 vide RDSO's letter No. MC/HAL/S/D/ dated 30-10-1979 to introduce the strengthened end structure in coaches produced by them as early as possible.

In view of the above, Railway Board do not a propose amending instructions on marshalling of BEML Coaches.

Para 9.2: Necessary action has been taken. Double ended entry for stabling Medical Relief Vans has been provided at all stations, as necessary, or Indian Railways except a few where also action has been initiated and progress is being watched.

Para 9.3: Instructions have been issued by the Railway Administration to ensure that Goods trains are worked with vacuum gauges in the guard's brakevans.

Suitable action will be taken by the Railway against the Guard for his failure to carry the vacuum gauge in this case.

24

RAILWAY ACCIDENT INVESTIGATION REPORT ON COLLISION BETWEEN 34 DOWN JAMMU TAWI MAIL AND LIGHT ENGINE AT DIWANA STATION ON NORTHERN RAILWAY ON AUGUST 15, 1979 — REPORT[1]

One Man Commission	Shri A.A. Rego
Officers Present	Shri R.K. Kamal; Shri R.K. Nair; Shri S.K. Gujrati; Shri Vijay Singh; Doctor O.P. Chugh; Shri L.C. Vaswani

Appointment

The Commission was constituted under Ministry of Tourism and Civil Aviation (Commission of Railway Safety) in accordance with Rule 4 of the Statutory Investigation into Railway Accidents Rules 1973 Vide Notification No. RS. 13-T(8)/71 dated April 19, 1973, on 15th August, 1979.

Terms of Reference

To investigate into the collision between 34 Down Jammu Tawi Mail and Light Engine at Diwana Station on Northern Railway on 15th August 1979.

Contents

Summary; Inspection and Inquiry; Relief Measures; The Trains; Local Conditions; Observations and Tests; Discussion; Conclusions; Remarks and Recommendations; Railway Board's Comments on

1. New Delhi, Ministry of Tourism and Civil Aviation (Commission of Railway Safety), Government of India, New Delhi; 1985, i + 28 p.

various paras of the Report; Annexures.

Conclusions

On careful consideration of the factual, material and circumstantial evidence and the basis of observations made/tests carried out, I have reached the following conclusions:

Cause of the Accident

The collision of 34 Dn Jammu Tawi Mail train with the light engine of Diwana Pilot at km. 80/10-11 on the Main line in the rear of the outer-most down facing point of Diwana station on the Ambala Cantt—Delhi B.K. single line section in Delhi Division of Northern Railway at 03.32 hrs. on 15-8-79 was the result of the inability of the Driver of the Mail train to control and bring his train to a halt in the rear of the Down Home signal, which was at danger, coupled with shunting of the light steam locomotive of Diwana Pilot being carried out outside the Down outermost facing point in face of an approaching train.

Responsibility

The responsibility for this accident devolves on—

(i) Shri Pearey Lal, the Driver of 34 Dn, for not paying immediate attention to passing the Down Home signal of Diwana station at danger. He violated the provisions of General Rule 76 and 78 (a)(i);

(ii) Shri Sat Pal Mittal, Assistant Station master of Diwana station for carrying out shunting outside the Down outer-most facing point in face of an approaching train. He violated the provision of General Rule 255A and 148, Subsidiary Rule 255-A/I and para 5(f) of the Station Working Rules of Diwana station;

(iii) Shri Gulzara, Diesel Assistant for not assisting his driver in correctly identifying the signals. He violated the provisions of General Rule 122 and Subsidiary Rule 22/1(a);

(iv) Shri Phool Singh, Leverman of Diwana station for carrying out shunting in face of an approaching train. He violated the provisions of General Rule 255A and Subsidiary Rule 255-A/1 and para 5(f) of the Station Working Rules of Diwana station; and

(v) Shri Santan Singh, Shunting Jamadar of Diwana station for carrying out shunting in face of an approaching train. He violated the provisions of General Rule 255A, Subsidiary Rule 255-A/1 and para 5(f) of the Station Working Rules of Diwana station.

Service Record of Persons Held Responsible

Shri Pearey lal, Driver joined service on 05/12/41 and worked as Fireman Gr 'C'/B till he was promoted as Shunter Gr 'B' in 10/55, Driver Gr 'C' on 20-6-60, Driver Gr 'B' on 04-8-68, Driver Gr 'A' on 01-1-76 and Special Gr 'A' Driver with effect from 21-7-1978 till date. He was censured once for a train parting in March 1962. His Accident Index is 152. He received 5 Awards during his long service and is $55^1/_2$ years of age (date of birth 17-3-24). He last attended a safety camp from 25-1-1979 to 30-1-1979.

Shri Satpal Mittal, Assistant Station Master is actually a Leave Reserve Assistant Station Master with headquarters at Panipat. He is a graduate and was appointed as a Signaller on 02-9-69 and has been working as a L.R. Assistant Station Master from 12-6-66 to date. He was punished twice on 22-5-74 and 26-11-74 for cases of detention. His Accident Index is 62. He passed his Refresher Course on 29-11-74 and last attended a Safety Camp on 07-5-77.

Shri Gulzara Munshi, Diesel Assistant was appointed on 18-7-79 as a Shed Cleaner. He was promoted as Fireman Gr 'C' on 31-1-65 and Fireman Gr. 'B' on 14-4-73. He passed the Diesel Assistant's Examination in July 1977 and has been working as a Diesel Assistant from 28-10-77 to date.

Shri Phool Singh, Leverman was appointed as Khalasi on 20-12-66. He worked as a Pointsman from 04-6-79 and was promoted as Leverman on 28-5-79 and is working in this capacity till date. His Accident Index is 92.

Shri Santan Singh, Shunting Jamadar was appointed as a Waterman on 27-2-60 and was promoted as Pointsman on 22-6-62, as Shuntman on 17-5-65 and as Shunting Jamadar from 28-8-78 to date. He was punished on 4 occasions according to his Accident record.

Relief Measures

The summoning of assistance, response thereto and the medical attention rendered to the injured at site by the Civil and Railway Doctors have been briefly set forth in section II of the report. The Medical Van stabled at Delhi left at 04.50 hrs., 55 minutes after it was ordered. This was 18 minutes in excess of the minimum time of 37 minutes stipulated by the Northern Railway for turning out Medical Vans vide correction slip No. 16 dated 09-8-73 of the Accident Manual 1960 of Northern Railway. At Panipat, where the ARME is stocked in a room on the station platform, action to remove the various packages, boxes and articles kept in the room, was taken only after the arrival of the ADMO Panipat at the station at 04.30 hrs. This is against extant instructions of the Northern Railway contained in para 18 of the Medical Manual 1960 where the initiative of removing various packages from the ARME room has to be taken by the SM/ASM on duty by breaking the glass of the box where a spare key is kept. Information of the accident was conveyed to the ASM Panipat at 03.40 hrs. yet the ADMO received first information only at 04.20 hrs. although his house is situated within 5 minutes walking distance from the station. There was therefore, avoidable delay in advising the ADMO Panipat by the ASM. The Medical Special ultimately left Panipat at 04.55 hrs, i.e., one hour and 15 minutes after first information was received by the ASM. This is considered to be on the high side.

I received three letters from the travellers of 34 Dn stating "inter-alia" that there was delay in arrival of the Doctors and the medical aid given at site was not adequate. My comments on these complaints have already been given in Para 2.2(d) above.

One traveller also complained about the transhipment arrangements made by the Railway. I was told by the Senior Divisional Commercial Superintendent that licensed porters from Panipat were made available at Diwana alongwith the Engineering labour and trollies to help the passengers during the transhipment and Vending Contractors were also brought from Panipat to arrange for tea, snacks and water for the passengers.

My inquiries indicate that the relief measures taken by the Railway were generally satisfactory subject to the comments regarding delay in the despatch of the Medical Van from Delhi and conveying first information of the accident to the nearest Railway Medical Officer, and giving unrealistic figures of the number of injuries to the Press.

Recommendations

9.1 No photographs were taken by the Railway Administration at the scene of accident. Fortunately the Director, Haryana Forensic Laboratory made up by producing a number of photographs, which enabled me to more or less re-construct the scene after the accident. Most of the photographs had been taken while restoration operations were in progress. While appreciating the initiative taken by the Police authorities, I am of the opinion that this action should have been independently taken by the Railway itself in the first instance. Panipat was quite close to the scene of the accident and professional or Railway photographers under the guidance of Railway officials could have covered various scenes particularly the position of signalling and interlocking gear, brakes, etc., better than the police and enabled me to get a complete picture of the scene after the accident. The Board may consider directing all Railway Administrations to take this action where feasible in the case of all serious accidents in future.

9.2 The Down Distant Signal post of Diwana station did not have the back light screen for the bottom yellow light with the result that the back light of the bottom yellow was visible even when the signal was in the 45° or 90° position. Arrangement may be made to make good this deficiency here and elsewhere.

9.3 The role of the Shunting Jamadar vis-a-vis the Guard in supervising the shunting operations in the two sidings of Diwana has not been spelt out in para 7 of the Station Working Rules. The Guard of Diwana Pilot sat at Diwana station practically nothing from 01.15 hrs. to 03.15 hrs., when a full train load of 20 = 25 units was pushed at night for a distance of approximately 3 kms with an engine which had not been fitted with a head-light on the tender in the rear. It is considered that in the case of the MFL siding, which is 3 kms in length and traverse 3 manned level crossings in-between, it is advisable for the Railway Administration to prescribe that the shunting be supervised by the Guard and the loads, which varies at times up to a maximum of 72 wagons, be pulled and not pushed to and from this siding. Necessary facilities may be provided by the Railway Administration to ensure this at an early date.

9.4 The Station Working Rules of Diwana station need revision on account of the deficiency in para 7 of the Rules as pointed out in para 9.3 above and also other shortcomings, some of which are given below:

(i) Same No. (91) has been given to 2 different keys at page no. 3, para 5(a)(ii);

(ii) The second sentence of para 5(b), sub-para (iv) at page 4 beginning with the words "The leverman on duty" is not happily worded and incomplete;

(iii) The 'Main Rules' referred to para 5(4) at page 6 do not figure anywhere in the Station Working Rules; and

(iv) The recent posting of Shunting Jamadar does not figure at para 8 of page 8.

There may be other shortcomings which the Railway may best look into by reviewing the entire Station Working Rules and updating them as necessary.

9.5 My inquiries reveal that between 15-5-79 to 15-8-79, Diwana Pilot was running without a brake-van on 6 occasions (inclusive of 15-8-79) in the Down direction and on 4 occasions in the Up direction, without proper authorisation and issue of special instructions, as required under General Rule 93. A similar irregularity was found in the running of the coaching pilot on 59 occasions between 15-5-79 to 15-8-79 in the Nizamuddin—New Delhi—Naya Azadpur section in the Delhi Area. Responsibility should be fixed and action taken against the Operating Officials responsible for these lapses on Delhi Division and other Divisions of Northern Railway as brought out in para 7.10.1 above. The Railway Administration should, if considered necessary, laid down special instructions for running of trains without brake-vans in the case of Diwana Pilot and other trains on Delhi Division and elsewhere and ensure stoppage of this unsafe practice hereafter.

9.6 Running of Diwana Pilots between Panipat and Diwana with engines without head-light on both sides should be prohibited as 15 engines on this link have been provided with tender head-lights and Diwana Pilot is not a daily train. Responsibility should be fixed for permitting a Steam locomotive without a tender head-light on 13-8-79 to leave on a link from Jind, when a head-light on the tender in rear was necessary to work the Diwana Pilot from Panipat on 15-8-79 and suitable action taken against the staff of Jind Loco Shed and Panipat for this lapse.

9.7 The purpose of the Vigilance Control Device on Engines will be lost if drivers can manipulate the device by placing a brick under the foot pedal to avoid being is vigilant as they are expected to be. The Railway Administration should take action against Drivers manipulating the Vigilance Device in any manner and make fool-proof arrangements to prevent this manipulation.

9.8 Medical Vans should be turned out within the time specified by the Railway and action take against individuals for the later turn-out from Delhi after this accident. Suitable action should also be taken against the staff responsible for taking extra time in conveying information the ADMO Panipat.

9.9 The Guard of Diwana Pilot did not sign the Complete Arrival Register maintained at Diwana station on the complete arrival of his train on 15-8-79 as required. Suitable action may be taken against the staff at fault.

Railway Board's Comments on Various Paras of the Report

Para 9.1: Necessary action has been taken by the Railway Administration in this regard. Instructions on the subject have also been issued to all the Railways.

Para 9.2: It has been advised by the Railway Administration that the back light screen for the bottom yellow light has since been provided and deficiency made good at all the affected stations on Delhi-Ambala section including Diwana station.

Para 9.3: As explained by the Railway Administration, Guards are not required to supervise shunting at terminating stations where shunting Jamadars are provided. However, Guards accompany full train loads placed in the National Fertilizer Ltd., siding under local instructions, which are being embodied in the Station Working Rules. Pulling of the goods rakes to and from the siding is not possible until remodelling of the station yard is completed.

Para 9.4: Action is being taken by the Railway Administration to review and update Station Working Rules of Diwana station. Instructions have been issued to other Railways also that Station Working Rules should be prepared with utmost care.

Para 9.5: Running of Diwana Pilots without brake vans has been stopped. The Railway Administration is reviewing the practice obtaining on other Divisions and sections in this regard, and special instructions, if found necessary, would be issued for running of goods trains without brakevans.

Para 9.6: Normally Diwana Pilot runs with head-light. On the day of the accident the link power fitted with headlight was put under repairs at the eleventh hour. Since no other power fitted with headlight on the tender was available, it became necessary to send a locomotive without head-light on the tender which is permissible under the rules.

This position has been noted by the Chief Commissioner of Railway Safety.

Para 9.7: Vigilance Control device cannot be manipulated by placing a brick under the foot pedal. The effect of the brick would be to reduce the travel of the foot pedal but the driver would still have to press/release the foot pedal to prove his vigilance. Thus it would be seen that by merely by placing a brick under the foot pedal, there cannot be any manipulation of the device, viz., to ensure vigilance of the driver by some activity is served.

Para 9.8: Remarks of this Ministry may please be seen against paras 8.8 and 2.2(d).

Relief Measures

Paras 2.2 and 8.8: The matter with regard to late departure of the Medical van from Delhi, delay in conveying information of the accident to the nearest Railway Medical Officer and giving of unrealistic figures of injuries to the press has been investigated by the Railway Administration and the position is given below:

1. *Late Start of the Medical Van from Delhi*

The first information about the accident was received by Delhi Control at 03.38 hrs. from ASM, Diwana immediately left the telephone to ascertain further details. This information was quite incomplete as at that time ASM, Diwana was under the impression that only the steam engine had derailed. This is evident from para 5.5 of the report which deals with the evidence of ASM, Diwana. Further details about the accident were received in Delhi Control at 3.55 hrs. when Delhi Accident Relief Train and Medical Van were ordered. The Medical Van however, left at 04.50 hrs., i.e., after 55 minutes which was 18 minutes in excess of the prescribed target of 37 minutes. This was due to non-availability of power at Delhi. The first power available was Subzimandi pilot which was rushed to Delhi. It reached Delhi at 4.28 hours after which the Medical Van was despatched at 4.50 hours.

2. *Delay in Conveying Information of the Accident to the Nearest Railway Medical Officer*

As per ADMO, Panipat's deposition vide para 5.21(a) of the CRS's report, the information about the accident was received by him at his residence at 4.20 hours and that he reached the station before 4.27 hours. It has also been brought out that since the P&T telephone in the TCR's office was defective, a callman was sent by the ASM, Panipat at ADMO's residence at 3.45 hours which was followed by a written message despatched at 3.50 hours. Since the ADMO's residence is located at a walking distance of about 5 minutes from the station and the ADMO had reached the station at 4.27 hours, it is obvious that the first information about the accident should have been received by him earlier than 4.20 hours. The Medical Special which left Panipat at 4.55 hours was not detained for the arrival of ADMO.

In his evidence given in para 5.18(b) of the report, the Dy. Chief Controller, New Delhi has stated that the medical van and ART from Delhi was ordered at 03.55 hours and from Ambala at 04.15 hours. The time of ordering of Medical Van and Accident Relief Train from Ambala, which has been mentioned as 04.35 hours in para 2.1 of the report, seems to be a typographial error and may please be corrected at 04.15 hours.

3. *Giving of Unrealistic Figures of Injuries to the Press*

As per extent rules, a member of the public is not to be considered an 'injured' persons when the injuries received the only petty abrasions or bruises or injuries which, in the opinion of the reporting officer, do not incapacitate the injured person from following the customary vocation or mode of life for a period of more than two days. This rule also applies to employees classed as 'passengers' or 'trespassers'.

According to the instructions issued by this Ministry in consultation with the Commission of Railway Safety, the Railway Administration concerned, while communicating information with respect to casualties involved in accident cases, to the offices of the Commission of Railway Safety or other outside agencies, should furnish information only in regard to the persons who die or sustain grievous or minor injuries. Cases of trivial injuries need not be reported. Though there has been a lapse in the strict compliance of these instructions, yet it is felt that release of incorrect figures of the number of injuries to the Press should not be taken as deficiency in the provision of relief measures. The phrase, "and giving unrealistic figures of the number of injuries to the Press" appearing at the end of para 8.8 of the report may, therefore, be deleted.

RAILWAY ACCIDENT INVESTIGATION REPORT ON COLLISION BETWEEN NO. 374 UP DELHI-PALWAL SHUTTLE TRAIN AND UP BAJWA SPECIAL GOODS TRAIN AT FARIDABAD STATION OF CENTRAL RAILWAY ON 5TH OCTOBER, 1979 — REPORT[1]

One Man Commission	Shri B.P. Sastry, Commissioner of Railway Safety, Central Circle, Bombay
Officer Present	Shri O.E. Oommen; Shri R. Balasubramanian; Shri S.P. Jain

Appointment

The Commission was constituted under Ministry of Tourism and Civil Aviation (Commission of Railway Safety) in accordance with Rule 4 of the Statutory Investigations into Railway Accidents Rules 1973 Vide Notification No. RS. 13-T(8)/71 dated October 5, 1979.

Terms of Reference

To investigate into the Collision between No. 374 Up Delhi-Palwal Shuttle Train and Up Bajwa Special Goods Train at Faridabad Station of Central Railway on 5th October, 1979.

Contents

Summary; Inspection and Inquiry; Relief Measures; The Trains, Local Features; Observations and Tests; Discussion; Conclusions; Remarks and Recommendations; Railway Board's Comments of Various Paras

1. Ministry of Tourism and Civil Aviation (Commission of Railway Safety), Government of India, New Delhi, 1985, i + 19 p.

of the Report; Annexures.

Conclusions

Cause of the Accident

Having carefully considered the factual, material and circumstantial evidence at my disposal, I have come to the conclusion that the accident which took place at Faridabad station on the evening of the 5th October was on account of the admission of No. 374 Up Shuttle on the Up loop line No. 3 while its path remained fouled by the rear portion of the Up Bajwa Special Goods which had a little earlier arrived on Up loop line No. 1.

Responsibility

I hold that primary responsibility for the occurrence has to be shared by Shri Rakesh Kumar Chaturvedi Guard of Up Bajwa Special Goods and Shri Swaroop Singh, Cabin Assistant Station Master, Faridabad who was on duty in 'B' Cabin at the time of the occurrence.

Shri Rakesh Kumar Chaturvedi, who has put in a service of about a year after his initial appointment as a Guard by the Western Railway, violated General Rule 135 inasmuch as he failed to ensure that the last vehicle of his train had cleared the fouling mark between Up loop lines 1 and 2 when his train came to a stand at the station and in spite of his being aware of that situation failed to inform the Cabin Assistant Station Master at once as required in the latter part of that Rule.

Shri Swaroop Singh, who has put in a service of about 14 years as an Assistant Station Master, violated the following Rules:

(i) General Rule 336 (b) and Para VII (b) of the Station Working Orders of Faridabad inasmuch as he failed to ensure that the Up Bajwa Special Goods train had completely arrived at the station and come to a stand clear of all fouling marks; and

(ii) General Rule 37 (a) (iii) inasmuch as he failed to ensure that the line over which No. 374 Up Shuttle train was to pass was clear and free from obstructions before he gave permission to take reception signals off for the train to be admitted on to Up loop line No. 3.

In adjudging the severity of the offence of Shri Swaroop Singh, the handicaps under which as Assistant Station Master in 'B' Cabin has to function during night shifts, as brought out in Para 7.5.5. have to be taken into account.

Shri Ramjilal B. Sharma, Driver of the Up Bajwa Special Goods contributed to the accident by his failure to stop the train at the proper place on the Up line No. 1 clear of fouling mark in the rear. He violated G.R. 136.

Relief Arrangements

I am satisfied with the relief arrangements. The Doctors of the Badshah Khan Hospital at Faridabad and other had promptly responded to the request of the Central Railway and taken adequate care of the injured.

I cannot, however, commend the Central Railway Administration for the undue delay in turning out the Medical Relief Van at Agra Cantonment and for the subsequent delay in despatching it to the site even after it was ready.

Recommendations

9.1 Yard interlocking arrangements at Faridabad station suffer from the following deficiencies:

(i) Up Goods loop lines 1 and 2 are not isolated from Up Passenger loop line No. 3. This is in violation of Para 145 of the IRSE Manual and corresponding provisions in Chapter VIII of the Rules for the Opening of a Railway or a Section of a Railway for the public Carriage of Passengers;

(ii) It is not possible for the Cabin Assistant Station Master of 'B' Cabin to estimate during dark house clearance of fouling points by incoming Up trains but no holding bars or other devices have been provided as stipulated in Para 153 of the Indian Railways Signal Engineering Manual and the corresponding provisions in Chapter VIII of the Rules for the Opening of a Railway or a Section of A Railway for the Public Carrier of Passengers; and

(iii) It is not possible for the Assistant Station Master to physically verify during night hours from his place of duty a major portion of the territory between the Up Home Signal and the 'B' Cabin which is not track circuited. He deals with 35-40 trains in a duty period of 8 hours and it is impossible for him to move out of the Cabin for the purpose. Hence compliance of General Rule 37(a) (iii) is not practicable at the station with the present arrangements.

9.1.2 It is recommended that these deficiencies may be made good expeditiously. It is also recommended that similar deficiencies, if any, at other stations on Indian Railways may be made good at the earliest.

9.2 The section between Junction Cabin and Mathura Junction – a length of about 115 kilometres is under the control of Central Railway Administration but sometimes trains are worked in the section by the crews of Western and Northern Railway Administrations. It appears that there are no rules under which such staff will be required to be conversant with the Subsidiary Rules and and other practices of Central Railway. This is a serious deficiency which the Railway Administrations concerned may be directed to make good early. Railway Board may also consider the desirability of prescribing uniform procedures in such vital matters like compliance of General Rule 135 by train Guards.

9.3 Subsidiary Rule 135-2 prescribed by the Central Railway Administration appears to be deficient in as much as it does not cover interlocked stations which form a major percentage of stations on that Railway. The Station Working Order, no doubt, makes good this deficiency in respect of Faridabad station but it would be desirable to have a Subsidiary Rule covering all such stations on the Railway. While doing so, the Railway Administration may review the effectiveness of the procedure itself.

9.4 Paras VI and VII of the Station Working Order of Faridabad have not been properly worded in the matter of defining the responsibility of various staff for compliance of G.R. 37(a) (iii) and G.R. 38 (a) (i). Similar vague wording is noticed at some other stations also. Central Railway Administration may be directed to pay attention to the necessity of precisely defining the responsibility of various staff in such matters.

9.5 The indifference with which the Medical Relief Van was turned out at Agra Cantonment and moved out to Faridabad would bring to light serious procedural deficiencies which the Central Railway Administration may be directed to review and make good.

9.6 It appears that through Goods trains originating in Northern

Railway area (even as far away as Jammu Tawi) on Ferozepur Division were not being examined at Tuglakabad but were being by passed to Central and Western Railways without ensuring adequate brake power. Northern Railway Administration may be directed to review the procedure with a view to ensure that safety of trains is fully taken care of.

9.7 It came to light that Central or Western Railway Drivers operating in the Automatic Signalling Territory of Northern Railway were not being equipped with Competency Certificates for working trains in such territories. The Railway Administrations concerned may be directed to make good this deficiency at the earliest.

9.8 One of the coaches involved in the accident, YSLR 05404 NR, marshalled second from the engine was a replaced coach. Besides being a vehicle which should not have been retained in service, it had also been wrongly marshalled in the train composition. With a large number of ICF coaches available on the train formation this wooden-bodied coach should not have been marshalled second from the engine. Due to the wrong marshalling, the body of the coach was reduced to smithereens accounting for most of the casualties of the accident. Northern Railway Administration may be directed to take such steps as would be necessary to avoid utilisation of replaced coaches in Passenger services and wrong marshalling of coaches on trains. Railway Board may also consider reiterating instructions to the Railway Administrations concerned to ensure strict enforcement of the Orders relating to replaced coaches issued in their letter No. 75/M(C)/650/10 dated 21-8-1975.

Railway Board's Comments on Various Paras of the Report

Para 9.1(i)—The Up loop lines No. 1 & 2 were not exclusively meant for goods trains only and as such provision of isolation on these lines from line No. 3 is not mandatory. However, since the lines do not have any platform face and local instructions in Station Working Order exist for not receiving passenger trains on loop lines 1 & 2, the Railway has been instructed to provide isolation of line No. 3 from lines No. 1 & 2.

Para 9.1(ii)—Para 153 refers not only to junctions but also to loop lines, siding connection, etc. Instructions have already been issued to the Railways to comply with para 153 where necessary.

Para 9.1(iii)—The Railway Administration have already demarcated the running lines suitably to see that the ASMs and Cabin

ASMs can ensure the vacancy of the running line by personal observation. The action taken by the Railway Administration has been noted by Chief Commissioner of Railway Safety.

Para 9.1.2—Instructions have been issued to the Railways, vide Board's circular letter No. 79/Safety (A&R)/1/2 dated 7-11-1979, that necessary remedial action as suggested by the Commissioner of Railway Safety should be taken at all those stations where such deficiencies exist.

Para 9.2—It is seen that Chief Commissioner of Railway Safety has noted the position explained by the Railway Administration, Instructions already exist that the train working staff of one railway who have to work as such on another railway must be examined in the Subsidiary Rules and local restrictions of the foreign railway concerned. These instructions have been reiterated vide Board's circular letter No. 80/Safety (A&R)/29/4 dated 14-3-1980, endorsing copies there of to the Chief Commissioner of Railway Safety.

Para 9.3—As explained by the Railway Administration, in terms of GR 135, the Guard has to inform the Station Master at once if the fouling marks of points and crossings are not cleared by his train. The Railway Administration are, however, amending their SR 135-2 to explicitly cover interlocked stations also.

Para 9.4—Instructions have been issued by the Railway Administration to precisely define in the Station Working Rules the responsibility of the various staff like Station Masters/ASMs/Cabin ASMs/ Switchmen, etc., in regard to compliance with GR 37(a)(iii) and GR 38(a)(i). Instructions on the subject have been issued to the other Railways also.

Paras 9.5 and 8.3 (Relief Measures)—It is noted that the Commissioner of Railway Safety is satisfied with the relief arrangements made in this case, and also that adequate care of the injured had been taken by the doctors of Badshah Khan Hospital at Faridabad, and others.

As for the delay in turning out of medical van at Agra Cantt., it may be mentioned that immediately on receipt of the information about the accident, medical vans from Agra Cantt. and Delhi, were ordered. At Agra Cantt. the medical van siding is not a double ended siding. It has existed only towards Bombay end and when the van is required to be despatched towards Delhi side, some more time is consumed in shunting the medical van and bringing it to the passenger yard for onwards, despatch in the down direction. The provision of double ended siding for the medical van at Agra Cantt. has already been programmed by the Railway.

In this case since the medical van was also ordered from Delhi, which is closer to the site of the accident than the Agra Cantt., the medical van from Agra Cantt. was meant only to supplement the medical facilities. Although medical van and the break-down train at Agra Cantt. was ready at 21-30 hours with a steam engine, it was detained to connect a diesel engine so that it could be rushed to the site earlier. It should, therefore, not be construed that there was any indifference in turning out the medical van from Agra.

As for the Medical Van from Delhi, it was ordered at 21-05 hours. It left for the site at 21-45 hours, i.e., within 40 minutes and reached the site at 22-55 hours, i.e., in one hour and 10 minutes. Northern Railway Administration is being asked to investigate as to why the time taken was excessive and also take action to avoid recurrence. Incidentally a team of doctors from Northern Railway Headquarters Hospital, New Delhi had reached the site a little after 22-00 hours, and coordinated with the Civil Hospital staff of the Badshah Khan in examining the injured and giving them further medical attention as mentioned in para 2.2.1. of the report.

Para 9.6—Instructions have been issued vide Board's letter No. 80M/N/951/13 dated 4-3-1980 for considering this issue and laying down the procedure for examination of inter railway goods trains. The matter will be pursued with the Railways.

Para 9.7—Instructions have been reiterated to the Railways vide Board's letter No. 80/Safety-I/25/3 dated 10-4-1980 that fresh competency certificates should be issued to the drivers/motormen in their knowledge of rules regarding Automatic Signalling and Absolute Permissive signalling territories after conducting systematic checks by qualified Inspectors at periods not exceeding one year.

Para 9.8—Instructions have been reiterated to the Railways vide Board's letter No. 80/M/(C)/650/ dated 19-7-1980 that special steps should be taken to take off the line, all the replaced unauthorized passenger coaches on condition basis immediately.

26

RAILWAY ACCIDENT INVESTIGATION REPORT ON THE REAR-END COLLISION BETWEEN ELECTRIC MULTIPLE UNIT TRAIN NO. E-65 AND NO. E-67 ON THE DOWN SUBURBAN LINE AT MADRAS EGMORE STATION ON MADRAS BEACH-TAMBARAM SUBURBAN METRE GAUGE SECTION OF SOUTHERN RAILWAY ON 26TH OCTOBER, 1979 — REPORT[1]

One Man Commission	Shri B.P. Sastry, Commissioner of Railway Safety, Southern Circle, Bangalore
Officers Present	Shri S.K. Nair; Shri N.V.S. Murthy; Shri M.N. Prasad; Shri S. Panchapakesan; Shri S. Narasimhan

Appointment

The Commission was constituted under Ministry of Tourism and Civil Aviation (Commission of Railway Safety) in accordance with Rule 4 of the statutory investigation into Railway Accidents Rules 1973 Vide Notification No. RS-13-T(8)/71 dated 26th October, 1979.

Terms of Reference

To inquire into the rear-end collision between electric multiple unit train No. E-65 and No. E-67 on the Down Suburban line at Madras Egmore Station on Madras Beach-Tambaram Suburban Metre Gauge Section of Southern Railway on 26th October, 1979.

---

1. Ministry of Tourism and Civil Aviation (Commissioner of Railway Safety), Government of India, New Delhi, 1984, i + 19 p.

Contents

Conclusions

Cause of the Accident

On a careful consideration of the factual, material and circumstantial evidence at my disposal, I have come to the conclusion that the collision had been brought about by the EMU train No. E-67 having been worked at a speed very much in excess of the Caution prescribed in G.R. 277, after the train passed the Automatic Signal MB-19 at 'ON' and the Motorman not having been able to stop short of the obstruction after sighting it.

Responsibility

I hold Shri T.K. Shanmugam, Motorman of E-67, responsible for the collision. He violated G.R. 277 and Southern Railway's Subsidiary Rule No. 277-I extracted at Annexure-I.

Shri Shanmugam who is 41 years of age was initially appointed in January 1956 as an Apprentice Fireman, promoted as a Driver in 1962. He was working as a Motorman of Electric Multiple Unit trains for nearly 3 years at the time of the accident. He was earlier punished twice for entering a Block section (under Absolute Block Working of Trains) without Authority and his Cumulative Accident Index prior to the present occurrence was computed as 518.

I hold that Shri M.K. Ravindran, Guard of E-67 had contributed to the collision. He violated G.R. 121 and G.R. 126 extracted at Annexure-I.

Relief Arrangements

I am satisfied that the relief arrangements were prompt and adequate.

Recommendations

9.1 G.R. 277 requires the Motorman to proceed at not more than 8 km./h. when, among other things, the line ahead cannot be seen clearly due to curvature of the track. Between Signal MB-19 and the next Signal MB-20 the Down line has three curves — a 4.75° curve at Signal MB-19 itself and two reverse curves of 6.78° and 6.2° between the Signal and the Platform. A Road-overbridge situated between the 4.75° curve and the 6.78° curve would also cause obstruction of view to a train approaching it. Thus nearly one half of the 940 metre spacing between the two signals warrants observance of a speed of 8 km./h. and the rest not more than 15 km./h. if the Motorman is to exercise "great caution so as to stop short of any obstruction", which, as amplified by Southern Railway's Subsidiary Rule 277(1), could be a broken or a displaced rail or any other cause. Considering that a Motorman would take nearly 8 minutes to reach the next Signal if he observes the Rule, thus starting a chain reaction for the following trains which the Railway Administration cannot afford in a rush hour due to the frequency of train services. I recommend breaking up of the inter-signal distance by introduction of another signal at a convenient location in between MB-19 and MB-20. A few more similar inconvenient locations exist in Madras Metre Gauge Suburban Section and my recommendation covers all such locations where visibility is restricted even during day light hours.

9.2 The fact that accidents continue to take place with alarming frequency due to non-compliance of General Rule 277 should be a sufficient reason for the Railway Administration to ruthlessly enforce its compliance in day-to-day working if accidents on account of such a failure are to be eliminated. This appears possible only by purposeful ambush checks and deterrent punishments to offenders of the Rule even when no accident has resulted from that violation, which does not appear to be the case at present. Southern Railway Administration may look into this aspect.

9.3 No Driver would like to endanger his own life by ignoring a Rule and if a large section of Driving staff choose to ignore General Rule 277 even after realising the possible serious consequences to themselves and to the travelling public, the reason perhaps is that it is not practicable for them to observe the Rule under the conditions in which they work. Railway Board may consider examining this aspect and give such directions to the Railway Administrations as may be warranted by the circumstances.

9.4 Provision of Auxiliary Warning System which prevents a speeding Driver attain speeds of over 15-20 km./h. after stopping at an Automatic Signal displaying DANGER aspect appears to be the only measure which would minimise the tragic consequences of accidents of this nature, even if it cannot altogether eliminate them. Railway Board may consider introducing the system in all Suburban Sections working on Automatic Signalling expeditiously.

9.5 The Guard of E-65 told me that fuses are not supplied to Guards of even Suburban Sections with Automatic Signalling Systems. This is against Railway Board's Policy and Southern Railway Administration may consider making good this inadequacy at an early date.

9.6 G.R. 113(b) requires the Guard of a train to satisfy himself "that the train is provided with the prescribed brake power" before it is despatched. In the case of EMU trains in the Metre Gauge Suburban System of Southern Railway, which are worked on Vacuum brakes, no method is prescribed for compliance of this Rule by the Guard unlike in the case of conventional trains, where a Brake Power Certificate is presented to him and his initials taken before it is issued to the Driver. Para 1270 of the Manual of AC Traction Maintenance and Operation and Article 6 of the Operating Manual — Part I for M/G AC-EMU prescribe a method of joint check of brakes by the Guard and Motorman. This procedure itself fails short of the requirement of G.R. 113(b) but even that procedure is not complied on the Metre Gauge Suburban System whenever Motormen and Guards change duties. It is recommended that Southern Railway Administration (and other Railway Administrations which may be following a similar practice) may be directed to take such action as would enable a Guard to comply with G.R. 113(b). Southern Railway Administration proposes to introduce a procedure under which the particulars of the Brake power of a rake as it comes out of the Car Shed in the morning for service is kept on record. Such a procedure will no doubt be in improvement on the current practice and may be accepted to start with but it will still be falling short of the requirements of the General Rule referred to above. The Rule can only be deemed to be complied with if copies of the Brake Power Certificate issued while the rake comes out of the Car Shed in the morning are in the hands of the Motorman and Guard who, while handing over the rake to their relievers may hand over the Brake Power Certificate also. Such a Brake Power Certificate should be valid for all trips on the date of issue unless the Motorman or the Guard has reasons to ask for a recheck to satisfy himself of the continued adequacy of the brake power. Railway Board may consider issuing suitable uniform instructions in this regard to all Railway Administrations operating EMU trains.

9.7 Had the Motorman of the train involved been subjected to an Alcohol test soon after the accident, it would have been possible to determine conclusively whether he was under the influence of liquor. At Madras Egmore there is a Health Unit and the Medical Officer was able to reach the site of accident within 8 minutes of the occurrence. The situation was thus an ideal one for subjecting the Motorman to an Alcohol test but the Medical Officer could not think of examining him for that purpose. It is recommended that clear instructions may be incorporated in the manual such that Medical Officers attending to accidents would consider this as one of their immediate duties on reaching the site.

9.8 On the Madras Suburban System, there is no procedure for recording the timings of movements of Suburban trains in the Control Office. While it may not be practicable for the Controller to keep track of the station to station movements of the large number of these trains running at short intervals, it may still be possible to keep a record of their departure from some important stations like Egmore, Mambalam and Guindy as is done on the Bombay Suburban System.

Again, there should be a procedure for keeping a record of trains detained due to Automatic Signals showing RED aspect of for other causes en-route. An analysis of the causes for Automatic Signals showing RED aspect and the time taken by such trains to reach the next signal would give an indication of whether the train crew faithfully observe the connected General Rules and would also help rectifying the causes for such display of RED aspect of Automatic Signals. Southern Railway Administration may consider adopting such a practice in the interests of safe operation of Suburban trains.

Railway Board's Comments on Various Paras of the Report

Remarks and Recommendations

Para 9.1: In the light of the position explained by the Railway Administration, it would not be correct to assume that speed of the trains for a part of the distance between Signals No. MB 19 and MB 20, where visibility is obstructed, will have to be restricted to 8 kmph and for the remaining portion to 15 kmph and that it would generally result in a chain reaction of a large number of suburban trains being hit by a single incident of signal showing red aspect. On the day in question there was queuing up of trains short of MB 23 which protects the level crossing gate between Madras-Egmore and Chetput, and which ceased to be automatic due to damage to the boom of the lifting barrier.

However, to reduce the time required for EMUs to cover the distance between MB 19 and MB 20, when MB 19 is RED, and also to give additional information to the driver, which is desirable from the safety point of view, the Railway Administration have proposed to introduce an additional signal at a distance of about 350 metres in rear of MB 20. Action is also being taken by the Railway to identify other inconvenient locations in the M.G. suburban section of checking up with the Motormen and also by foot-plate in inspections, whereafter additional signals, if considered necessary, will be provided. Instructions on the subject are also being issued to the other Railways.

Para 9.2: This has been accepted by the Railway Administration. In fact the Railway had already carried out a number of ambush checks in the past and taken up with the offenders of GR 277. The Railway will also carry out additional checks with regard to the speed attained by the drivers after stopping at the signals, particularly at those location where line ahead presents problems of visibility.

Para 9.3: It would not be correct to assume that it is impracticable for the drivers to observe the provisions of GR 277 because of the circumstances in which they have to work, and that GR 277 has ceased to be a rule (as contended by Commissioner of Railway Safety in para 7.4.6) commanding respect of a large section of motormen/drivers in automatic signalling territories. It has been advised by the Railway Administration that past record of the Motormen working in the MG suburban section between Madras Beach and Tambaram has been very good, and that there has not been a single case of collision in this section during the last ten years.

The Ministry of Railways have recently reiterated the instructions regarding regular counselling of the drivers/motormen working in the automatic signalling territories. The Railways have been advised to conduct one day's intensive course once in six months. Further, the drivers/motormen working in the automatic block and absolute permissive signalling section should be in possession in competency certificate which should be issued after thorough testing of their knowledge about rules for working of trains in such sections, and also these certificates should be renewed after a period of one year. Five copies of the instructions are enclosed for Chief Commissioner of Railway Safety's information.

Instructions are also being issued to the Railways to intensify ambush checks in automatic signalling territories to ensure that there is no laxity amongst drivers/motormen in regard to rigid compliance of provisions of G.Rs. 277 and 279.

In view of the fact that an analysis of all the accidents on suburban sections attributable to lapses on the part of driving staff during the last 10 years may be a very voluminous task for the psycho-technical wing of the RDSO, that organisation is being asked to undertake a study on all the collisions caused by violation of G.Rs 277/279 during the last 3 years.

Para 9.4: A survey is already in progress for provision of automatic warning system on the suburban section of Southern Railway. This would also include the automatic signalling section and would provide the necessary check to prevent over-speeding beyond 20 kmph after a train passed a automatic signal at 'ON' till the train passes the next signal at 'OFF'.

Para 9.5: As advised by the Railway Administration, fusees have already been supplied to Drivers and Guards working in automatic signalling territories. Instructions with regard to usage of the fusees have also been reiterated to the Railways.

Para 9.6.: As for ensuring the adequacy of brake power of EMU trains before commencement of journey on the same pattern as is done in the case of conventional stock, it may be mentioned that the operating conditions of EMU locals and loco-hauled trains are not identical Some of the differences are given below:

Loco-hauled trains	EMU locals
1	2
1. In case of conventional trains, the locomotive is maintained separately from the rolling stock and is attached to and detached from the load on a number of occasions.	1. In the case of EMU locals, the entire formation is maintained by one agency.

1	2
2. The operation of the train is not confined to a particular Division and it may have to traverse over a number of Divisions and even Railways in the course of its journey.	2. The operation is limited to one Division only.
3. The conventional train is subjected to attachment, detachment and similar reformation during the course of its journey.	3. After leaving the car shed, the rake is not subjected to any reformation enroute.

There is already elaborate system for checking the continuity of air pressure and the level of air pressure both in the main reservoir pipe as well as the brake pipe.

In so far as effective brake cylinders are concerned, the arrangement is somewhat different in the case of EMU wherein a complete bogie is isolated and effectiveness is counted in terms of the number of bogies having brake power. In a rake consisting of 18 bogies (i.e., 9 coaches × 2 = 10) not more than 3 bogies at a time are allowed to be ineffective. In the event of the 4th bogie becoming ineffective, the rake is withdrawn and sent to car shed. Apart from the continuity test and the extent of isolation being stipulated on the EMUs, the actual brake power is required to be tested by the motormen during the course of the journey. To aid them in such tests, the marker boards have been provided along side the track. These guidelines coupled with the motormen's own subjective reaction which he looks the defect card are considered sufficient for ensuring adequate brake power on the EMU rakes.

The provisions of GR 113(b) cannot be practically applied to EMU trains particularly in respect of a number of rakes which are stabled overnight at stations other than the car shed to start the morning services. In the event of brake power certificate not being available, the crew may refuse to start the train. Also, the procedure would involve handling over and taking over at the terminals which may create difficulties and cause avoidable delays particularly during peak hours.

CRS has already noted the position in case of rear-end collision between No. C-35 Down and No. T-81 Down Suburban Trains between Matunga and Sion station of Central Railway on 14-11-1979. In this connection attention is also invited to this Ministry's office Memorandum No. 79/Safety(A&R)/1/28 dated 19-10-1980.

Para 9.7: Instructions on the subject have been issued to the Railways, vide Board's circular letter No. 80/Safety-I/12/6 dated 27-2-1980, and a copy thereof is enclosed for Chief Commissioner of Railway Safety's information.

Para 9.8: The records of actual timings of the trains during the peak hours are already being maintained at important stations such as Madras Beach, Madras Egmore, Mambalam, Saidapet, Guindy and Tambaram. Records of timings of the suburban trains at important stations are also now being maintained in the control office.

Regarding suggestion for keeping a record of trains detained due to automatic signals showing 'RED' aspect or other causes enroute and the time taken by such trains to reach the next signal, it is considered that even if such a record is maintained by the drivers, it will not help inasmuch as the Administration will have to depend on the version of the driver regarding the time taken to cover the inter signal distances. No organisation exists at present for such a check, and introduction of any procedure for this purpose would need additional staff without commensurate advantage as the Administration has necessarily to depend on the driver's version in this regard.

27

REVIEW COMMITTEE ON THE NATIONAL ADULT EDUCATION PROGRAMME, 1979 — REPORT[1]

Chairman	Prof. D.S. Kothari
Members	Dr. M.S. Adiseshiah; Smt. Ela Bhatt; Shri J.P. Naik; Shri V. Siddharthacharry; Dr. Surajit Sinha; Shri Habib Tanvir; Shri B.G. Verghese
M. Secy.	Shri Anil Bordia

Appointment

The Review Committee on the National Adult Education Programme was appointed by the Ministry of Education and Culture, Government of India in October 1979.

Terms of Reference

(a) To review the working of the NAEP in all its aspects, and to recommend any modifications that would improve its implementation, quality and impact;

(b) to recommend any changes in the priority assigned to adult education that may be called for in the light of the review by the Committee; and

(c) to examine if any economy could be effected in the allocations for the NAEP by better implementation and more effective participation of educational institutions and non-official agencies.

Contents

Letter from the Chairman to the Union Education Minister; Members

1. New Delhi, Ministry of Education and Culture, Government of India, 1980, 127 p.

of the Review Committee; Introduction; Adult Education: Objectives and Organisation; The Role of Adult Education in Educational System; Adult Education for Development; Preconditions for Organisation of a National wide Adult Education Programme; The National Adult Education Programme: A Review; Early efforts; Development since independence; The National Adult Education Programme (1978); Progress of the NAEP (1978-80); Recommendations; The Future Programme: Scope and Organization; Magnitude of the Programme and Annual Projections; Widening and Deepening of the Content; Motivation; Participation of Priority Groups; Organization; Evaluation, Monitoring and Research; Implementing Agencies: Resources Development and Media; Implementing Agencies; The Instructor; Supervisors and Project Officers; Resource Centres; Production of Instructional Materials; Communication and Culture; Finance and Implementation; Conclusions and Recommendations; Appendix – State Resource Centres as on 31-3-1980; Statistical Tables from IA to IE and IIA to IIH.

Recommendations

7.1 In the modern world, education and development, and indeed survival, go together. Good education promotes development – economic, social and moral. Bad education is counter-productive and can seriously harm national interest and welfare, Mahatma Gandhi assigned the first place in education to character-building. The education of the people was upper-most in the mind of Jawaharlal Nehru. He said: "The country cannot make progress worth the name till we are able to remove illiteracy from among our masses."

7.2 There is an increasing realisation of the crucial importance of adult education. Yet in determination and effort for its promotion has been hardly commensurate with the colossal magnitude and extreme urgency of the task. The literacy rate for the country is still only 35 per cent. Even if a hundred million people were covered by the NAEP in five years – an extremely difficult task – the national literacy percentage would still be below 60 per cent.

7.3 A preliminary review of the NAEP, as operating at present, shows that it has evoked an encouraging response. Nothing should be done to undermine this. The present programme has both strengths and shortcomings. Despite commendable work done in several areas, the review also brings out many weaknesses. For instance, more careful preparation is needed in the formulation of State and district plans, preparation of annual projections, training of instructors, and greater participation of all priority groups. The duration of the programme is too short and provision for follow-up activities is inadequate. The link between the education and development components of the programme is lacking. The feasibility of the programme and the tangible benefits flowing from it are not clear. *An uncertain programme cannot be a mass movement.* The more crucial a programme for national development, the greater is the need for thorough preparation.

7.4 The Programme needs to be radically modified and strengthened. Our specific recommendations are:

(1) *Priority*

(a) In the plans of national development, along with universalisation of primary education, adult education should receive the highest priority. Adult education should be an integral part of the Basic Minimum Needs Programme (Paras 2.13 and 2.16)

(b) All illiterate persons of the age group of about 15 to 35 should be covered in the shortest time possible by a programme of adult education. Nothing should be done to weaken the momentum generated for the NAEP. The Programme should be continued, and steps taken to radically modify and strengthen it.

(2) *The Future Adult Education Programme*

(a) State and district plans of adult education and annual projections should be prepared. With determined effort, most States and many districts in all States would be able to complete the programme in five years. Some would take longer. But even in these areas the programme should be completed in not more than ten years.

(b) Pending the finalisation of the plans, the number of illiterate persons to be covered in the year 1980-81 may be retained for the present at nine million, as visualised in the NAEP.

(c) The content of the programme – consisting of literacy, functionality, and awareness – should be deepened and widened. An adequate level of literacy should be insisted upon with emphasis on the learners improving their vocational skills and taking organised action for the improvement of their condition.

(d) Sustained effort should be made to link literacy with development.

(e) The duration of the programme should be about three years, divided into three stages of about a year each.

(f) The programme should be flexible and closely related to the needs of the learners and the local environment (Paras 4.2 to 4.11).

(3) *Participation*

(a) In organisation of the programme special attention should be paid to creation and sustenance of motivation among the learners.

(b) Emphasis should be laid on participation of women in the programme. Measures should be taken which would influence social attitudes and remove practical difficulties which women face in attending adult education classes. It would be desirable to arrange adult education for women as part of their work.

(c) Women should be adequately represented on advisory committees at all levels. Their recruitment as instructors and at other levels should be substantially raised.

(d) The programme for the Scheduled Castes should pay attention to their special problems. Adult education centres common to all are desirable, and efforts should be made to move in that direction. Where necessary, separate classes for the Scheduled Castes should be organised in their localities.

(e) The adult education programmes for the Scheduled Tribes should use tribal languages where necessary and pay special attention to their special cultural heritage and crafts.

(f) The involvement of Scheduled Castes and Scheduled Tribes should be emphasised. They should be made aware of the Government schemes for their amelioration and be enabled to utilize them.

(g) The Scheduled Castes and Scheduled Tribes should be represented on all advisory committees. Their recruitment as instructors and at other levels should be encouraged in every possible way

(h) Special attention should be paid to the organisation of adult education programmes for the physically handicapped (Paras

4.13-4.27).

(4) *National Board of Adult Education*

The National Board of Adult Education should be autonomous, with the Union Education Minister as Chairman. There should be a whole time Vice-Chairman and two or three other whole-time members. It should be responsible for planning, financing and implementation of the Programme at the Centre and for giving it the necessary leadership and support. The NBAE's responsibility would also include support to and development of the SRCs, monitoring, evaluation and research and, generally, improvement of the quality and coverage of the Programme. The funds provided in the Central budget for adult education should be placed at its disposal. The Board should make an annual report to the Parliament (Paras 4.28-4.29 and 4.39 to 4.42).

(5) *State Boards of Adult Education*

Autonomous Boards of Adult Education (SBAE) should be established in every State. They should be responsible for planning, financing and implementing the Programme and for its coordination at the State level. They should make more intensive efforts to expand and improve the Programme (Para 4.30).

(6) *District and Field Organisation*

(a) Every district should have an Adult Education Committee.
(b) The District Adult Education Officers should be responsible to the SBAE. Their duties would include planning and implementation of the Programme. They should have adequate powers and support for the purpose.
(c) The Project should be smaller in size than at present, ordinarily consisting of 100 to 200 centres. The project officers should have wider powers than at present.
(d) The organisation of the adult education centres should be flexible enough to suit the learners' needs, local conditions and availability of resources (Paras 4.31 to 4.36).

(7) *Implementing Agencies*

A number of agencies are making or could make an important contribution to the Programme. In respect of them, we recommend as follows:

(a) *Voluntary Agencies*: The association with the programme of voluntary agencies engaged in social service, education, rural development, village industries, health-care and such other activities, should be continued and they should be given all encouragement and assistance. Whether they should continue to be assisted directly from the Centre or through the State Governments would need further examination by the National Board of Adult Education (Paras 5.11 to 5.13).

(b) *Universities and Colleges*: Universities and colleges should be involved to the greatest possible extent, through NSS or otherwise. Involvement of Women's colleges would help in increasing the participation of women learners in the Programme. In the long run, participation in social service, including adult education, should become a part of the academic course (Paras 2.14, 5.14 and 5.15).

(c) *Schools*: Involvement of Schools should be increased. Eventually every school should be developed into a community centre for the education of children as well as adults (Para 5.16).

(d) *Panchayati Raj Institutions and Municipalities*: Panchayati Raj Institutions and Municipalities should be involved in the programme, wherever and howsoever possible. They should also take responsibility for running reading rooms and libraries (Para 5.9).

(e) *Cooperatives*: The NBAE should prepare, in consultation with the National Cooperative Union of India, a detailed programme for participation in adult education of the members of cooperative societies and also of their families, if possible (Para 5.10).

(g) *Employers*: Employers in the organised sector, public and private, should be required to provide adult education facilities for all their employees, and if possible, for the members of their families. A lead should be given by Government and the public sector undertakings. In this, trade unions and Central Board of Workers' Education should be associated (Para 5.17).

(h) *Individuals and other groups*: Every effort should be made to involve dedicated individuals, housewives and youth clubs,

Mahila Mandals and Sainik Boards, and other interested organizations (Para 5.18).

(8) *Involvement of Political Parties and certain other Organisations*

The NBAE should examine, as soon as possible, the question of ineligibility of political parties and certain other organisations – such as trade unions, associations of teachers and students, all-India cultural organisations, etc., to receive grants from Government. Till then the present practice may continue (Paras 5.19 and 5.20).

(9) *Need for Vigilance*

Appropriate mechanisms should be evolved for ensuring that misuse of funds for adult education is prevented (Para 5.21).

(10) *The Instructor*

Every effort should be made to attract the best possible persons as instructors. Steps should be taken to increase the pool of persons available for recruitment as instructors, especially in remote and backward areas. Training of instructors should be improved and the best available persons should be involved in it. The honorarium of the instructor should be raised to Rs. 75 per months in Stage I and to Rs. 100 and Rs. 125 per month respectively for Stages II and III. The appointment of instructors should be for the duration of the project (i.e., 3 or 4 years), subject to satisfactory work. There should be adequate opportunities for their advancement (Paras 5.22 to 5.29).

(11) *Supervisors and Project Officers*

There is need to improve the opportunities of advancement for supervisors and project officers. The gap between the remuneration of instructors, supervisors and project officers should be reduced (Paras 5.30 and 5.31).

(12) *Resource Centres*

The Central Directorate of Adult Education and the SRCs should be strengthened. A Resource Centre, should be established for the North-

Eastern Region. District Resource Units should be established. Full use should be made of universities and other institutions for resource development (Paras 5.32 to 5.36).

(13) *Instructional Material*

Material of good quality, including teaching aids, need to be produced in larger numbers for the instructional programme, especially for functionality and awareness and for Stages II and III. Materials are also needed for training of instructors, supervisors and project officers, and for promotional and motivational purposes. While production of material is a responsibility of the Central Directorate of Adult Education and the SRCs, there is need for serious involvement of universities and other institutions of proven capability (Paras 5.37 – 5.40).

(14) *Traditional and Folk Media*

A programme of people's education should lead to a renaissance of the people's culture. There is need to support traditional and folk arts *per se* and also for their fuller and wider use in the furtherance of literacy and adult education programmes. Suitable schemes for this purpose should be prepared (Paras 5.42 and 5.43).

(15) *The Modern Media*

The potential of the electronic media and film should be exploited for the Programme. This needs close collaboration between the authorities concerned with education, INSAT, Films, Doordarshan and AIR. The National and State Boards should have Media Councils and the AIR and Doordarshan should have adult education and distance learning cells at their national and regional headquarters (Paras 5.44 to 5.49).

(16) *Libraries and Continuing Education*

Steps should be taken to produce literature needed for post-literacy and continuing education. A nation-wide network of libraries should be organised and linked closely to the adult education programme (Paras 5.50 to 5.52).

(17) *Finance*

(a) The cost per person covered under the modified programme, on a rough estimate, works out to Rs. 150. The present figure is a little over Rs. 100 (Para 6.8).

(b) On the above basis, the total cost of the Programme for 100 million persons will be Rs. 15,000 million (or Rs. 1500 crores). Of this, the amount needed in the next five years would be about Rs. 9,000 million (or Rs. 900 crores).

(c) A major part of this sum of Rs. 9,000 million should be provided in the Plan of the Education Sector. The rest should be in the other sectors of development to enable the development agencies to include a component of adult education in their programmes. It should be earmarked for adult education.

(d) The existing arrangement of equal sharing of expenditure between the Central and State Plans should continue. However, special additional provision should be made in the Central Plan to provide support for tribal hill and desert regions and for such priority groups as women. Scheduled Castes, Scheduled Tribes, and the physically handicapped (Para 6.9).

(18) *Financial Procedures*

(a) There should be no diversion of funds provided for adult education to any other stage of education or to any other sector of development.

(b) It is essential to devise procedures which will ensure that funds reach the project agencies in time and to delegate adequate financial powers to the project officer to enable him to deal effectively with the day-to-day problems (Para 6.10).

(19) *Economy*

An important method of economy is to improve the efficiency and quality of the programmes. Other means would include the involvement of the community and harnessing the idealism, dedication and commitment of the people, especially the youth (Para 6.11).

(20) *Implementation*

The first step should be a statement by the Government regarding acceptance of the main recommendations contained in the Report. The National Board of Adult Education should be set up as early as possible to give effect to the modifications needed in the Programme. Meanwhile, action should be taken to implement recommendations such as improvement of training of instructors and instructional material, special attention to priority groups, greater involvement of voluntary agencies and local bodies, cooperatives, and employers and expansion of the participation of teachers and students. (Paras 6.12 to 6.15).

APPENDIX

State Resource Centres (as on 31-3-1980)

Address of the Institution	*States Covered*
1	2
1. Department of Continuing Adult Education Osmania University, Hyderabad	Andhra Pradesh
2. Deepayatan 32-A, New Srikrishnapuri, Patna	Bihar
3. Gujarat Vidyapeeth, Ahmedabad	Gujarat
4. State Resource Centre, Chandigarh	Haryana
5. Centre for Continuing Education Panjab University, Chandigarh	Himachal Pradesh Punjab UT of Chandigarh
6. Department of Education University of Kashmir, Srinagar	Jammu & Kashmir
7. Karnataka State Adult Education Council Krishnamurthipuram, Mysore.	Karnataka
8. Kerala Association for Non-formal Education and Development, Trivandrum	Kerala
9. Indian Institute of Education 168/2 Karve Road Kothrud, Pune	Maharashtra
10. Utkal Navjeevan Mandal Angul Distt. Dhankanal	Orissa
11. Rajasthan Adult Education Association 38, Jobner Bagh, Jaipur	Rajasthan
12. Tamil Nadu Board of Continuing Education 2, Adams Road, Madras	Tamil Nadu
13. Literacy House, P.O. Alambagh, Lucknow	Uttar Pradesh
14. Bengal Social Service League 1/6, Raja Dinendra Street Calcutta	West Bengal

RAILWAY ACCIDENT INVESTIGATION REPORT ON THE REAR-END COLLISION BETWEEN C-35 AND T-81 DOWN SUBURBAN LOCAL TRAIN ON THE DOWN SUBURBAN LINE BETWEEN MATUNGA AND SION STATIONS ON BOMBAY V.T. – KALYAN ELECTRIFIED SECTION OF CENTRAL RAILWAY ON NOVEMBER 14, 1979 — REPORT[1]

One Man Commission Shri B.P. Sastry

Appointment

The Commission was constituted under Ministry of Tourism and Civil Aviation (Commission on Railway Safety) in accordance with Rule 4 of the Statutory Investigation into Railway Accidents Rules 1973 Vide Notification No. RS.13-T(8)/71 dated April 19, 1973 on November 14, 1979.

Terms of Reference

To enquire into the Rear-end Collision between C-35 and T-81 Down Suburban Local Train on the Down Suburban Line Between Matunga and Sion Stations on Bombay V.T. – Kalyan Electrified Section of Central Railway on November 14, 1979.

Contents

Summary; Inspection and Inquiry; Relief Arrangements; Local Features; Summary of Evidence; Tests and Observations; Discussion;

1. Delhi, Controller of Publications, 1982, 18 p.

Conclusions; Remarks and Recommendations; Railway Board's Comment on various paras of the Report.

Conclusions

Cause of the Accident

On a careful consideration of the factual, material and circumstantial evidence at my disposal, I have come to the conclusion that the tragedy which overtook Down EMU trains T-81 and C-35 between Matunga and Sion Stations on the 14th November 1979 had, in all probability, been brought about due to a sudden disability suffered by the Motorman of the colliding train No. T-81, late Shri H. Dey, either due to his having suddenly taken ill or on account of stones thrown at him by an outside or outsiders having hit him, at about the time he was approaching the stationary train No. C-35 and the Automatic Signal No. L-1111 after leading Matunga station.

Responsibility

I do not hold the deceased Motorman, late Shri Dey, responsible for the occurrence.

Relief Arrangements

I am satisfied with the relief arrangements. Medical help reached the site promptly and in an adequate measure, thanks to the spontaneous response of the Doctors and other Staff of the nearby Lokmanya Tilak Memorial Municipal Hospital, Sion, when contacted. The Police and the Fire Services had reached the site within minutes of the occurrence and taken charge of the situation, bringing relief to the injured who needed speedy hospitalisation.

Recommendations

9.1 Great concern has been voiced by the Press and the public in regard to this tragic occurrence. One of the points made out was that the Motormen of Suburban trains in Bombay area were over-worked. While I am clear in my mind, as brought out already, that exhaustion or long hours of work of the Motorman was not the cause of the accident,

I consider that there is a case for review of the working hours of Motormen in Bombay area. Driving an EMU train on Bombay Suburban System carrying up to 4000 highly sensitive commuters during rush hours is a responsible job requiring a high degree of concentration during almost every minute of the period spent by the Motorman in the Cab. Picking up signals at the average rate of nearly one a minute and understanding their implications, negotiating curves and other obstructions which are numerous within the short distance negotiated by the train, continuous trespassing by pedestrians in view of the fact that the Railway line is not walled at all places and runs alongside residential areas in the heart of the densely populated city, and last but not the least the volatile nature of the commuters for whom every minute of delay means a substantial loss are something which require of the Motorman continued alertness and concentration, quick reflexes and capacity to keep cool under provocative circumstances and, above all, driving skill. It is, perhaps, not correct to compare the tough job which a Motorman has to perform with the functions of a Driver of a long distance train and subject them to the same rules as regards hours of duty. It is true that Motormen are not required to work more than 108 hours in a fortnight as per their current classification (as continuous workers) or in excess of 92 hours in actual practice in a large number of cases as per published schedules but the concentration they are required to display is much more than what an average Driver of a long distance train is required to display and it appears there is a case for reviewing their classification with a view to see if their functions come under 'intensive' category of workers. I have had the opportunity of travelling a few lines on the foot plate of the Diesel locomotive hauling Rajdhani Express on the Delhi-Howrah route and I consider that the degree of concentration shouldered by a Motorman on Bombay Suburban Section is in no way less than that of the Driver of the prestigious Express train despite the fact that the operating speed of the EMU trains is much less. The Driver of the Express train has a colleague by his side (a qualified Driver) during his 5 or 6 hours run to share his responsibilities which the Motorman of Bombay Suburban System has to perform alone.

9.2 Another aspect of the working of the Central Railway Suburban Services of which the Press and the public are critical is their efficiency. Even the Railway Officials in informal discussions concede this charge and it appears desirable to go into the reasons for the disparity between the quality of service rendered by the two contiguous systems of the same Indian Railway family. A direction in which improvement appears to be called for is the maintenance of the rakes and the consequent reliability of the services. Figures furnished in respect of the P.O.H. of EMU rakes would indicate a high percentage of arrears. One of the rakes involved in the collision was noticed to be over-due POH by about 3 months. Its brake system also was an item of frequent complaints. Rejection of a rake by Motormen while taking up duty is also not infrequent. There may be several causes for this position, one of which being the high percentage of wastage of imported rakes due to non-availability of spares and other causes as mentioned by Engineers concerned during informal discussions. While clarifying the point that the collision of 14th November had nothing to do with the aspect discussed in this paragraph, I would all the same suggest a detailed review of the situation with a view to improve the quality of the services.

9.3.1 General Rule 113(b) requires the Guard of a train to satisfy himself about the adequacy of brake power on his train before commencing the journey and this is complied in case of conventional trains by the issue of a Brake Power Certificate by the train examining staff. The Certificate is required to be initialled by the Guard in token of his acceptance as to the adequacy of Brake power on his train before it is made over to the Driver. The latter keeps it in his possession for the entire journey and makes it over to his reliever along with the locomotive if he is relieved enroute destination. Such a procedure is not in vogue on the Suburban System, not only on the Central Railway but on some other Railways as well. The arguments advanced in the matter are that each rake is thoroughly checked and its fitness recorded before it is put into service every day and since the trains are required to stop at short intervals, the efficacy of brakes is tested by the Motorman frequently on the run. While the procedure might have been working fairly satisfactorily all these years, it gives no guarantee or assurance to the Motormen that the brake system is satisfactory. Human nature being what it is, no procedure which is not subjected to checks and cross checks can be considered fool-proof, particularly in the present state of discipline and devotion to duty in our system. Examples are not wanting where a rake subjected to a check by the examining staff had been rejected by the Motorman at the time to taking it over. Even the rake of T-81 Down which was on 5-11-1979 checked and certified fit by the Train Examining Staff was declared unfit in the following terms by the Motorman after working it only for about half an hour after it was put in service after testing.

"Brake Power Very Poor not Holding at All"

Earlier on 23-10-1979 two Motormen had recorded in respect of the same rake as under"

"Brake Power Very Poor" (S-6 Up) "Brake Power is very Poor from Bombay end, Motormen Please be Careful while Stopping your Train" (T-44).

Again, on 29-10-1979 two Motormen had recorded as under:

"Brake Power Poor from Bombay end" (T-64) "E.P. Brakes from BB end Poor. The Train Does not Come Under Control Unless Brakes are Applied in Full" (A-41).

9.3.2 Para 1270 of the A.C. Traction Manual – Operation and Maintenance, prescribes a joint test of brakes by the Guard and Motorman. The check prescribed therein does not cover the effectiveness of brake cylinders and even such an incomplete test is not in vogue on Madras Suburban Sections which work on 25 kV A.C. Traction and on Bombay Suburban Sections which work on 1500 V DC Traction. It is suggested that the adequacy of current practices of various Railways in the matter of brake power of Suburban trains may be reviewed and a procedure consistent with safety of trains and in compliance of General Rule 113(b) may be introduced.

9.4 Another point given expression to by a witness who deposed before me and by another who addressed a letter to me was that the Motorman of the ill-fated train had once before fainted while on duty requiring a replacement. I questioned the Divisional Medical Officer of Byculla Railway Hospital and called for particulars of the alleged incident from the Divisional Administration but without success. Even if the allegation is not true it underlines the need to ensure that Motormen are thoroughly fit physically and mentally and their continued fitness is subjected to a check periodically. Periodical Medical Examinations every 12 months are prescribed in case of staff who cross the age of 45 and 36 months in respect of those below 45 but what is desired in case of Motormen, who are subjected to functions requiring a high degree of mental alertness and quick reflexes, is a thorough periodical check-up, to rule out even the remotest possibility of a person, not quite fit to work as a Motorman, being missed. It is suggested that the present procedures for periodical medical examination of staff in such sensitive assignments may be reviewed by the appropriate medical authorities and revisions as warranted may be introduced.

9.5 While the efficient functioning of the man behind the machine is important, it is necessary that gadgets brought about by advancement in science and technology are introduced to reduce our dependence on man as much as possible particularly in situations like the operation of Suburban trains in Bombay. In this context the proposal of the Indian Railways to introduce Auxiliary Warning System of train control in heavily worked routes, deserves to be implemented without further delay. I was told by the Chief Signal and Telecommunication Engineer, Central Railway, that an approved work for introduction of Auxiliary Warning System on the Bombay-Kalyan Section appears in the Pink Book of the Railways. It is recommended that expeditious implementation of this work be looked into in all seriousness without permitting constraints like financial resources standing in its way. While it may not prevent a Motorman attaining a speed of 15-20 km. per hr. after stopping at an Automatic Signal at 'ON', it will certainly prevent an accident of the type which overtook trains C-35 and T-81 on the 14th November.

9.6 A pre-requisite for a statutory inquiry of this nature to be successful is that all relevant clues relating to the accident are preserved and made available to the investigating officer. While clear cut procedure for joint recording of track, conventional signalling installations and rolling stock exists and is generally complied with, there do not appear to be similar instructions available in the matter of sophisticated signalling installations and Electric Multiple Units involved in accidents. In Automatic Signalling System and at stations worked on route relay interlocking, unless the position of the relays of the relevant circuits at the moment of occurrence of the accident is kept on record, vital clues get lost and sealing of Relay Rooms and Location Boxes serve no purpose once the signals operate for further movement of trains. In this particular case, had the "picked up" or "dropped" position of relays relating to Automatic Signal L-1111 been preserved, the exact position of the signal for the ill-fated train could have been inferred from the position of the relays. Considering that no traffic moved past Signal L-1111 for several hours, this could not have been difficult had the Senior Officials of different Departments who reached the scene of the accident tried to do so. Similarly, the position of the Master Controller, reversing handle and Electric Pneumatic Brake handle in the driving Cab as it existed after the collision (even admitting that the Cab had been damaged) would have given some idea of the action taken by the Motorman prior to collision. It had not been possible for me to elicit the information as to whether the brake blocks of the unaffected coaches were in applied or released position just after the collision because a authentic joint survey was done only after about 3 hours and the brake blocks of the air brake system got released in the meantime due to exposure to atmospheric pressure. It is recommended that suitable guidelines for action to be taken by the officials who visit the site immediately after the occurrence may be drawn up by the Railway Administration and placed in the Accident Manual and the Manuals of the relevant Technical Departments, viz., Signal Engineering and Traction Departments for guidance when accidents of this nature take place.

9.7 It is recommended that the look-out glass and the window glass panes of all driving Cabs in the Suburban Sections be immediately replaced by splinter-proof toughened glass, against the present practice of replacing only the affected look-out glass by splinter-proof glass. It is also desirable that the protective screen in front of the the look-out glass is of a properly designed and fixed material such that it does not cause strain to the Motorman and at the same time protects him from vandalism. The tendency of the Motormen to drop the protective screen should be discouraged by making it fixed as is done on the Suburban Sections in Madras City. The practice of keeping open the entrance door of the far side of the Motorman's driving controls may also be prohibited which would increase the degree of protection to the Motorman from vandalism.

9.8 In the densely built up areas of the City, through which the line passes, it would be desirable to wall up the Railway boundary to prevent trespassing as much as possible. In particular, such a step would be a positive aid to safe operation if the boundary near slums like the one between Matunga and Sion is walled up. It is, accordingly, recommended that Central Railway Administration may have the matter examined in detail and steps taken to wall up the boundary wherever feasible and possible.

9.9 Due to curved alignment of tracks at a number of places it becomes difficult for a Motorman to identify a standing train in front of him and determine whether it is on his own line or on an adjoining line.

A suggestion made by one of the Motormen in his evidence was to give a conspicuous paint of a uniform design on the rear Cab. During day time the Motorman of a following train will be in a position to know from the design of the rear portion from a distance if the train ahead of him is on his own line or on the adjoining line. But the design will have to be covered when the rear Cab becomes the front Cab in the opposite direction. A conspicuous design of about 0.6 m. dia. with a covering arrangement to be used as necessary will serve the intended purpose during day light hours. During night time the red tail lamp in the rear of a train in the same direction as distinguished from the head light of a train in the opposite direction would serve that purpose. Central Railway Administration may consider implementation of this useful suggestion from one of their Motormen.

Railway Board's Comments on Various Paras of the Report

Para 9.1: The recommendations made by the Commissioner of Railway Safety that there is a case for reviewing the existing 'Continuous' classification of Motormen with a view to see that their functions come under the 'Intensive' classification under the Hours of Employment Regulations, has been carefully examined in the light of all the existing relevant factors as well as the rules. A High-powered Committee appointed by the Railway Board, known as the Committee on Running Allowances, 1980, have only recently completed a detailed study, *inter alia*, of working conditions of Running staff, but the said Committee have not recommended change of classification of any category of Running staff, from 'Continuous' to 'Intensive' under the Hours of Employment Regulations. From the point of view of the nature of duty of Motormen working in EMUs in suburban sections also, it is considered that there is no justification for any change in the existing procedures for the following reasons: –

(a) It is not correct to say that sighting of signals frequently constitutes additional strain since Automatic signalling provides advance warning and this tends to ease the tension on the Motormen. Even in non-suburban sections where automatic signalling is provided, the conditions are same;
(b) EMUs are fitted with air-brakes which give better control to the Motormen as compared with vacuum braked trains. The EMU rakes are also of 8 or 9 coaches and as such the braking distances

are less; and

(c) Hours of employment of Motormen on the Central Railway are generally 91 hours in a fortnight, i.e., almost the same as prescribed for 'Intensive' classified staff, but with distinct breaks at the end of each trip, as against the statutory limit of 108 hours as prescribed for 'Continuous' staff. The duty hours of Motormen are also limited to 8 hours a day from 'signing on' to 'signing off' as against the 10-hours limit prescribed for other Running Staff, though in actual practice, a motorman generally performs duties for 6-30 on an average.

In view of this position, there is no justification for reclassifying Motormen working in suburban sections in Bombay area as 'Intensive' under the Hours of Employment Regulations.

Para 9.2: Arrangements have been made to allot the required new EMU stock to C. Rly. This will not only facilitate replacement of old imported stock but would enable the railways to introduce additional suburban trains. In regard to POH, centralisation of facilities in Matunga Workshops have been approved with a view to improve quality of POH work as well as its frequency.

Para 9.3: This is under examination.

Para 9.4: The existing rules providing for medical examination of the employees in categories A1, A2 and A3 at an interval of 3 years in the case of those below 45 years of age, are considered quite adequate. Apart from the periodical medical examination at the stated intervals, an employee can be sent for special examination if his controlling officer considers is necessary. The periodical medical examination includes general physical examination in addition to examination to determine acuity of vision. In the event of suspicion of a disease, the employee is subjected to further investigations as considered necessary. As regards the aspect of mental alertness, it may be mentioned that the Railways have already been advised vide Board's letter No. 69/Safety-1/RAIC-68/Item/88 (Pt. B), dated 22-12-1979 to introduce a scheme of periodical psychological check up of drivers over 45 years of age for counselling purpose. This scheme envisages psycho-motor testing once in 2 years after the age of 45 years and counselling of those drivers who are found to be wanting in respect of the abilities tested. This is a purely welfare oriented safety programme, the purpose of which is to make the drivers aware of the changes in two significant abilities – Form Perception capacity and Reaction Time – and make them familiar with the likely job hazards arising out of these changes and counsel them within a well-defined specific framework.

Para 9.5: Tenders for the work of providing Automatic Warning System on the Suburban Scction of Central Railway are to be invited shortly. The work will be expedited so that the benefits of the system are available to the motormen at an early date. The system will incorporate all essential features enumerated in the I.R.S. specification S. 38/70 for Automatic Warning System.

Para 9.6: As mentioned by the Railway, instructions already exist that the condition of all the driving equipments, electrical controls, brake equipment, etc., should be recorded jointly by a Committee of 3 Supervisors/Officers on the accident spot. The position of Master Control reversing handle is also normally recorded after the accident. In this particular accident the driving cab was so badly smashed that it was not possible for anyone either to enter it or record/observe the position of the equipment although efforts were made in this regard. Noting the position of the Relays jointly with the officers/supervisors of departments other than the S&T is difficult as the other Department's representative available may not be able to understand the implications. Sealing of the apparatus cases is considered adequate since full functional tests are carried out as soon as possible before traffic is restored.

Para 9.7: As advised by Railway administration, look-out glasses of the driving cabs are being replaced by toughened splinter-proof glasses on a programmed basis during POH and quarterly inspection schedules. Regarding side window panes, these are normally kept open by motormen for ventilation. In case any protection is required, venetian shutters can be raised immediately. Provision of splinter proof glasses on side window panes is not considered necessary.

As for suggestion that protection cover outside the the look-out glass should be made permanently fixed, it is considered that this would cause strain on the motorman's eyes. The Railway Administration has, therefore, developed a protective cover with an arrangement to get it in position by motorman himself from inside the Cab quickly and when required while on run. Necessary instructions on the subject are also being issued to all the Railways.

Para 9.8: Railway boundary along Bombay suburban lines has been walled/fenced over considerable length but its maintenance/ rebuilding has been posing serious problems. In Bombay area, there is problem of breaking of wall/fencing by the public, the commuters and the hutment dwellers in various forms. The commuters break open the boundary walls near the ends of the platforms of suburban stations for easy access to the platform. The hutment dwellers also break open the boundary walls either for using the railway land as open lavatories or at times taking away the building materials for their own use. The public also break open walls at certain important locations for short cut approaches for places on the other side of the track. Inspite of these constraints, the Railway is taking action to repair the damaged portions of boundary walls at vulnerable places at times by R.P.F. staff. However, at many places boundary walls cannot be rebuilt unless the hutment-dwellers are pushed back and are made to have their access opening into the private land. As the hutments under reference are regular confused hutments, their shifting will have be processed through the State Government which is likely to take some time. It will be appreciated that so long as the hutment dwellers are not entirely removed and people/commuters become more responsible, the Railway will have to live with this problem inspite of all the efforts put in this direction.

Para 9.9: Detailed instructions in this regard have already been issued to RDSO/Railways vide Board's Circular letter No. 77/(Electrical) TRS/445/20, dated 26-3-1980. Copies of the said circular are enclosed for CCRS's information.

29

REVIEW COMMITTEE ON INDIAN INSTITUTE OF MANAGEMENT (AHMEDABAD, BANGALORE, CALCUTTA) AND PROMOTION AND DEVELOPMENT OF MANAGEMENT EDUCATION 1979 — REPORT[1]

Chairman Shri H.P. Nanda

Members Dr. S. Varadarajan; Shri Mohd. Fazal; Shri Ajit Kerkar; Prof. G.R. Damodaran; Dr. P.K. Narayanaswamy; Shri Prem Pandhi; Shri J. Sen Gupta, Shri K.R. Sivaramakrishnan (during his absence on leave Shri S.R. Chopra attended the meetings); Dr. S. Muthukumaran.

Appointment

The Government of India had in Collaboration with State Governments of West Bengal, Gujarat and Karnataka set up earlier, three IIMS at Calcutta, Ahmedabad and Bangalore respectively to provide education, training, research and consultancy in Management Sciences. These institutes were registered under the Societies Registration Act. Clause 5 of the Memorandum of Association of these institutes Vests the Government of India with powers to appoint at any time in consultation with the respective State Government, one or more persons to review the work and progress of the institutes and to hold an inquiry into its affairs.

According to the Government of India have Constituted a Review Committee Vide D.O. No. F. 5-2/79-T.1 dated November 26, 1979.

Terms of Reference

(i) To review the working of Indian Institute of Management in

1. New Delhi, Ministry of Education and Culture, 1982, xii, 69 p.

all respects since their establishment as centres for advanced education and research in management.

(ii) To report on their organisational and administrative structures in relation to the aims and objects with which the institutes have been established; and

(iii) To advise on the broad lines of future development of the institutes and to make recommendation on any other aspects regarding development of management, education, training and research.

Contents

List of Abbreviation; Preface; Summary and Recommendations; Preamble; Institutes – Their Establishment and Growth; Review of the Working of the Institutes; Future Strategy; Annexures.

Recommendations

Review

In November 1979, the Government of India appointed a Committee to review the working of the three Indian Institutes of Management set up by it earlier in collaboration with the respective State Governments at Calcutta, Ahmedabad and Bangalore and also to make recommendations regarding the development of management education, training and research. The Committee met on several occasions and also visited the three Institutes. It also met and discussed with several persons connected with the Institutes and interested in management education. The Committee collected factual information, self-evaluation and opinions on several vital issues from the Institutes and also comments from several others who are associated with or interested in management education. These discussions, comments and notes collected are utilised in the preparation of this report.

The report deals with the establishment, growth and review of the working of these three Institutes. It also gives recommendations on future strategy for these Institutes in particular and outlines the possible approach to development of management education in the country. The main findings and recommendations are briefly summarised in the following:

General

1. The setting up of the Calcutta Institute had been delayed mainly due to difficult side conditions at the campus. However, in recent years it has moved to its own campus at Joka and within the next few years, it would have created the necessary infrastructure. Thereafter, it would be possible for this Institute to increase the intake in PGP to the planned extent and undertake on a larger scale, the fellowship programme and research activities. (Para 2.2.2)

2. The Ahmedabad Institute had established itself as per its original schedule. Its growth has been steady. It has adequate physical facilities and other infrastructure. Its annual PGP intake and academic activities are the maximum. (Para 2.2.3)

3. The Bangalore Institute will be moving to its permanent campus by the end of the first decade of its existence, at slightly behind the original scheduled due to unavoidable reasons. To some extent, this delay has hampered its growth. However, before the end of the Sixth Plan, it is expected that this Institute would have built basic facilities and would be on the road to consolidation and further growth. (Para 2.2.4)

4. These three Institutes have, since their establishment, pioneered and contributed substantially to the advancement of management education in the country. They have generally met the objectives with which they have been set up and deserve every encouragement for future growth on the lines suggested by this Committee. (Para 3.8)

Post-Graduate Programmes

5. The two-year post-graduate programme in Management of these three Institutes is a major activity and is valuable. Nearly a quarter of the output of management post-graduates of this country are from these three institutes. The Committee recommends that these programmes should be continued and the present intake may also be raised to 180 at Calcutta and Bangalore. (Para 3.1.5)

6. Each of these Institutes has developed its post-graduate programme with some special characteristics. The present freedom and initiative found in the formulation of the courses should continue to receive encouragement. In addition to developing courses in the general management area, it would be desirable for each Institute to identify its strengths and develop a degree of specialisation in specified

areas. (Para 3.1.5)

7. Many employers opined that the post-graduates of these institutes are good in their understanding of management principles and theories, but are generally reluctant to undertake line jobs. They do not have tolerance and do not know how to respect the views of other employees. The Committee also noticed that these post-graduates do not take to self-employment and do not seek or desire employment in nationally important tasks. The Committee, therefore, recommends that apart from the presently existing subjects in the post-graduate programmes, training and education may be included to appropriately develop entrepreneurship, leadership qualities and a spirit of national service in the students. Education and training of the most gifted graduates, from these best equipped and sought after institutions; while providing a very sound understanding of the techniques, systems and methods prevalent in modern professional management should, in a developing country, with large sections of the poor, aim also to inculcate a strong sense of obligation of the privileged towards the uplift and betterment of their follow citizens. A commitment to place their talents, knowledge and experience in the service of the society and the country, as well as a sense of pride in the Country's culture and history and an aspiration for participation in the nation's destiny. (Paras 3.1.5. and 3.1.6)

8. There is a need to develop basic teaching materials for the post-graduate programmes based upon relevant and contemporary Indian experience. These Institutes may develop such teaching materials and make them available not only to their own students but also to universities and other educational institutions offering post-graduate management programmes. (Para 3.1.5)

9. The present common admission test serves the purpose of identifying suitable candidates and should continue. The Committee is of the view that work experience prior to undertaking the study of management programme is desirable, as such individuals can better appreciate management techniques. Further interest participation in extra-curricular activities give ample scope for team work. In view, of these factors, the Institutes may consider giving due weightage for work experience and participation in extra-curricular activities. The Committee also observed that the final selection process consumes a lot of faculty time. It would therefore, recommend that, with a view to lessening the burden on the faculty in the final selection process, a modified procedure may be adopted which may have some common

and shared features. (Para 3.1.7).

10. Persons with engineering education followed by management education are better suited for certain types of managerial positions than persons from non-engineering backgrounds. There are other areas where management graduates with other backgrounds are required. There should therefore, be a mix of students of varying backgrounds as now exists. However, at present, it is not necessary to reserve seats for different entry qualifications. (Para 3.1.8)

11. Considering that a certain proportion of the PGP students leave without completing the programme, the Institutes may ensure that the out-turn is of a satisfactory number by taking necessary steps, such as keeping a sufficiently long waiting list, and admitting a slightly larger number than the approved intake to allow for the anticipated early drop-outs. (Para 3.1.9)

12. It is observed that in the present circumstances, opportunities are provided to post-graduates of these institutes mainly by the private sector. The Institutes may discuss with the public sector organisations and concerned authorities, and suggest suitable modifications in the recruitment procedures of the organisations so that the post-graduates of these institutes are given opportunities to serve the public sector. It may also be necessary to suggest as a result of such discussions, appropriate actions and procedures for bringing about the necessary climate in the public sector organisations and for motivating the post-graduates of these institutes to join and stay in the public sector. (Para 3.1.10).

13. The Ahmedabad and Bangalore Institutes have specialised programmes for training young persons to take up management positions in Government and in public utility organisations. However, these trained or educated persons are generally not taking up such positions because of the lack of opportunities to induct such persons at the middle management positions. A suitable climate will have to be created in this connection by perhaps bringing the concerned authorities in a forum for discussing this issue so that the post-graduates of these Institutes who had undergone sectoral specialisation are beneficially utilised in the respective sectors. (Para 3.1.10)

14. The financial burden on the individual in pursuing a post-graduate programme at these institutes is substantial. Since the best students are admitted from among a large number of applicants, once admission is offered, a student should not be denied the opportunity of joining and pursuing the course owing to financial difficulties. The In-

stitutes should, therefore, provide a sufficient number of scholarships and loans. The Ahmedabad Institute has started providing such loans. All the Institutes should arrange for providing an adequate number of stipends and loans. (Para 3.1.11)

15. It is noted that special assistance is being given to Scheduled Caste/Scheduled Tribe students to pursue and complete the courses. In addition to this special assistance, it may be desirable to consider, in specific instances, allowing of a longer course period as has been done by the Bangalore Institute. (Para 3.1.12)

16. There is a necessity for students-counselling and also for setting up an effective mechanism for students to express their requirements, grievances, and problems. The Committee recommends that the Institutes may establish, where it does not already exist, a suitable consultation mechanism to appreciate and respond to the requirements of individuals or groups of students or alternatively to activate the mechanism, if it exists already. (Para 3.1.13)

Fellowship Programmes

17. The Calcutta and Ahmedabad Institutes have been offering a fellowship programme from 1971. The Bangalore Institute started this programme in 1976. Till now, about 60 students have successfully completed the fellowship programme in these three Institutes. This activity requires to be strengthened considerably. It is recommended that the intake into the fellowship programmes may be increased to at least 15 to 20 students per year at each Institute. At the same time, the Institute may provide the necessary single, as well as married accommodation for the fellowship students. (Para 3.2.5)

Other Educational Programmes

18. An important function of these Institutes is the providing of training in management subjects to persons from industry to equip them thoroughly in their areas of specialisation. This function will be fulfilled by the Institutes organising full-time condensed general management programmes and post-graduate programmes by correspondence and full-time condensed functional management programmes. It is, however, recommended that these Institutes offer these programmes only to a limited extent so as to develop the necessary packages and encourage other institutions to undertake such ac-

tivities. (Para 3.3.6)

Training Programmes

19. These Institutes are offering training programmes to satisfy the specific objective of providing training in management and related subjects to persons already employed in managerial positions. It is noted that these programmes have been successful and in good demand. Such training programmes greatly benefit practising managers as they have an excellent appreciation of the organisational and personal needs. These programmes also provide opportunities for understanding professional management by those who did not have formal management education. In addition, these programmes offer an excellent opportunity for the faculty to come into contact with real field issues. It is recommended that this activity is increased and continued. However, each Institute may annually review its training programmes and delete programmes which can be or are being offered by other training organisations and add original or novel programmes and new programmes based upon the national needs. Further, it is recommended that each Institute may concentrate in certain identified special areas, sectors or organisations so that its training programmes are more effective. (Para 3.4.5)

Faculty

20. The mode of selection of faculty at these institutes varies from being wholly internal to being similar to the procedure commonly adopted by universities. The Committee suggests, that to give the necessary appearance of fairness and impartiality, and also to ensure the selection of high calibre faculty, the selection committees may include outstanding academics and experts, not only from the Institute but also from outside. The Institutes may suitably modify their procedure. (Para 3.5.1.)

21. It is recommended that the Institutes may draw up systematic training programmes for their newly recruited faculty members and devise methods of assessing periodically, the training needs of the faculty members, plan and send them for such training. (Para 3.5.2)

22. It is recommended that the faculty of these Institutes may assess their present work-load and account for the total number of hours spent at the Institute by each faculty member. Thereafter, the Faculty may

lay down criteria for work-load and ensure that the maximum targeted amount of time is devoted to teaching and research. (Para 3.5.3)

23. The record of the Ahmedabad Institute in terms of cases collected and publications, is good. The three Institutes should aim at adding substantially, and up-dating every year. Indian teaching materials including case studies, books and research articles so that the country as a whole, is benefited. (Para 3.5.4)

Research Activities

24. In the academic community, the position of a university is evaluated by its record of output of original research of high order, the quality of which is judged by its peers in the wider academic community. Faculty members are appointed and advanced, based largely, upon their research achievements and original publications. A high-level institute is distinguished from other institutions by the importance it gives to research by its faculty. Since these institutions are institutes of higher learning, they may attach special importance to the pursuit of basic and applied research, evolve a future perspective and undertake research as an institute activity. Adequate funding for research should be provided so that research can be pursued in its own right without soliciting project funding and consultancy. (Para 3.6.4)

25. Research in the basic disciplines supported by applied research in Management Sciences may be pursued as is research in basic disciplines such as economics, psychology, behavioural sciences, etc., which helps in raising academic standards and the pursuit of applied research as well as teaching. (Para 3.6.4)

26. As these Institutes have pioneered and are premier institutions in management education in the country, their educational programmes are of a high order and require continuous modifications effected as a product and corollary of research. It is, therefore, essential that every faculty member is directly engaged in research in addition to guiding research fellows and scholars. All necessary steps may be taken to foster a climate for research and to establish a high reputation for the Institute in research output. For this purpose, it would be desirable to study the pattern and policy followed by reputed institutions such as the Harvard Business School, (M.I.T.) Sloan School, etc., which will provide the basis for research activity in these institutes. Such policies, if vigorously followed and supported, would greatly enhance the standing of these institutes in the country and internationally. It will also

help to attract renowned faculty and post-doctoral research scholars, thereby providing excellent bridges to other high level institutes and university departments in the country. The Committee recommends special funding for the purpose of exchange of research faculty with other institutes in the country and with universities abroad. Since students in these institutes are among the very best in the country, the pursuit of high order research and the presence of visiting research professors, will help to provide a sufficiently challenging course-content and also establish values in the minds of the young students and develop them to leadership positions. (Para 3.6.4)

Consultancy

27. As management teaching is enriched by blending theory with practice, it is useful if faculty members engage themselves in consultancy work. However, the danger of faculty members becoming preoccupied in consultancy must be avoided. Consultancy activity should be subsidiary to teaching and research. Each Institute may therefore, frame a policy regulating the quantum of consultancy, and the acceptance of short-term projects taking into consideration that consultancy not only helps the organisation but also the faculty members and the institute. (Para 3.7.4)

IIM Societies

28. The Societies of the respective Institutes are essentially similar to the respective Boards of Governors except in the case of the Ahmedabad Society, which has a wider membership. As it would be advantageous to have a society with a broader base including persons belonging to the user groups, academics, professionals and scientists; it is recommended that membership in the societies may be made flexible to allow for differential subscription. The societies must be active and act as promoters of major policies towards achieving relevance and excellence (Para 4.1.2)

Board of Governors

29. The Board of Governors may be reconstituted at fixed intervals of, say, 5 years with a composition suggested in para 4.1.4. The Chairman of the Board should be one who is a successful manager with

proven commitment and interest in educational organisations, a distinguished academic with administrative experience or an administrator with experience in educational management, who is committed to the furtherance of management education and research and has adequate time to spare. Those who are co-opted should be persons connected with the management profession by being professional managers or employers or the post-graduates of the Institute, a user of the research output or connected with management education or profession in any other manner or a person connected with a related subject or profession. The cooption should permit the inclusion of persons in areas that are not adequately represented otherwise. (Para 4.1.4)

30. A locally-based member of the Board who is interested in the subject of management education and training and is able to devote his time to attend meetings and the work connected with the Institute may be nominated by the Chairman as the Vice-Chairman of the Board of Governors. It would be advantageous if a Managing Committee of not more than 10 members of the Board is constituted. This committee may meet at the instance of the Director as often as necessary between board meetings. The powers of the Board in regard to many of the routine administrative matters may be delegated to this Managing Committee so that the Board is free to spend more of its time in reviewing the academic work. the Managing Committee may be chaired by the Vice-Chairman of the Board. (Para 4.1.4.)

Other Authorities

31. Apart from the existing committees and the managing committee recommended earlier, an academic committee may also be constituted which will be the advisory body of the Board of Governors in all academic matters including research. In order to ensure quality in academic matters, including identification of potential faculty members, visiting professorships and promotion of specific areas of research, it would be advisable to have small advisory bodies for special subject areas especially during the periods of development of such subject areas. (Para 4.1.6)

Administration

32. The Institutes may have to formalise their administrative procedures so as to minimise the time spent by faculty on non-academic ac-

tivities. (Para 4.1.10)

33. The Institutes should review their organisational structure from time to time keeping in view the basic principle that administration should subserve the needs of education and research. (Para 4.1.10)

34. The Institutes must have well defined rules and regulations and have a suitable mechanism for dealing with grievances and welfare, etc., of non-teaching staff. Not only should rules be framed but also disseminated. (Para 4.1.11)

Research Staff

35. There could be two categories of research staff. The first, designated as Project staff engaged in assisting in specific projects and may be paid a fixed monthly emolument. The other, classified as Research Scholars engaged in long term research, paid a time-scale of pay and trained to become faculty members in the same Institute or in other educational institutions. (Para 4.1.12)

Objectives and Powers

36. In order to enable these Institutes to formulate new programmes to meet their changing roles and the changing environment and to implement their programmes effectively, it is necessary to include in the objectives the training and educating of managers of public utilities and services. The training and educating of management teachers and powers to award degrees, and to create cadres which are broadly in line with the Central Government cadres, etc. (Para 4.2.5)

Role of IIMs

37. The role of these Institutes should not be the same as that of a department of management studies in a university. These Institutes should concentrate in those activities which will lead to a multiplier effect in carrying the message of modern methods of management such as generating faculty members for other institutions which offer post-graduate programmes in management, setting up of such institutions and institutions offering training programmes in management subjects. In other words they should act as mother Institutes and foster the growth of other management Institutions in the country. (Para 4.3.6)

Autonomy

38. Educational Institutions live by self-regulation. The Government control should be minimal and should be only to the extent required to ensure economical use of public funds towards fulfilling the objectives of the Institutes. The autonomy now enjoyed by these institutes should in no way be curtailed. There is room for progressive reduction of Government control as each Institute becomes more and more self reliant. (Para 4.4.4)

Status of IIMs

39. These three Institutes are pioneering institutions in the field of Management Education and have demonstrated their ability in fulfilling the needs in this area successfully as evidenced by the manner in which they have attracted outstanding students. They have a national character and have the potential to develop into institutes of national importance. In the field of engineering and technology, the Government of India has set up five institutions of national importance. There are two institutions of national importance in the field of medicine but there are no such institutions in the field of Management Education. To bring about the necessary discipline the self-reliance in the country's economic, social and public administration activities with a view to improving productivity, it is necessary to effectively apply modern management principles. The Indian Institutes of Management are playing and will continue to play a vital role in this national effort to develop and channelise human resources. Therefore, the Government of India should take early necessary steps to declare these three institutes as institutes of national importance with a flexible institutional framework. (Para 4.5.6)

Coordination of Activities of IIMs

40. While the individual character and autonomy of these Institutes are to be maintained, it is desirable to develop an informal forum for periodic exchange of experience and information in planning for development in new special areas, and possibly in the role of these institutes in developing faculty for themselves and for other Institutions. This forum could also help in exchange of faculty, in resolving problems pertaining to administrative and organisational structures,

etc. (Para 4.6.6)

Industry — IIM Cooperation

41. Industry-Institute Cooperation may be fostered by encouraging the sending of teachers to the industry or relevant Government organisations for field training, urging the industries and Government departments to institute Chairs at the Institutes, encouraging the writing of books jointly by faculty members and practising managers, exchanging of faculty with managers, etc. (Para 4.7.2)

IIMs – Linkages with other Institutions

42. One of the objectives of these Institutes is to develop linkages with the educational and research institutes having similar objectives. Linkages will have to be brought about both upward and downward. There are some informal linkages with the management departments of the universities in this country and elsewhere. These Institutes should be encouraged to formalise such linkages and also form new linkages with special research or training institutes such as IIFT, etc. (Para 4.8.4)

Additional IIMs

43. The demand for seats in these Institutes is in excess of their present and potential capacity. In view of the continuous expansion of business activity and planned economic growth, the demand for education in IIMs will continue to increase. As a large expansion in these Institutes is not desirable, the committee recommends that two more IIMs – one in the Northern region and the other in the Central region may be established early. (Para 4.9.3)

Management Programme at University and other Educational Institutions

44. The management courses offered at over 40 university departments and affiliated colleges are of widely varying standard. There is need to regulate such programmes. Haphazard starting of post-graduate programmes by universities and colleges should be avoided and they should be advised to start such programmes only with prior approval of

AICTE. There is an urgent need to improve and consolidate the existing and approved programmes. High priority may be given to the consolidation of existing courses and increasing the quantum of financial assistance to satisfactory levels so as to enable them to improve qualitatively, as such selective financial assistance would make a good contribution to the overall economy of the country by improving managerial efficiency. Further, the university departments and affiliated colleges may be linked with the IIM of the region in a network system by a special Central Government scheme similar to the institutional network scheme now being implemented in the technical education system. (Paras 4.10.3, 4.3.6 and 4.8.4)

45. To remedy the present situation where a large number of universities are attempting to start management educational programmes with or without AICTE approval and to avoid rush of engineering graduates to the IIMs, it is recommended that a one-year management course in continuation of the Engineering Degree Course specially designed to suit the engineers with particular emphasis on production, technical and engineering management may be offered by the IITs and other well-established Engineering Colleges with adequate number of seats. (Para 4.10.3).

46. An important function of the IIMs is to provide training in Management Subjects for persons from institutions to equip them to instruct others in the practice of management. The Ahmedabad Institute has recently started a faculty development programme. The Bangalore Institute has offered a teacher training programme to the faculty of two state training institutions. All the three Institutes may start such programmes in order to fulfil this objective. The Government of India may also consider instituting a QIP for management teachers apart from the one now existing for technical teachers so as to enable the IIMs to offer with freedom a QIP to suit the special requirements of management teacher. (Para 3.3.6. and 3.2.5.)

Future Management Education Scene

47. Apart from the necessity to spread management concepts to public utilities, as brought out elsewhere, there is an urgent necessity to develop expertise in International management due to a growing number of Indian companies spreading their operations abroad, creation of facilities and offering of educational and training programmes in International management should be encouraged. (Para 4.11.1)

48. There is a great and growing demand for management education as evidenced by a large number of institutions with grossly inadequate facilities coming up throughout the country to cater to the unsatisfied demand, thereby creating a substandard management education of dubious value. To remedy this, the concept of management education may be broadened by recognising management qualifications in different functional areas and at different levels. In order to reduce the cost to the exchequer, the offering of suitable educational programmes by professionals and professional associations and the starting of institutes by voluntary non-profit viable educational societies may be encouraged by the Government. Further, as earlier recommended by AICTE, management education may be integrated with professional/technical education. (Para 4.11.3)

30

RAILWAY ACCIDENT INVESTIGATION REPORT ON COLLISION OF 26 DOWN GAUHATI – DHUBRI PASSENGER TRAIN WITH 1 DOWN AVADH – TRIHUT MAIL AT KM 87/11-12 BETWEEN PATHSHALA AND SORUPETA STATIONS ON BONGAIGAON – CHANGSARI CTC METRE GAUGE SECTION IN ALIPURDUAR DIVISION OF N.F. RAILWAY ON 23rd DECEMBER, 1979 — REPORT[1]

One Man Commission	Shri K. Ganapati, Commissioner of Railway Safety, South Eastern Circle, Calcutta
Officers Present	Dr. C.M. Kulshreshtha; Shri A.N. Perumal; Shri S. Sen; Shri I.P. Phookan; Shri D. Bora

Appointment

The Commission was constituted under the Ministry of Tourism and Civil Aviation (Commission of Railway Safety) in accordance with Rule 4 of the Statutory Investigation into the Railway Accidents Rules 1973 vide Notification No. R.S. 13-T (8)/71 dated April 19, 1973 on December 23, 1979.

Terms of Reference

To enquire into the Collision of 26 Down Gauhati – Dhubri Passenger Train with 1 Down Avadh – Tirhut Mail at km 87/11-12 between Pathshala and Sorupeta Stations on Bongaigaon – Changsari CTC Metre Gauge Section in Alipurduar Division on December 23, 1979.

---

1. Ministry of Tourism and Civil Aviation (Commission of Railway Safety), Government of India, New Delhi, 1982, 21 p.

Contents

Summary; Inspection and Inquiry; Relief Measures; The Trains; Local Conditions; Summary of Evidence; Tests and Observations; Discussion; Conclusions; Remarks and Recommendations; Annexure; Railway Board's Comments on Various Paras of the Report.

Conclusions

Cause of the Accident

On careful consideration of the factual material and circumstantial evidence, I have come to the conclusion that the rear end collision of 26 Down Passenger with 1 Down A.T. Mail at km/87/11-12 between Pathshala and Sorupeta Stations on Bongaigaon Changsari C.T.C. Metre Gauge Section on Alipurduar Division of N.F. Railway at 2.50 hours on 23-12-1979 was caused by the Driver of 26 Down Passenger having not exercised great caution after Passing the Permissive Signal No. 8502 in the 'On' position.

Responsibility

(a) Sri Kalipada Shome, deceased Driver of 26 Down is mainly responsible for not having exercised great caution after passing AP Signal No. 8502 in the 'On' position. He violated G.R. 436 (ii) (iii) & (iv).

(b) In defence of the deceased Driver, it is stated that he was somewhat handicapped by the non-functioning of the telephones at the foot of AP Signal envisaged in G.R. 436(i).

Service Record

Sri Kalipada Shome, born on 4-1-1926, joined the railway as a cleaner on 17-1-1944. He was promoted as a 2nd Fireman on 30-1-1945, as Fireman 'B' grade on 1-9-1950, as Shunter on 22-8-1959, as Driver 'C' grade on 22-11-1962, as Driver 'C' grade special on 1-12-1978 and as Driver 'B' grade on 13-12-1979. He was drawing a pay of Rs. 530 in Rs. 425–600 grade. He was last medically examined on 24-3-1979 and passed in category A/1 with glass. He attended last refresher course on 20-12-1978. His increment was withheld for 2 years on

12-1-1970 for engine failure. His increment was again withheld for 12 months on 16-8-1976 for causing heavy detention to goods train; otherwise his record was free from blame.

Note: The Railway Administration has accepted the above conclusions.

Relief Arrangements and Medical Attention

I am satisfied with the relief arrangements and medical attention given.

Recommendations

9.1 *Competency Certificate*

It appears that stoppage of a train in the C.T.C. Section on red aspect of AP signals is a rare occurrence with the result that the drivers are not readily conversant with the rules. My own inference was that the driver of the ill-fated 26 Down was not clear in his mind about the rules as brought out in para 7.5 (a) above. It is understood that the position is more or less same in respect of at least 40 per cent of the drivers working on the C.T.C. Section. Further there is no procedure on the N.F. Railway to issue competency certificate at intervals not exceeding one year in terms of Railway Board's letter No. 73/Safety-1/24/1 dated 23-11-73. At present the railway is issuing competency certificates once in 3 years. It is, therefore, necessary that all drivers working in C.T.C. Section on the N.F. Railway should be again thoroughly examined, educated in relevant rules and issued with fresh competency certificate which should be renewed at intervals not exceeding one year after conducting systematic check by qualified inspectors in terms of the extant orders of the Railway Board.

9.2 *Telephones to be Commissioned*

It is unfortunate that telephone at the foot of AP signal which is an integral part of the C.T.C. working, has been mostly abandoned after 1976 without proper appreciation of the handicap that this will cause to the driver. No alternative precautionary arrangements were also resorted to by the Railway Administration when they found themselves not in a position to maintain the telephone link. The Railway

Administration should make really serious efforts to restore all telephones in working condition at the foot of all the APB signals as early as possible.

Note: The Railway expect to recommission all the telephones latest by June 1980.

9.3 *Slack Working in Many Respects*

The following minor irregularities were noticed:

(a) The Guard of 1 Down did not carry emergency lighting equipment;
(b) The Guard of 26 Down did not carry any fusee, fire extinguisher and emergency train lighting equipment;
(c) There was no vacuum gauge in the SLR of 1 down;
(d) The vacuum gauge in the SLR of 26 Down was not working; and
(e) From the Return Date on VPL 1606 NE (1st coach on 1 Down A.T. Mail) it is seen that the VPL was intended to be used on other than Mail and Express trains. If the VPL is to be used regularly on Mail and Express trains the Return Date should have been 6/80.

The above minor irregularities in train working do not have a direct bearing on the cause of the present accident. On the other hand it cannot also be claimed that the minor irregularities have any connection with the General Law and order situation prevailing in the area. The only show slack supervision at various levels and poor procurement of stores. The Railway may take necessary action to tighten the supervision and ensure better compliance to the safety rules.

9.4 *Marshalling Order Violations*

The marshalling order of 26 Down and 1 Down rakes involved in the accident revealed violations of standing marshalling orders. The Railway Administration explained that they are unable to comply with the marshalling instructions in view of the fact that a very high percentage of A.T. SLRs are sick. According to the Railway Administration 50 SLRs were sick, out of a total holding of 216

(23.1%) as on 28-1-1980. Evidently the Railway Administration appears to have taken the view that it is better to run the train violating marshalling order rules rather than cancel the trains for want of an A.T. SLR. In view of the above I can only suggest that the railway should either procure more number of A.T. SLRs to enable them to conform to the marshalling order rules or take measures to keep down the percentage of sick SLRs.

9.5 *Inadequate Tail Lamp*

One of the factors contributing to the present accident is the disparity in the visibility distances of the AP signal and the tail lamp; whereas the green aspect of AP signal was visible at a distance of over 3 kms., the visibility of the tail lamp was only 151 m. If the visibility of a tail lamp were about 1 km. this accident would probably have been averted. In view of the above the necessity for increasing the visibility of the tail lamp is apparent. Time and again the Commission has pointed out the inadequacy of the present tail lamp and the necessity of providing a rear warning system suitable to present day speed and traffic. Para 102 of Naini Accident Report may be referred to for further details.

9.6 *Working Time Table*

Working Time tables of all railways generally give the kilometres of all stations to two decimal places in addition to giving the inter distances between stations. However, in the case of N.F. Railway it is seen that the kilometrage of all stations have been rounded up to the nearest integer while the inter distances between the stations are not given. The procedure followed by the N.F. Railway appears to have no special advantage vis-a-vis the procedure followed on other railways. On the other hand the procedure followed by the N.F. Railway may give misleading information to the driver and guard in regard to the kilometerage of the station and inter-station distances. It is therefore suggested that the N.F. Railway should fall in line with the other railways in regard to this matter.

9.7 *Amendment to Relevant Rules*

(a) In view of what is stated in para 7.7(b) above the N.F. Railway should ensure a speed restriction of 15 kmph during day time and 10 kmph during night time and under conditions of poor visibility when a Driver passes an AP signal in the 'On' position. This may be ensured by a suitable SR till GR 436 is revised.

Note: The Railway have issued a suitable SR to the above effect on 13-2-1980.

(b) Apropos to para 7.7(b) above the Railway Board may consider dual control by Guard by suitably amending GR 436 in order to provide a second line of defence. In the event of the Driver violating a speed restriction under GR436 the Guard should be enjoined to draw the attention of the Driver and/or stop the train by applying the vacuum brake; and

(c) Apropos to para 7.7(c) above the GRs 280 and 442 should be amended to provide rear protection when the detention in block section exceeds or likely to exceed 5 minutes, irrespective of the cause of stoppage, viz., the position as obtaining prior to the issue of Notification No. 66/Safety (II)/29/1 dated 18-12-67 should be restored. The same view has been expressed by the CCRS, Lucknow in his Note on the Collision of K. 121 Up with the rear of 3 Up on 18-5-79 on South Eastern Railway vide para 6.A(c) page 11 of his letter No. RS. 21-T(6)/79 dated 22-9-79.

Railway Board's Comments on Various Paras of the Report

Para 9.1 As explained by the Railway Administration, stoppage of trains in the C.T.C. Section on red aspect of a signal is not a rare occurrence. In fact trains follow in quick succession on the heavily occupied Changsari-Bongaigaon section. Also the Drivers working on C.T.C. Section are given adequate road learning before being put to work. Even the deceased Driver of 26 Down had been worked as a Driver since 1962 on Alipurduar-Siliguri section in the Down direction and Alipurduar-Bongaigaon-Gauhati in the Up direction with headquarters at Alipurduar. Further, this Driver had also undergone refresher course training on 20-12-1978. Regular checks are being conducted on the C.T.C. Section by Officers/Inspectors to watch the performance of Drivers.

Under the circumstances, it would not be correct to assume that stoppage of a train in C.T.C. Section is uncommon and that the Drivers are not conversant with the rules pertaining to the working of trains in C.T.C. Section.

Instructions have been emphasised on the Railways vide letter No. 80/Safety-I/25/3 dated 10-4-1980 that Drivers/Motormen working in automatic/absolute permissive block and C.T.C. Sections should be counselled regularly and subjected to one day's intensive course once in six months and that fresh competency certificates should be issued to the Drivers/Motormen in the knowledge of rules after conducting systematic checks by qualified inspectors at an interval of not exceeding one year. Further, Drivers/ Motormen should not be allowed to operate on such sections unless they are in possession of valid certificates.

Regarding the practice followed by N.F. Railway for issuing the competency certificates to the Drivers working in C.T.C. Sections, after a period of 3 years, contrary to Board's directive contained in their letter No. 73/Safety-I/24/1 dated 23-11-1973, the matter has been taken up with the Railway.

Para 9.2: Most of the telephones provided at the foot of the APB signals in C.T.C. Section had either been damaged or stolen by the miscreants from the cast iron boxes to the apparatus case by the side of the signal post. The deficiency has, however, since been made good by the Railway.

Para 9.3(a): Regarding non-availability of emergency train lighting box, the matter has been taken up with the Railway. The Railway Administration has been asked to fix responsibility and take up with defaulting staff. Instructions have been issued in December, 1980 that the Railway should ensure that trains do not run without portable lighting equipment and take action to provide spare train lighting equipments at out-stations so that in the event of equipment having not received in the terminating station, the train do not run without train lighting equipment in originating trip.

Para 9.3(b): Instructions with regard to supply/usage of fusees have been issued to the Railways.

The non-availability of the fire extinguisher on the train, as advised by the Railway Administration, was due to the fact that a number of fire extinguishers were lying an discharged condition at Gauhati and efforts made by the Railway to procure the stock did not prove fruitful. Instructions have since been issued to N.F. Railway to arrange for the refills on priority and avoid such cases in future. It may also be mentioned here that instructions have recently been issued to the Railways to provide four fire extinguishers on Mail/Express trains – two in the Guards Brakevan and two in the front Brakevan.

Regarding non-availability of the emergency lighting equipment on 26 Down Passenger, the remarks against para above may please be referred to.

Paras 9.3(c) & 9.3(d): Suitable instruction have been issued to N.F. Railway in this regard.

Para 9.3(e): Instructions have already been issued to the Railways that OCVs meant for Mail/Express trains should also be given POH at intervals of 12 months, vide Railway Board's letter No. 72M(W)/814/60 dated 29-11-1979. These instructions have since been reiterated. Railways have also been advised that in case of non-availability of Mail/Express OCVs, Passenger fit OCVs, which are within 12 months of their last POH should preferably be used for Mail/Express services. It has also been stipulated that in all cases of using passenger fit OVC coaches on Mail/Express trains, the coaches should be specially checked and certified by C&W Maintenance Staff for their fitness to work in Main/Express trains, before they are used.

Para 9.4: Due to high percentage of ineffective anti-telescopic SLRs, it could not be possible to comply with the safety marshalling instructions. Action has been taken by the railway to see that the percentage of damages is kept to the minimum by gearing up the work in the sick lines and also turning out such SLRs from the workshops on priority basis. Also 14 newly built SLRs have been allotted to the N.F. Railway on replacement account.

Para 9.5: As already advised in this Ministry's O.M. No. 77/Safety (A&R)/1/26, dated 29-8-1980, the matter is already receiving the attention of the RDSO. The position, as advised in the said O.M., is given below: –

> "The matter is already receiving the attention of the RDSO. For use on Mail/Express and Passenger trains, electric tail lamp of 24 V auto bulb or reflector assembly, (which uses power from the train battery) has been developed by the RDSO. This would give much better visibility and is expected to give sufficient warning to the Drivers of approaching trains in time. The tail lamp developed has given a good account in preliminary trials. Further trails under various adverse conditions are being planned and it would be possible to arrive at the decision after these trials are completed.
>
> As for Goods trains, the development of a suitable tail lamp by drawing energy from the portable lead acid rechargeable battery is in progress. It may be mentioned that the development of flasher

unit for tail light is also under consideration."

Para 9.6: This recommendation has been noted by the Railway Administration for compliance.

Para 9.7(a): The Railway Accidents Enquiry Committee, 1978, vide item No. 160(i) of recommendations contained in Part-II of their report, have recommended that a speed limit of 20 kmph should be specified under normal conditions of visibility under "Stop and Proceed" Rules in automatic signalling and C.T.C. territories. This recommendation has been accepted and necessary instructions issued to the Railways.

Para 9.7(b): The matter with regard to amendment of G.R. 436 enjoining on the Guard to draw the attention of the Driver and/or stop the train by applying the vacuum brake, when he observes that the Driver is exceeding the speed restriction, has been examined but not found feasible due to following considerations: –

(a) Such a rule would enjoin upon the Guard to see that Driver observes all speed restrictions including cautious driving. It will not be possible for the Guard to either check the speed at which the train is running (as brakevans are not fitted with speedometers) or to ensure whether the train is passing through the cautious driving area;

(b) In many cases, the Guard is unaware of the reasons for stopping and restarting, as the trains stop for various reasons including trespassing, cattle on track, etc.; and

(c) It is also felt that it is entirely the Driver's responsibility to ensure observance of proper speed limits and any attempt to involve any other person may make the Driver complacent in the performance of his duties.

Para 9.7(c): With regard to amendment of G.R. 280 and G.R. 436 to provide for rear-protection when the detention in block section exceeds or likely to exceed 5 minutes, irrespective of the causes of the stoppage, it may be mentioned that the issue has already been considered in the inquiry report of the CRS on the collision between 121 Up Local and 3 Up Mail between Chengail and Bauria stations of S.E. Railway on 18-5-1979. In the connection, this Ministry's remarks communicated vide O.M. No. 79/Safety (A&R)/1/15 dated 18-6-1980 would be relevant. These are re-produced below for ready reference:

"While furnishing their comments on the revised General Rules, the Commission of Railway Safety vide their D.O. letter No. RS.3-T(4)/74 dated 16-1-1975 categorically stated that the question protecting a train in the automatic block system should not normally arise, as it is impracticable and dilutes the responsibility of the Driver who becomes complacent and gets a false sense of safety. The Commission considered that it should be made clear that the entire responsibility in such cases rests squarely on the Driver/Motorman. The General Rules, have, therefore, been amended to stipulate that protection will be resorted to only when the train stops in an automatic block signal section on account of accidents, failure or obstruction, and the train cannot proceed. If the train stops in automatic signal section for short duration for any other season, there is no need to protect the train. Under the circumstances, no amendment of G.R. 280 is considered necessary".

CHAIRMAN INDEX OF COMMITTEES & COMMISSIONS IN INDIA 1947-79

Volumes 1 to 17